Federal Judicial Center National, Case-Based Civil Rules Survey

Preliminary Report to the Judicial Conference Advisory Committee on Civil Rules

Emery G. Lee III & Thomas E. Willging

Federal Judicial Center

October 2009

This Federal Judicial Center publication was undertaken in furtherance of the Center's statutory mission to conduct and stimulate research and development for the improvement of judicial administration. While the Center regards the content as responsible and valuable, it does not reflect policy or recommendations of the Board of the Federal Judicial Center.

Table of Contents

Executive Summary, 1

I. Introduction, 5

II. Discovery Activity in the Closed Cases, 7

III. Electronic Discovery Activity in the Closed Cases, 15

IV. Attorneys' Evaluation of Discovery in the Closed Cases, 27

V. Attorney Estimates of Costs in the Closed Cases, 35

VI. Reform Proposals, 45

VII. The Federal Rules, 57

Appendix A: Methods, 77

Appendix B: Attorney Characteristics, 79

Appendix C: Survey Instrument, 83

Appendix D: Attorney Comments, 109

Executive Summary

This report presents preliminary findings from a survey of attorneys in recently closed civil cases which the Federal Judicial Center conducted in May and June of 2009. Nearly half of the attorneys invited to participate responded. The report covers discovery activities and case management in the closed cases; electronic discovery activity in the closed cases; attorney evaluations of discovery in the closed cases; the costs of litigation and discovery; and attorney attitudes toward specific reform proposals and, more generally, the Federal Rules of Civil Procedure.

Discovery activity and case management

The parties conferred to plan discovery in more than 80 percent of cases in which respondents reported at least one type of discovery out of 12 types queried. Most commonly reported were interrogatories and requests for production of documents, followed by initial disclosures and informal exchanges of documents. The median number of types of discovery per case was 5.

The court adopted a discovery plan in more than 70 percent of respondents' cases. The most common case management activities reported by respondents were conferring to plan discovery and limiting the time for completion of discovery. The median time imposed for completion of discovery was 6 months.

Courts ruled on at least one summary judgment motion in more than a quarter of respondents' cases. Rule 12(b)(6) motions were ruled on in more than 10 percent.

Electronic discovery

Issues related to electronically stored information ("ESI") were discussed by the parties in more than 30 percent of the discovery planning conferences. The most common issues discussed were the parties' routine practices regarding retention of ESI and the format of production of ESI. Approximately 50 percent of parties eventually producing ESI instituted a litigation "freeze."

Respondents reported a request for production of ESI in 30 to 40 percent of cases with any discovery. In the ESI cases, plaintiffs tended to be requesting parties and defendants tended to be producing parties, but more than 40 percent of plaintiff attorneys and more than 50 percent of defendant attorneys reported representing both a producing and requesting party in the closed cases.

Problems relating to ESI occurred in about a quarter of the cases with a request for production of ESI. The most common problem was a dispute that could not be resolved without court action over the burden of production of ESI.

The most common uses of ESI produced in discovery in the closed cases were in preparing and deposing witnesses, in interviewing clients or clients' employees, and in evaluating cases for settlement. The ESI was reportedly not used in approximately 1 in 5 cases.

Attorney evaluation of discovery in the closed cases

More than 60 percent of respondents (and 2 out of 3 defendant attorneys) reported that the disclosure and discovery in the closed cases generated the "right amount" of information. More than half reported that the costs of discovery were the "right amount" in proportion to their client's stakes in the closed cases.

A majority of respondents reported that the parties were able to reduce the cost and burden of discovery by cooperating. A majority also reported that the costs of discovery had "no effect" on the likelihood of settlement in the closed cases.

Costs of litigation

For the closed cases included in the sample, the median cost, including attorney fees, was $15,000 for plaintiffs and $20,000 for defendants. For plaintiffs, reported costs ranged from $1,600 at the 10th percentile to $280,000 at the 95th percentile; for defendants, the range was from $5,000 at the 10th percentile to $300,000 at the 95th percentile. Median costs were higher in cases with electronic discovery (especially if the client was both a producing and requesting party) and in cases with more reported types of discovery.

The median estimate of the percentage of litigation costs incurred in discovery was 20 percent for plaintiffs and 27 percent for defendants. Electronic discovery costs accounted for 5 percent of the costs of discovery, at the median, in plaintiff attorneys' cases with discovery of ESI, and 10 percent, at the median, in defendant attorneys' cases with discovery of ESI.

The median estimate of the stakes in the litigation for plaintiffs was $160,000; estimates ranged from less than $15,000 at the 10th percentile to almost $4 million at the 95th percentile. The median estimate of the stakes for defendant attorneys was $200,000; estimates ranged from $15,000 at the 10th percentile to $5 million at the 95th percentile.

Reported expenditures for discovery, including attorney fees, amounted to, at the median, 1.6 percent of the reported stakes for plaintiff attorneys and 3.3 percent of the reported stakes for defendant attorneys.

Reform proposals

When asked at what point in litigation the central issues are narrowed and framed for resolution in the typical case, respondents most commonly identified "after fact discovery." In the closed case itself, over half of the respondents reported that the central issues were narrowed and framed for resolution after initial disclosure of non-expert documents. For plaintiff attorneys, the most common response in the closed case was at the initial complaint.

Respondents representing primarily defendants tended to favor raising pleading standards, and those representing primarily plaintiffs tended to disfavor raising pleading standards. Respondents representing plaintiffs and defendants about equally were divided on the issue.

Respondents were somewhat open to the general idea of testing simplified procedures, with all parties' consent, in a limited number of districts.

The Rules in general

Respondents were asked several questions about the operation of the Rules and potential changes to the Rules. When respondents were asked to compare the costs of litigation and discovery in the federal and state courts, the responses were mixed; a narrow plurality tended to disagree that litigation and discovery are more expensive in the federal courts than in the state courts.

When asked whether the Rules should be revised to limit electronic discovery specifically, respondents representing primarily plaintiffs tended to disagree and those representing primarily defendants tended to agree. On the other hand, those representing plaintiffs and defendants about equally were opposed to limiting discovery in general but divided about evenly on the specific question of limiting electronic discovery.

A majority of respondents in all three groups supported revising the Rules to enforce discovery obligations more effectively.

More than two-thirds of respondents agreed with the statement that "the procedures employed in the federal courts are generally fair," and a majority disagreed with the statement that "discovery is abused in almost every case in federal court."

Respondents seemed relatively satisfied with current levels of judicial case management in the federal courts.

I. Introduction[1]

In late 2008, the Honorable Mark R. Kravitz, chair of the Judicial Conference's Advisory Committee on Civil Rules ("the Committee"), requested that the Federal Judicial Center ("the Center") conduct research to support the Committee's planned May 2010 conference on civil litigation at Duke University Law School. Judge Kravitz's request indicated that the Committee's "priority is to examine the costs of discovery and to identify successes and problems related to electronic discovery under the revised rules."[2] Judge Kravitz appointed District Judge John Koeltl to chair a planning committee for the 2010 conference. In response to the Committee's request and in consultation with Judges Kravitz and Koeltl and the Committee's reporters, Professors Edward Cooper and Richard Marcus, the Center designed and administered a national, case-based survey of attorneys. The survey was designed to parallel, in several key respects, one previously conducted for the Committee.[3]

This report presents preliminary findings from the survey. A large sample of attorneys listed as counsel in federal civil cases terminated in the last quarter of 2008 were invited to participate; most of the survey questions focused on respondents' experiences in the recently terminated cases. The survey was administered in May and June of 2009. Nearly half of the attorneys invited to participate responded (approximately 47 percent).

The sampling procedures and the attorneys in the sample are described in detail in Appendices A and B of this report. The survey instrument is reproduced in Appendix C. Hundreds of attorneys offered written comments regarding federal practice and the survey; Appendix D of this report reproduces those respondents' comments, which were edited only to protect the confidentiality of respondents.

Section II reports findings on the frequency of various activities related to discovery in general, from the planning stage through the types of discovery permitted under the Federal Rules of Civil Procedure ("the Rules"). It also reports findings on the case management activities of judicial officers in respondents' cases, including the setting of time limits for the completion of discovery and ruling on discovery-related motions. Section III reports findings on electronic discovery activities in respondents' cases, including the frequency of requests for discovery of electronically stored information (ESI) in those cases. Section IV reports findings on respondents' overall evaluations of discovery in the closed cases, including any effect discovery may have had on choice of forum, settlement, and the fairness of the case outcome.

---

[1] We acknowledge the valuable assistance of a number of Center staff members in various stages of preparing and conducting the survey and drafting this report: Jared Bataillon, Joe Cecil, George Cort, Carolyn Dubay, James Eaglin, Meghan Dunn, Christina Fuentes, Jill Gloekler, Donna Stienstra, and Margaret Williams. Several members of the Committee also commented on the survey instrument. Ken Withers of the Sedona Conference provided useful comments on the instrument in general and especially on the electronic discovery questions.

[2] Letter from Honorable Mark R. Kravitz to Honorable Barbara J. Rothstein, Center Director, dated December 4, 2008.

[3] Thomas E. Willging, John Shapard, Donna Stienstra, and Dean Miletich, *Discovery and Disclosure Practice, Problems, and Proposals for Change: A Case-based National Survey of Counsel in Closed Federal Civil Cases* (Federal Judicial Center, 1997) (hereinafter *Discovery and Disclosure*).

Section V reports findings on the costs of the closed cases as estimated by respondents. Costs are then analyzed in relation to the amount at stake in the litigation—including nonmonetary costs—and attorney opinions on the relationship between costs and the stakes of the litigation. Sections VI and VII report findings on respondents' opinions on various topics with respect to federal practice and the operation of the Rules, in general, including proposals to adopt fact pleading and/or simplified procedures in certain kinds of cases.

This report is preliminary. It does not include multivariate analysis of costs, nor does it come close to exhausting the potential of the data collected to shed light on a great range of topics. As readers will see, in many ways the report raises as many questions as it answers. It is intended, more or less, as a framework for discussion for the October meeting of the Committee and for participants in the 2010 conference. The follow-up report to the Committee in March 2010 will seek to address questions raised in the course of that discussion.

II. Discovery Activity in the Closed Cases

Question 1 of the survey asked respondents whether the parties in the closed case conferred to plan for discovery. If only respondents reporting discovery events are included, as shown in Figure 1, 82.4 percent of plaintiff attorneys and 82.6 percent of defendant attorneys reported a conference to plan discovery; 13.3 and 12.9 percent, respectively, reported no conference; and 4.2 and 4.5 percent, respectively, declined to answer ("I can't say").[4]

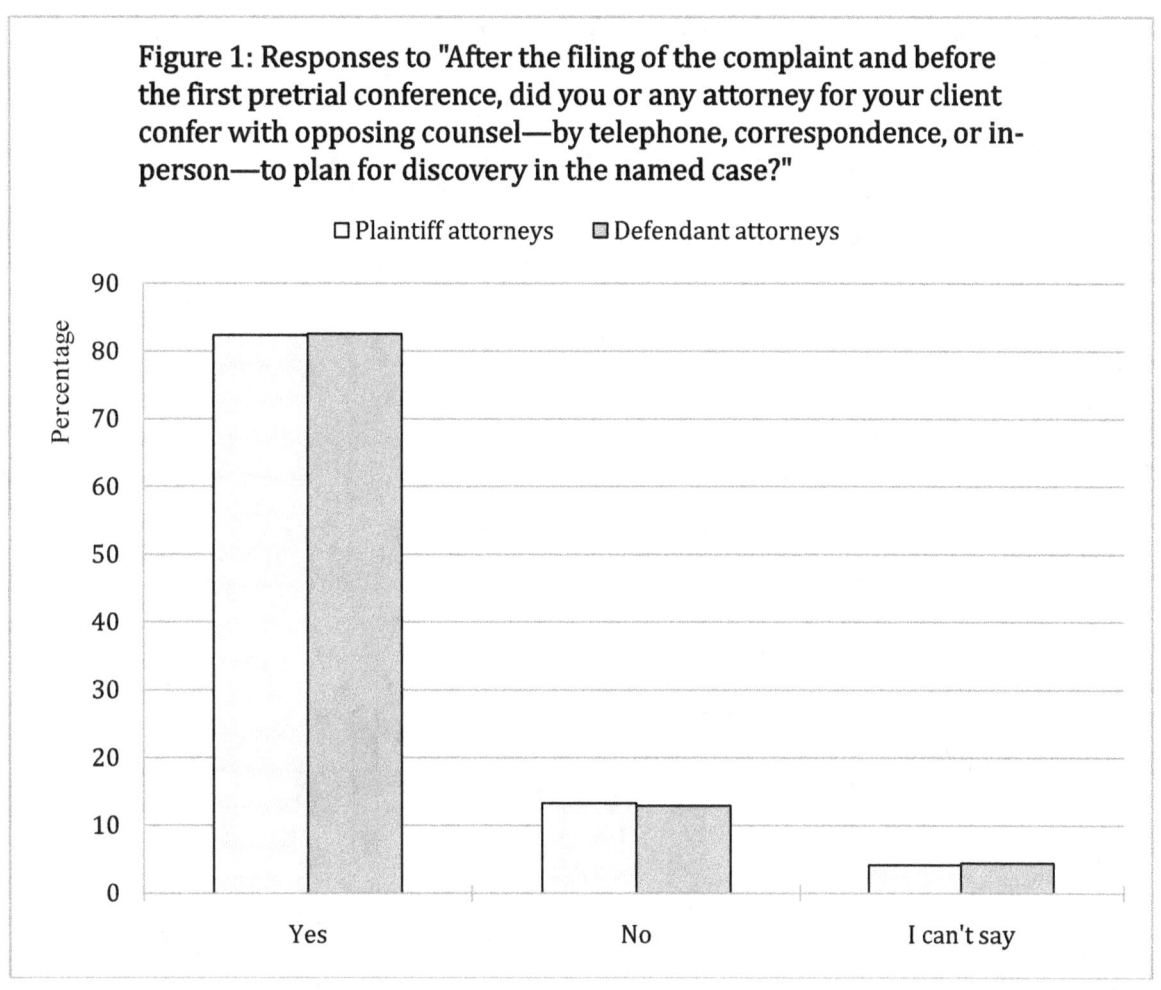

[4] Restricting the analysis to those reporting one or more types of discovery, there were 2,371 total respondents (unweighted), of which 1,183 were attorneys representing a plaintiff in the closed case ("plaintiff attorney") and 1,188 were attorneys representing a defendant in the closed case ("defendant attorney"). The designation of "plaintiff attorney" and "defendant attorney" used in this report is based on how the attorney was designated in the courts' Case Management/Electronic Case Files (CM/ECF) system. In the questions that follow, the number of respondents varies slightly, given non-responses. The weighting of cases is discussed in Appendix A, *infra*.

In question 9, the survey asked respondents whether the following types of discovery occurred in the closed case (in the order presented in the figure): initial disclosure of non-expert documents; informal exchange of documents; informal exchange of other materials; interrogatories; request for production of documents; disclosure of expert reports; deposition of experts; deposition of non-experts; requests for admission; physical or mental examination; inspection of property, computer equipment or media, or designated object; and third-party subpoena. When questions used the term "documents," they specified that it included electronically stored documents. Figure 2 displays the percentage of plaintiff and defendant attorneys responding that a particular type of discovery occurred in the closed case. Fully 86.3 percent of all respondents—89.3 percent of plaintiff attorneys and 83.6 percent of defendant attorneys—reported at least one of the types of discovery in the closed case.

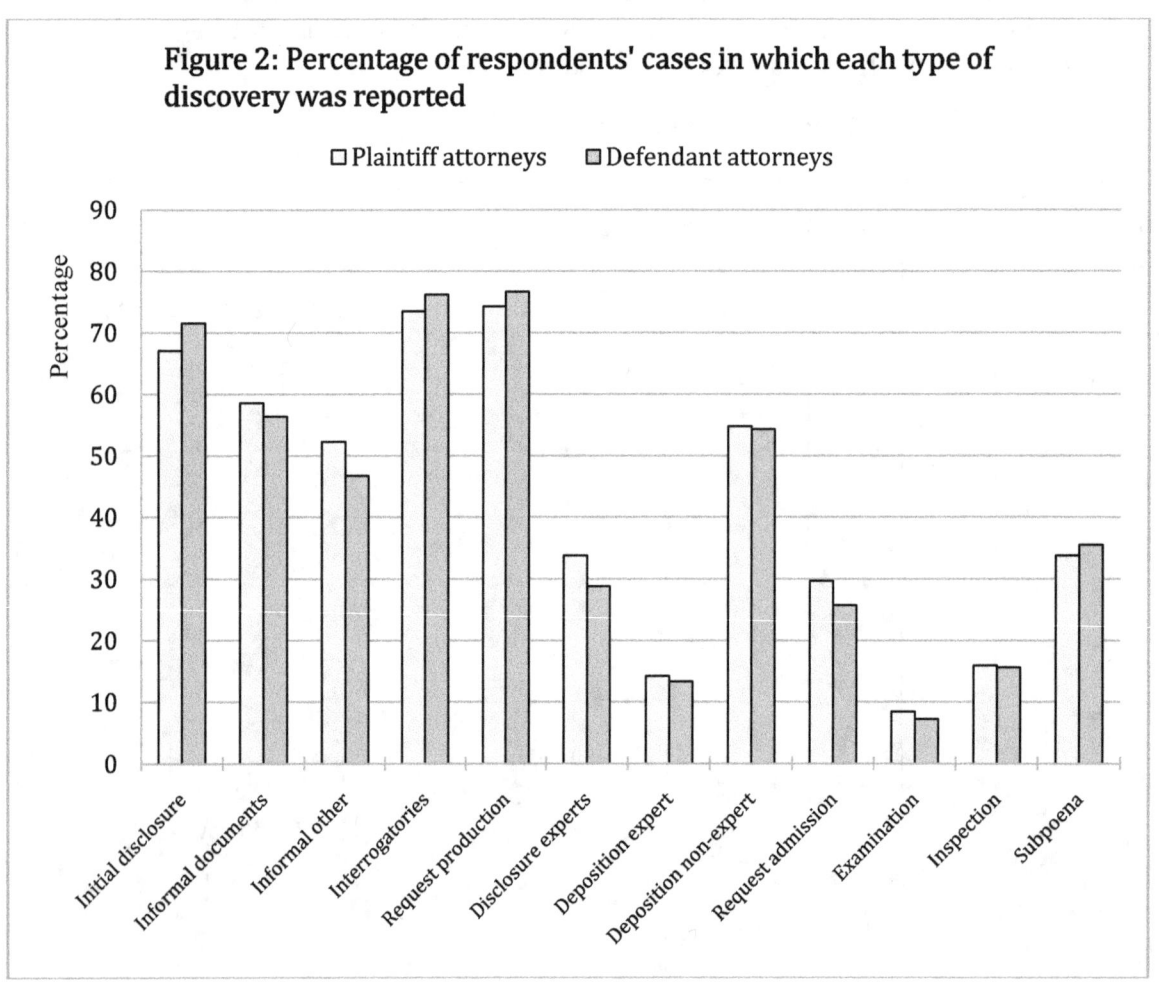

Initial disclosure of non-expert documents. As shown in Figure 2, initial disclosure of non-expert documents(including electronically stored documents) was reported by more than two-thirds of respondents. Fully 67.1 percent of plaintiff attorneys and 71.6 percent of defendant attorneys reported that there was initial disclosure of non-expert documents; 27.8 and 23.3 percent, respectively, reported that there was not initial disclosure, and 5.0 and 5.1 percent, respectively, declined to answer.

Informal exchange of documents. Informal exchange of documents was reported by a majority of respondents, as shown in Figure 2. Fully 58.6 percent of plaintiff attorneys and 56.4 percent of defendant attorneys reported that there had been informal exchange of documents; 37.8 and 38.4 percent, respectively, reported no informal exchange of documents, and 3.6 and 5.2 percent, respectively, declined to answer.

Among those indicating that there was no informal exchange of documents, 27.3 percent of plaintiff attorneys and 21.8 percent of defendant attorneys reported that they discussed making an informal exchange with the other side, even though no such exchange occurred. However, most attorneys in cases without an informal exchange did not discuss making one—67.2 and 73.2 percent, respectively; 5.5 and 4.9 percent, respectively, declined to answer.

Informal exchange of other materials. A majority of plaintiff attorney respondents and slightly less than a majority of defendant attorney respondents reported informal exchange of other materials—52.3 and 46.8 percent, respectively. Fully 43.2 and 46.9 percent of respondents, respectively, reported no informal exchange of other materials, and 4.6 and 6.4 percent, respectively, declined to answer.

Interrogatories. As shown in Figure 2, about three-quarters of respondents reported interrogatories in the closed case, 73.5 percent of plaintiff attorneys and 76.2 percent of defendant attorneys; 24.8 and 21.8 percent, respectively, reported no interrogatories and 1.8 and 2.1 percent, respectively, declined to answer.

Request for production of documents. About three-quarters of respondents reported a request for production of documents, including electronically stored documents, 74.3 percent of plaintiff attorneys and 76.7 percent of defendant attorneys; 22.9 and 21.1 percent, respectively, reported no such requests, and 2.8 and 2.2 percent, respectively, declined to answer.

Disclosure of expert reports. Slightly less than one-third of all respondents reported disclosure of expert reports, 33.8 percent of plaintiff attorneys and 28.8 percent of defendant attorneys; 64.7 and 68.9 percent, respectively, reported no disclosure of expert reports, and 1.5 and 2.3 percent, respectively, declined to answer.

Respondents were also asked how many experts both sides in the closed case identified. The following figures are limited to respondents reporting disclosure of at least one expert witness by one party. As reported by plaintiff attorneys ($n = 444$), the mean number of experts disclosed by plaintiffs was 2.2, and the median was 2; the mean number identified by the defendants, as reported by plaintiff attorneys, was 1.7, and the median was 1. As reported by defendant attorneys ($n = 406$), the mean number reported by defendants was 2.0, and the median was 1; defendant attorneys reported a mean of 2.2 experts disclosed by plaintiffs, and the median was 2.

Deposition of experts. Fewer than 1 respondent in 7 reported any deposition of an expert in the closed case, 14.2 percent of plaintiff attorneys and 13.3 percent of defendant attorneys; 84.8 and 85.5 percent, respectively, reported no expert depositions, and 0.9 and 1.2 percent, respectively, declined to answer.

Respondents were also asked how many experts each side deposed and how many of these depositions lasted more than 7 hours. The following figures are limited to respondents reporting at least one expert deposition by at least one side. The mean number of expert depositions by plaintiffs reported by plaintiff attorneys ($n = 238$) was 1.4 (median = 1); plaintiff attorneys reported a mean of 1.7 expert depositions by defendants (median = 1). The median number of depositions per case lasting more than 7 hours reported by plaintiff attorneys was 0 (zero), and the mean was 0.2. The mean number of expert depositions taken by defendants reported by defendant attorneys ($n = 235$) was 2.1 (median= 1). The mean number of expert depositions taken by plaintiffs reported by defendants was 1.2, and the median was 1. The median number of expert depositions lasting more than 7 hours per case was 0 (zero), and the mean was 0.3.

Deposition of non-experts. A majority of plaintiff attorneys (54.8 percent) and defendant attorneys (54.3 percent) reported one or more depositions of non-experts in the closed case; 44.6 and 44.7 percent, respectively, reported no non-expert depositions, and 0.6 and 1.0 percent, respectively, declined to answer.

Respondents were also asked how many non-experts each side deposed and how many of these depositions lasted more than 7 hours. The following figures are limited to respondents reporting at least one non-expert deposition by at least one side. The mean number of non-expert depositions taken by plaintiffs reported by plaintiff attorneys ($n = 724$) was 3.8, and the median was 3; the mean number of non-expert depositions taken by defendants reported by plaintiff attorneys was 2.8, and the median was 2. The median number of non-expert depositions per case reported by plaintiff attorneys as lasting more than 7 hours was 0 (zero), and the mean number was 0.8. The mean number of non-expert depositions taken by defendants reported by defendant attorneys ($n = 730$) was 2.6, and the median was 2. The mean number of non-expert depositions taken by plaintiffs reported by defendant attorneys was 3.1, and the median was 2. The median number of non-expert depositions per case reported by defendant attorneys as lasting more than 7 hours was 0 (zero), and the mean number was 0.3.

Requests for admission. More than one-quarter of respondents reported requests for admissions in the closed case, 29.7 percent of plaintiff attorneys and 25.7 percent of defendant attorneys; 64.9 and 67.4 percent, respectively, reported no requests for admission, and 5.4 and 6.9 percent, respectively, declined to answer.

Respondents were also asked how many such requests each side propounded to the other. The following figures are limited to cases with at least one request propounded by at least one side. Plaintiff attorneys ($n = 344$) reported a mean number of requests for admission propounded by plaintiffs of 22 per case, and a median of 15, and a mean number of requests propounded by defendants of 20.8, and a median of 0 (zero). Defendant attorneys ($n = 296$) reported a mean number of requests propounded by defendants of 13.2 per case, and a median of 9, and a mean number of requests propounded by plaintiffs of 21.9 per case, and a median of 4.

Physical or mental examination. Fewer than 1 in 10 respondents reported a physical or mental examination in the closed case, 8.4 percent of plaintiff attorneys and 7.2 percent of defendant attorneys; 90.6 and 91.7 percent, respectively, reported no such examination, and 1.0 and 1.1 percent, respectively, declined to answer.

Inspection of property, computer equipment or media, or designated objects. Fully 15.9 percent of plaintiff attorneys and 15.6 percent of defendant attorneys reported an inspection of property, including computer equipment, in the closed case; 82.9 and 83.4 percent, respectively, reported no inspection, and 1.1 and 1.0 percent, respectively, declined to answer.

Third-party subpoena. More than 1 in 3 respondents reported a third-party subpoena in the closed case, 33.8 percent of plaintiff attorneys and 35.5 percent of defendant attorneys; 62.9 and 59.7 percent, respectively, reported no subpoena, and 3.3 and 4.8 percent, respectively, declined to answer.

Respondents were also asked how many third-party subpoenas were issued by each side. The following figures are limited to respondents reporting at least one third-party subpoena by one side in the closed case. Plaintiff attorneys ($n = 437$) reported a mean number of subpoenas issued by plaintiffs of 3.3 per case, and a median of 1; plaintiff attorneys reported a mean number of subpoenas issued by defendants of 3.9 per case, and a median of 1. Defendant attorneys ($n = 468$) reported a mean number of subpoenas issued by defendants of 3.8 per case, and a median of 3; defendant attorneys reported a mean number of subpoenas issued by plaintiffs of 1.1, and a median of 0 (zero).

In order to measure (in a fairly rough fashion) the volume of discovery in each closed case, we calculated a simple additive index. For example, a case in which the respondent reported only an informal exchange of documents would receive a score of 1, a case with an informal exchange of documents and an informal exchange of other materials would receive a score of 2, and so on. The maximum score is 12, for the few cases in which every type of discovery asked about in the survey(and as displayed in Figure 2) was reported to have occurred. In cases with at least one reported discovery type, the mean number of discovery types for plaintiff attorneys ($n = 1,184$) and defendant attorneys ($n = 1,193$) was 5.1 per closed case, and the median for both groups was 5 types of discovery per case.

Respondents were asked in question 50 to estimate, in general, what percentage of their practice is spent in discovery-related activities. Not surprisingly, respondents representing primarily defendants, in general, reported that a greater percentage of their time was consumed by discovery-related activities than did those representing primarily plaintiffs or those reporting that they represent plaintiffs and defendants about equally. Respondents representing primarily plaintiffs gave a median response of 40 percent of their practice spent in discovery-related activities, and a mean of 42.7 percent. The 10th percentile response was 10 percent, and the 95th percentile was 85 percent ($n = 759$). Respondents representing plaintiffs and defendants about equally in their practice reported a median of 30 percent, and a mean of 36.4 percent. The 10th percentile was 10 percent, and the 95th percentile was 75 percent ($n = 548$). Respondents representing primarily defendants reported a median of 50 percent of their practice time spent in discovery-related activities, and a mean of 47.7 percent. The 10th percentile for this group was 20 percent, and the 95th percentile was 85 percent ($n = 1,002$).

Question 6 asked respondents whether the court adopted a discovery plan in the closed case. As shown in Figure 3, about three-quarters of respondents in closed cases with at least one type of discovery reported that the court had adopted a discovery plan. Fully 72.6 percent of plaintiff attorneys and 75.6 percent of defendant attorneys reporting some discovery activity in the case indicated that the court adopted a plan; 22.4 and 18.5 percent, respectively, reported that the court did not adopt a plan; and 5.0 and 5.9 percent, respectively, declined to answer.

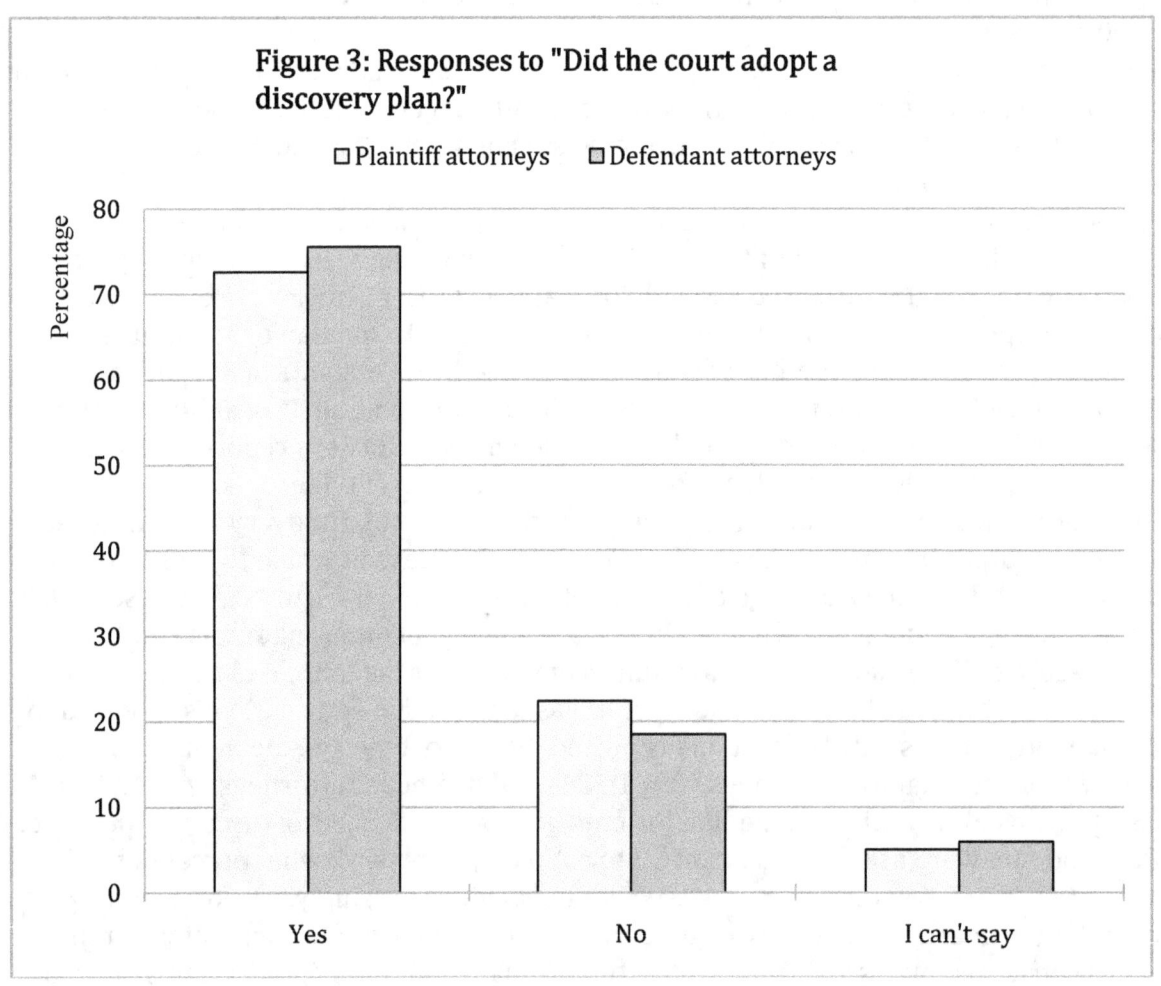

Respondents were asked, in question 20, whether a judicial officer (including a special master or other neutral) performed various actions that have been grouped under the heading "case management." As shown in Figure 4, one of the most common responses, reported by 45.2 percent of plaintiff attorneys and 44.6 percent of defendant attorneys, was to limit the time for completion of discovery.[5] Plaintiff attorneys ($n = 466$) and defendant attorneys ($n = 483$) reported the same median (6 months) and mean (7.3 months) time limitations.

---

[5] In cases with one or more reported discovery events (weighted); $n = 2,379$, with 1,193 plaintiff attorneys and 1,184 defendant attorneys responding.

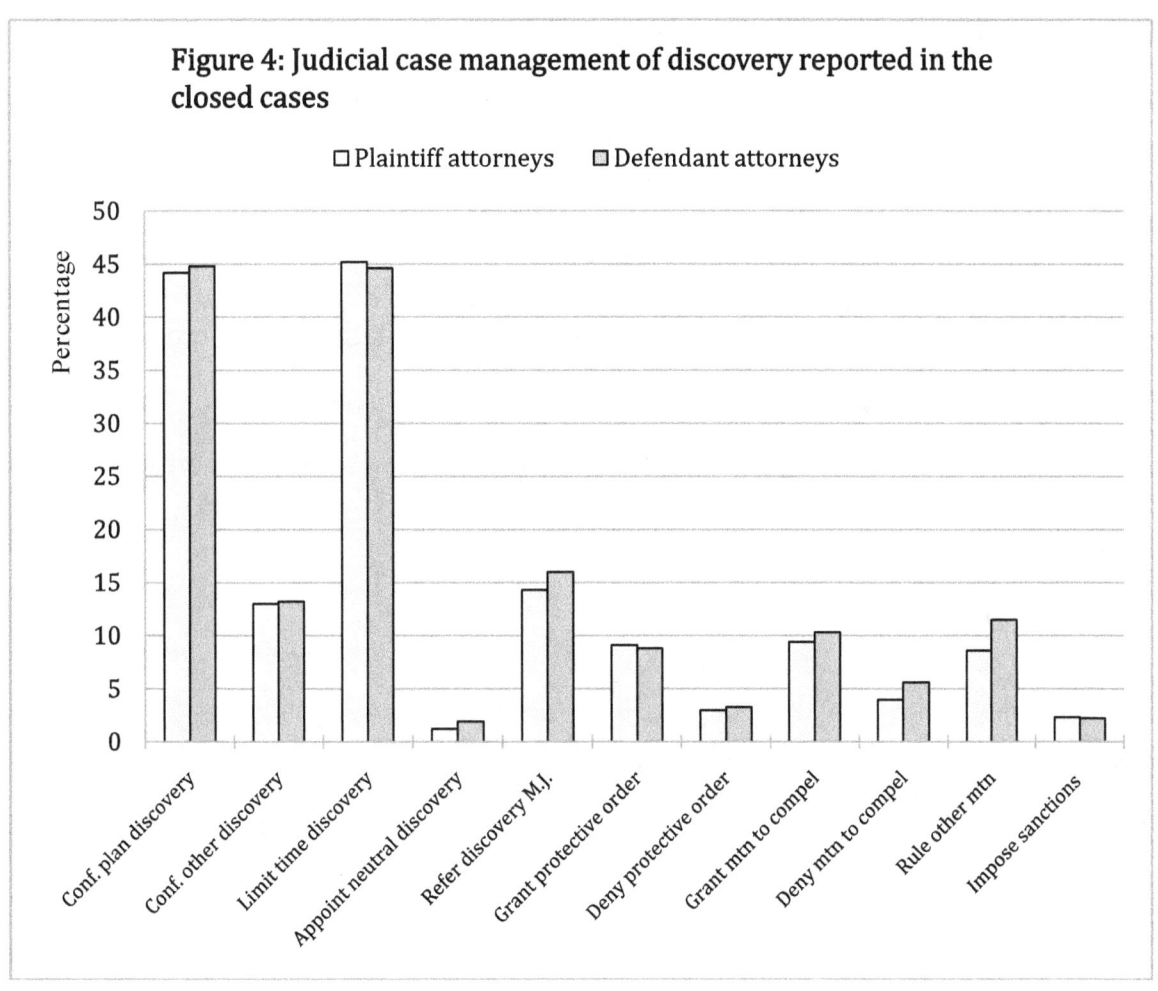

Figure 4: Judicial case management of discovery reported in the closed cases

The other most common response was the judicial officer held a conference (by telephone, correspondence, or in-person) to consider a plan for discovery. Fully 44.2 percent of defendant attorneys and 44.8 percent of plaintiff attorneys reported that a judicial officer held such a conference. No other action was reported by more than 20 percent of respondents. The district judge in the closed case referred a discovery issue to a magistrate judge in 14.3 percent of plaintiff attorneys' cases and in 16.0 percent of defendant attorneys' cases. Few cases saw the appointment of a neutral to oversee discovery matters; this was reported by 1.2 percent of plaintiff attorneys and 1.9 percent of defendant attorneys.

The court granted motions to compel discovery in 9.4 percent of plaintiff attorneys' cases and in 10.3 percent of defendant attorneys' cases, and denied motions to compel in 4.0 and 5.6 percent, respectively. The court granted a protective order in 9.1 percent of plaintiff attorneys' cases and in 8.8 percent of defendant attorneys' cases, and denied a motion for a protective order in 3.0 and 3.3 percent, respectively. The court also ruled on another discovery-related motion in 8.6 and 11.5 percent of cases, respectively. A discovery conference, other than to plan for discovery, was held in 13 and 13.2 percent of cases, respectively.

Sanctions related to discovery were reported in 2.3 percent of the plaintiff attorneys' cases and 2.2 percent of the defendant attorneys' cases.

Respondents were also asked whether the court ruled on various types of motions. The responses are summarized in Table 1. Rulings on Rule 56 summary judgment motions were reported by more than a quarter of respondents—by 25.1 percent of plaintiff attorneys and 27.7 percent of defendant attorneys.[6] Rulings on Rule 12(b)(6) motions to dismiss for failure to state a claim were reported by 11.0 and 13.2 percent, respectively. Rulings on other Rule 12(b) motions to dismiss were reported by 7.5 and 7.8 percent, respectively. Rulings on Rule 12(c) and 12(e) motions were relatively uncommon.

Table 1: Rulings on motions, cases with at least one reported type of discovery

Type of Motion	Plaintiff attorneys (%)	Defendant attorneys (%)
Rule 12(b)(6)	11.0	13.2
Other Rule 12(b)	7.5	7.8
Rule 12(c)	1.6	1.7
Rule 12(e)	1.2	1.1
Rule 56	25.1	27.7
Can't say	7.7	7.3
N	1,176	1,193

---

[6] Rulings on summary judgment motions were much more common in the cases terminated by trial (67.1 percent of all respondents in such cases) and in the long-pending cases (62.5 percent) than in cases selected at random (23.8 percent). See Appendix A for more information on these cases.

III. Electronic Discovery Activity in the Closed Cases

Respondents were asked, in question 2, whether the conference to plan discovery included discussion of ESI. About 1 in 3 respondents reported that the conference included discussion of ESI, 34.8 percent of plaintiff attorneys and 33.0 percent of defendant attorneys.[7] More than half of all respondents reported that the conference to plan for discovery did not include discussion of ESI—57.6 percent of plaintiff attorneys and 57.4 percent of defendant attorneys; 7.6 and 9.6 percent, respectively, declined to answer. The distribution of responses is displayed in Figure 5.

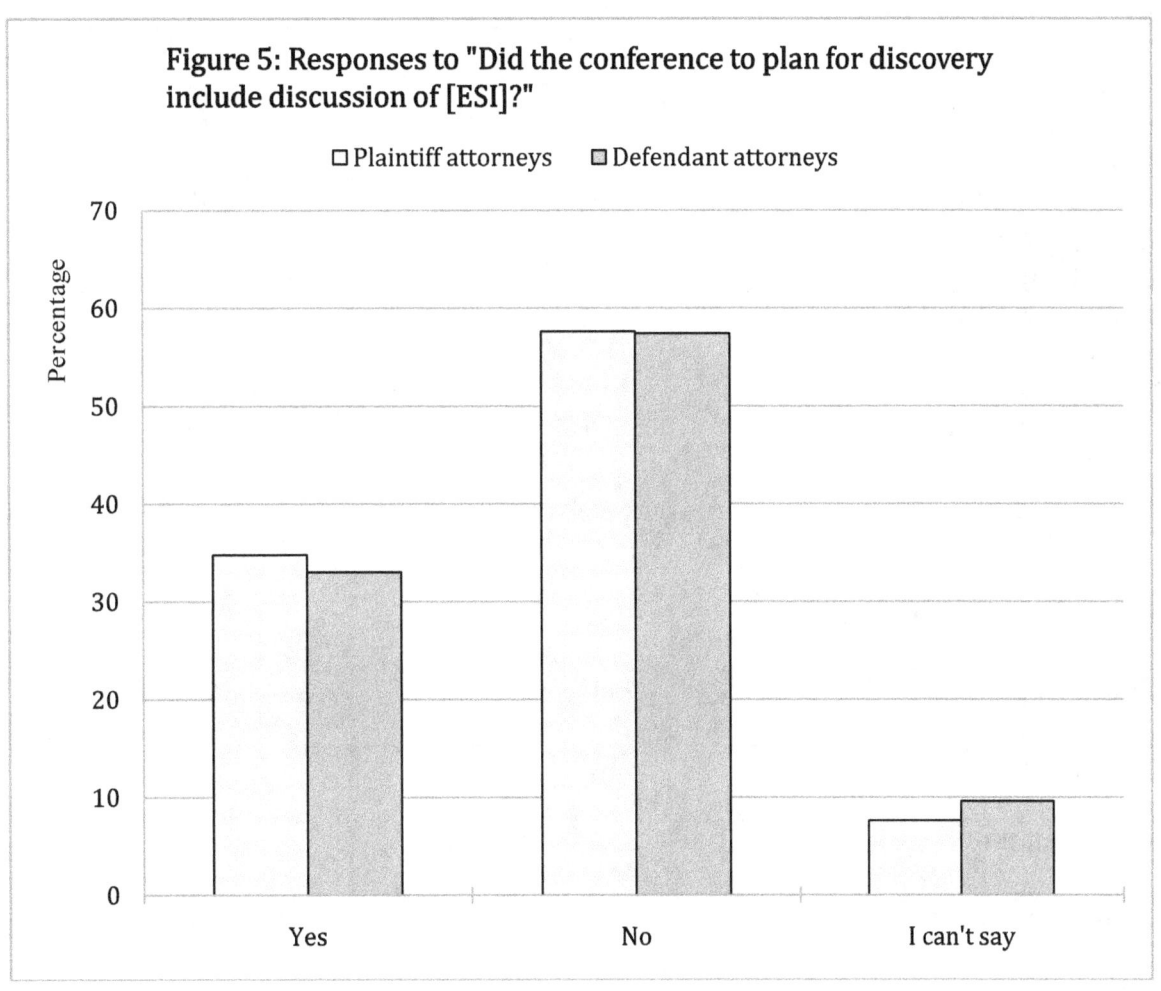

Figure 5: Responses to "Did the conference to plan for discovery include discussion of [ESI]?"

---

[7] In cases in which a conference to plan discovery was reported, there were 1,926 total respondents, composed of 959 attorneys representing plaintiffs in the closed case and 967 attorneys representing defendants in the closed case.

Only about 1 respondent in 5 reported that the discovery plan adopted by the court included provisions related to ESI—20.1 percent of plaintiff attorneys and 22.5 percent of defendant attorneys (question 7).

In closed cases in which the conference to plan for discovery included discussion of ESI, respondents were asked to identify which of a series of potential issues were discussed (questions 3 and 4). Question 3 focused on issues related to the collection of ESI. The distribution of responses to question 3 is summarized in Table 2.

Table 2: Reported issues related to collection of ESI, in cases where ESI issues were discussed at discovery conference

Issue	Plaintiff attorneys (%)	Defendant attorneys (%)
Parties' practices re: retention of ESI	46.5	55.5
Scope, method, duration of preserving ESI	36.1	37.5
Potential cost or burden of collecting, reviewing, and producing ESI	34.4	36.0
Restricting scope or altogether avoiding discovery of ESI	32.8	41.9
Whether ESI stored or in format "not reasonably accessible"	22.0	15.6
Methods of searching by topic	17.1	18.7
Methods of searching by custodian	19.3	18.5
Possibility of phased discovery of ESI	12.0	10.3
Possibility of sampling	3.8	6.0
Culling techniques	8.5	11.2
Dynamic database issues	2.5	4.2
Voicemail, etc.	6.8	6.3
N	316	312

For both plaintiff and defendant attorneys, the most common reported issue related to collection was the parties' practices with respect to retention of ESI, reported by 46.5 percent of plaintiff attorneys and 55.5 percent of defendant attorneys. For plaintiff attorneys, the next most common topics were the scope, cost, method, or duration of preserving ESI (36.1 percent); the potential cost or burden of collecting, reviewing, and producing ESI (34.4 percent); restricting the scope or avoiding altogether the discovery of ESI (32.8 percent); and whether potentially responsive information was stored on a device or in a format that a party considered "not reasonably accessible" (22.0 percent). For defendant attorneys, the next most common responses were restricting the scope or avoiding altogether the discovery of ESI (41.9 percent); the scope, cost, method, or duration of preserving ESI (37.5 percent); and the potential cost or burden of collecting, reviewing, and producing ESI (36 percent).

No other issue related to collection of ESI was reported to have been discussed by more than 20 percent of either plaintiff or defendant attorneys in closed cases in which the discovery conference included discussion of ESI. Defendant attorneys reported discussing whether potentially responsive information was stored on a device or in a format that a party considered "not reasonably accessible" 15.6 percent of the time. Parties reported discussing methods of searching for or reducing the scope of responsive documents by topic, including search terms—by 17.1 percent of plaintiff attorneys and 18.7 percent of defendant attorneys—and methods of searching for or reducing the scope of responsive documents by custodian, in 19.3 and 18.5 percent, respectively. Discussion of the possibility of phased discovery of ESI was reported by 12 and 10.3 percent, respectively; discussion of the possibility of sampling to determine whether production was justified, by 3.8 and 6 percent, respectively; and discussion of the use of culling techniques such as date ranges or file extensions, by 8.5 and 11.2 percent, respectively. Issues related to information contained in dynamic databases was reported discussed by 2.5 percent of plaintiff attorneys and 4.2 percent of defendant attorneys, and issues related to Instant Messaging, Voicemail, and the like, by 6.8 and 6.3 percent, respectively.

Question 4 focused on issues related to the production of ESI. The distribution of responses is summarized in Table 3. The most common response for both plaintiff attorneys (51.1 percent of those reporting that the discovery conference included discussion of ESI) and defendant attorneys (46.1 percent) was the format of production of ESI (e.g., pdf, tiff, native format). The next most common responses for both groups were methods of handling confidential or trade secret information, confidential communications, or information subject to work-product privilege, reported by 38.3 percent of plaintiff attorneys and 36.5 percent of defendant attorneys, and the media of production of ESI (e.g., paper printouts, compact disks, hard drives), reported by 31.9 and 36.7 percent, respectively. Fully 29.1 percent of plaintiff attorneys and 26.4 percent of defendant attorneys reported discussing privilege log issues, and 27.7 and 26.2 percent, respectively, reported discussing the media on which the parties routinely maintain their ESI.

Table 3: Reported issues related to production of ESI, in cases where ESI issues were discussed at discovery conference

Issue	Plaintiff attorneys (%)	Defendant attorneys (%)
Format of production of ESI (pdf, tiff, native format)	51.1	46.1
Confidential, trade secret, privileged communications	38.3	36.5
Media of production of ESI	31.9	36.7
Privilege log issues	29.1	26.4
Media/how parties routinely maintain ESI	27.7	26.2
Indexing/organizing responsive documents	14.1	12.8
"Claw back" agreements	13.6	17.4
Production of metadata	11.2	13.6
Load files	10.9	8.7
"Quick peek" agreements	3.6	2.1
N	316	312

Other issues related to production of ESI were reported less often: document indexing or other methods of organizing responsive electronic documents (14.1 percent of plaintiff attorneys and 12.8 percent of defendant attorneys); so-called "claw back" agreements (13.6 and 17.4 percent, respectively); the production of metadata (11.2 and 13.6 percent, respectively); the need for, or content of, accompanying load files (10.9 and 8.7 percent, respectively); and so-called "quick peek" agreements (3.6 and 2.1 percent, respectively).

Respondents were asked, in question 5, whether their client in the closed case had placed a litigation hold or "freeze" on deletion of ESI in anticipation of or in response to the filing of the complaint. The distribution of responses, in cases with one or more reported discovery events, is displayed in Figure 6. Fully 18.7 percent of plaintiff attorneys and 40.6 percent of defendant attorneys reported that their client in the closed case had initiated such a hold; 63 and 37 percent, respectively, reported no such hold; and 18.3 and 22.4 percent, respectively, declined to answer. The much higher percentage of defendant attorneys reporting litigation holds makes sense in light of the expectation—supported below—that defendants are more likely to be producing parties than are plaintiffs.

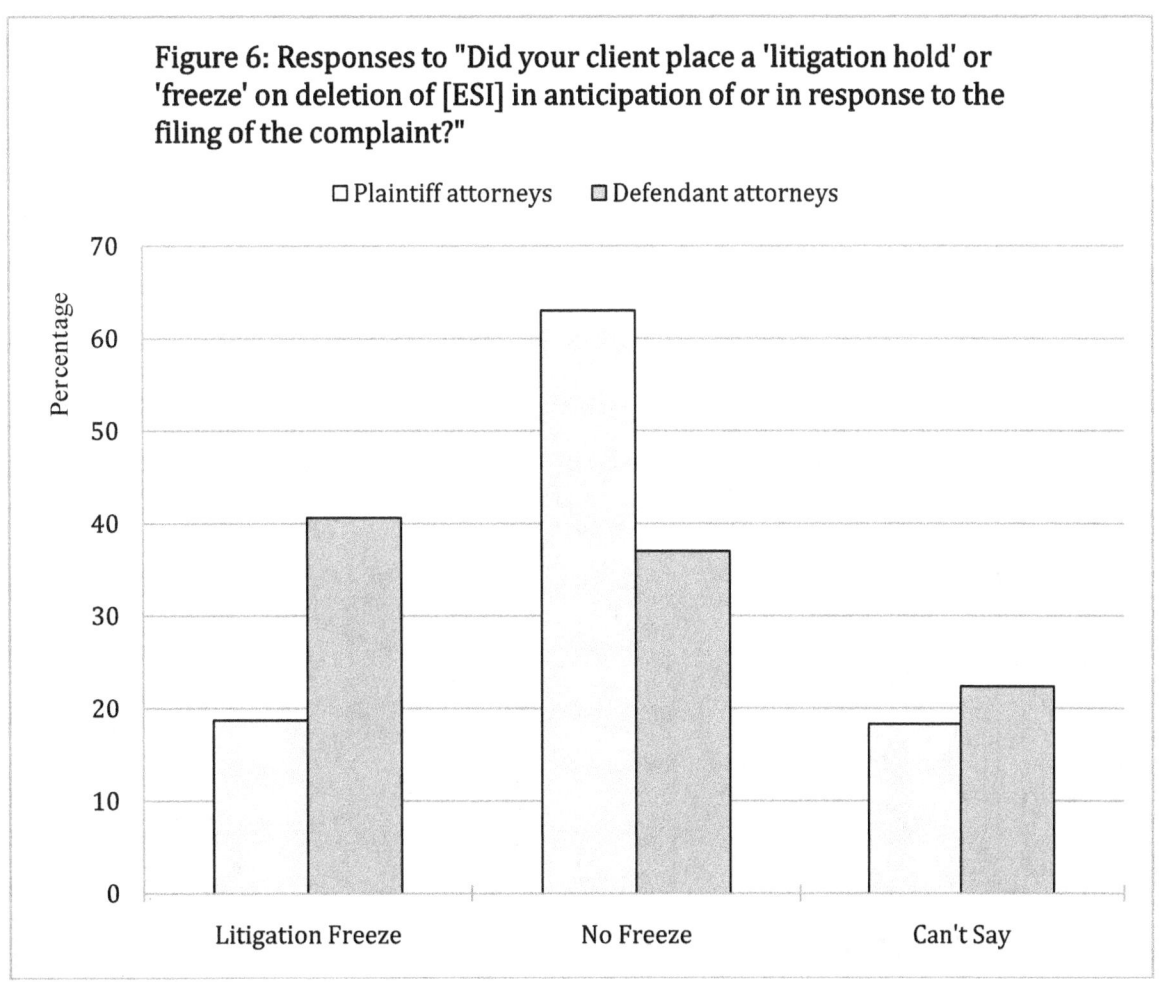

Figure 6: Responses to "Did your client place a 'litigation hold' or 'freeze' on deletion of [ESI] in anticipation of or in response to the filing of the complaint?"

As displayed in Figure 7, requests for production of ESI were reported by 36.1 percent of respondents—38.9 percent of plaintiff attorneys and 33.4 percent of defendant attorneys. Again, a majority of respondents—54.1 percent of plaintiff attorneys and 59.1 percent of defendant attorneys—reported that no party requested production of ESI in discovery in the closed case. In more than a quarter of cases with a request for production of ESI, respondents reported no discussion of ESI at the conference to plan for discovery (25.5 and 29.8 percent, respectively).

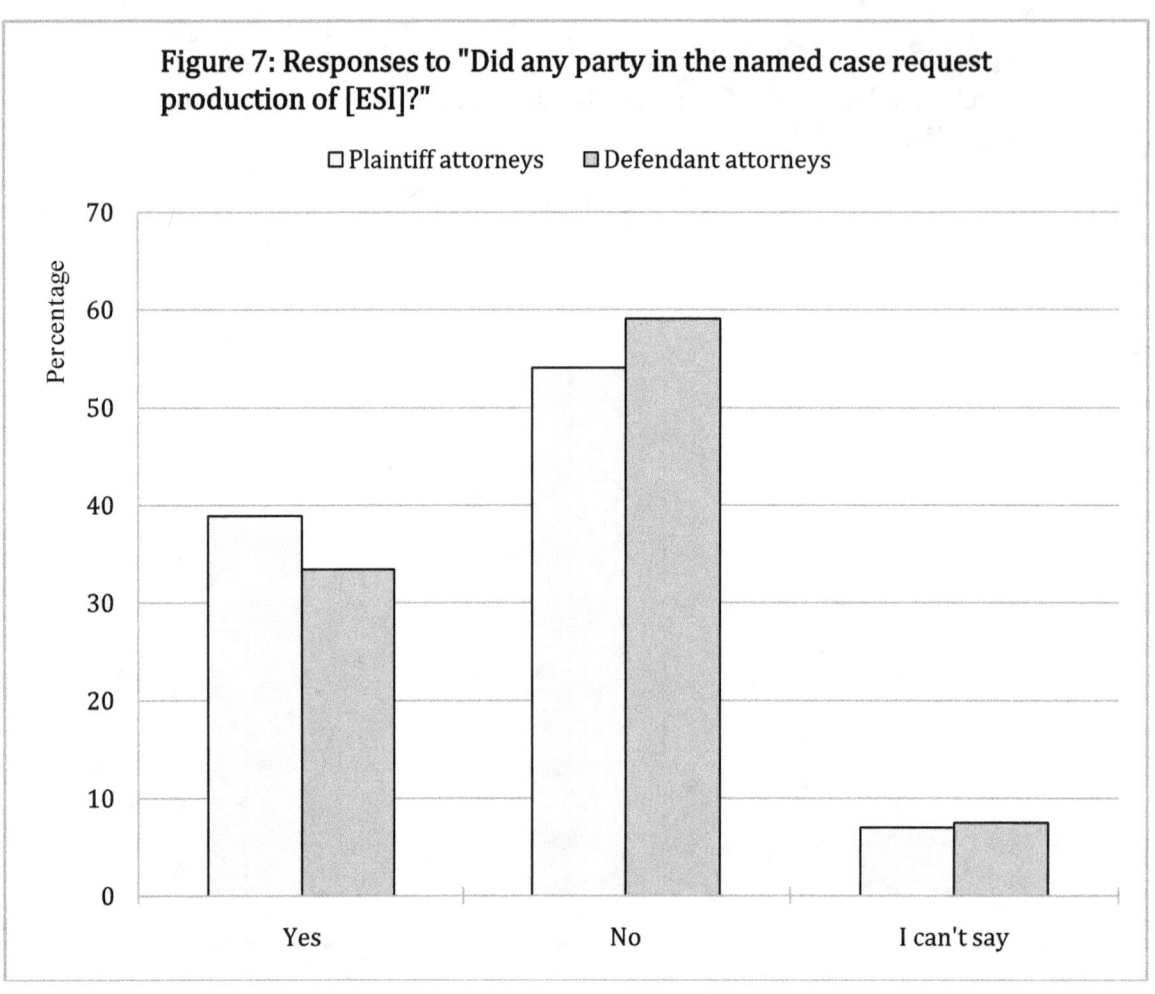

Figure 7: Responses to "Did any party in the named case request production of [ESI]?"

Respondents reporting a request for production of ESI in the closed case were asked whether their clients were producing parties, requesting parties, or both producing and requesting parties (question 11). The distribution of responses is displayed in Figure 8. As one would expect, plaintiff attorneys were more likely to be requesting parties (55.1 percent) than producing parties (4.0 percent), although a sizeable proportion of plaintiff attorneys reported that, in the closed case, their client was both a producing and requesting party (41.0 percent). In other words, plaintiff attorneys reported requesting status in 96 percent of cases in which they reported a request for ESI. Defendant attorneys were less likely to be requesting parties (12.7 percent) than producing parties (34.7 percent), but in cases with electronic discovery they most often reported being both a producing and requesting party (52.7 percent). Somewhat surprisingly, defendant attorneys reported requesting status in 65.4 percent of cases in which they reported a request for ESI. The majority of ESI cases in the sample, then, involved requests for production of ESI from both sides of the litigation.

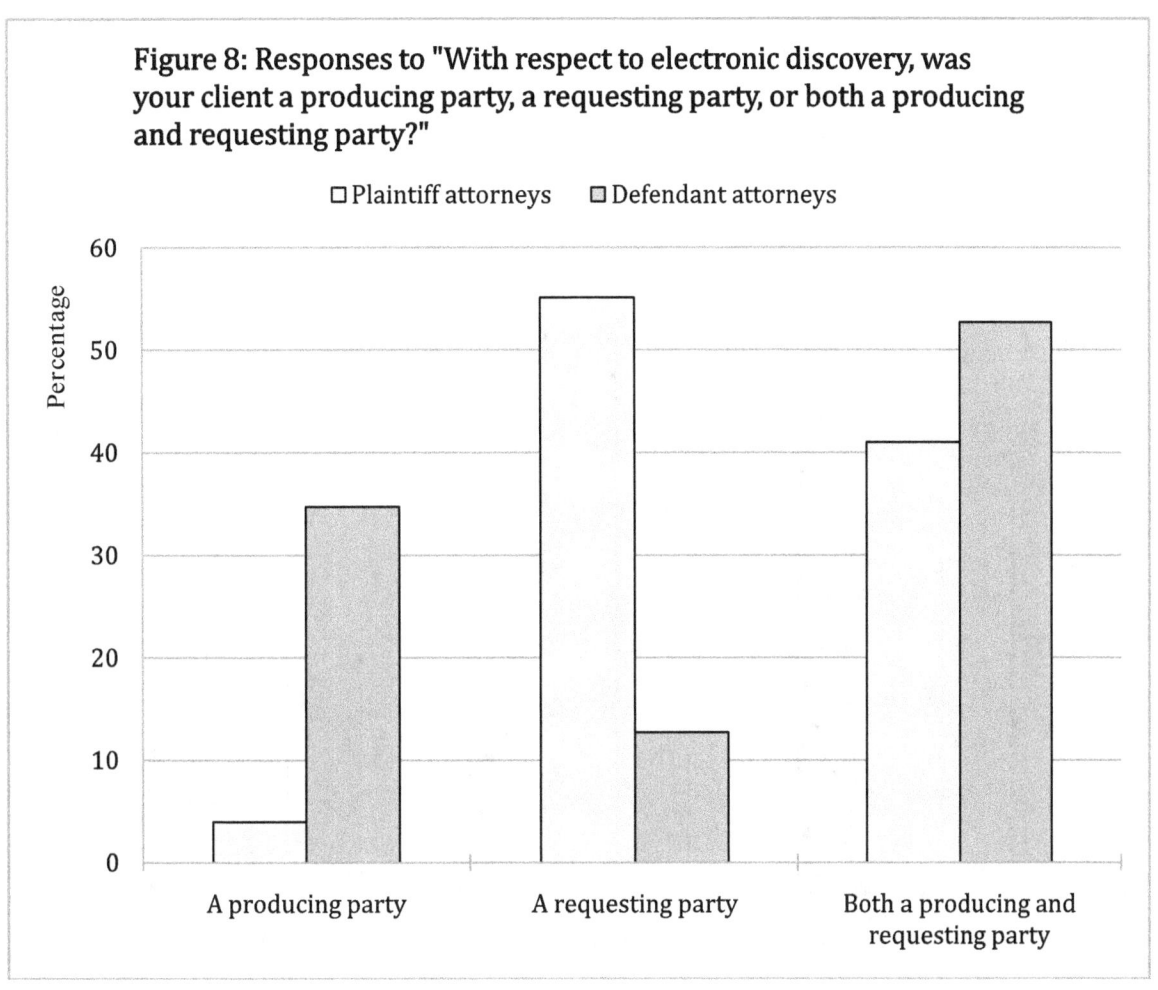

Figure 8: Responses to "With respect to electronic discovery, was your client a producing party, a requesting party, or both a producing and requesting party?"

Producing parties, including parties that requested and produced ESI, were more likely to have initiated a litigation freeze. The distribution of these responses is displayed in Figure 9. Parties that both produced and requested ESI reported litigation freezes in 52.6 percent of cases, and parties that produced only reported initiated freezes in 47.5 percent of cases. Requesting only parties, by contrast, initiated litigation freezes in just 21.4 percent of cases and reported no such freeze in 60.3 percent of cases. Again, relatively high levels of respondents declined to answer the question—26.1 percent of producing parties, 18.3 percent of requesting parties, and 15.8 percent of parties both producing and requesting ESI. In short, the actual incidence of litigation freezes may be higher than shown in the figure.

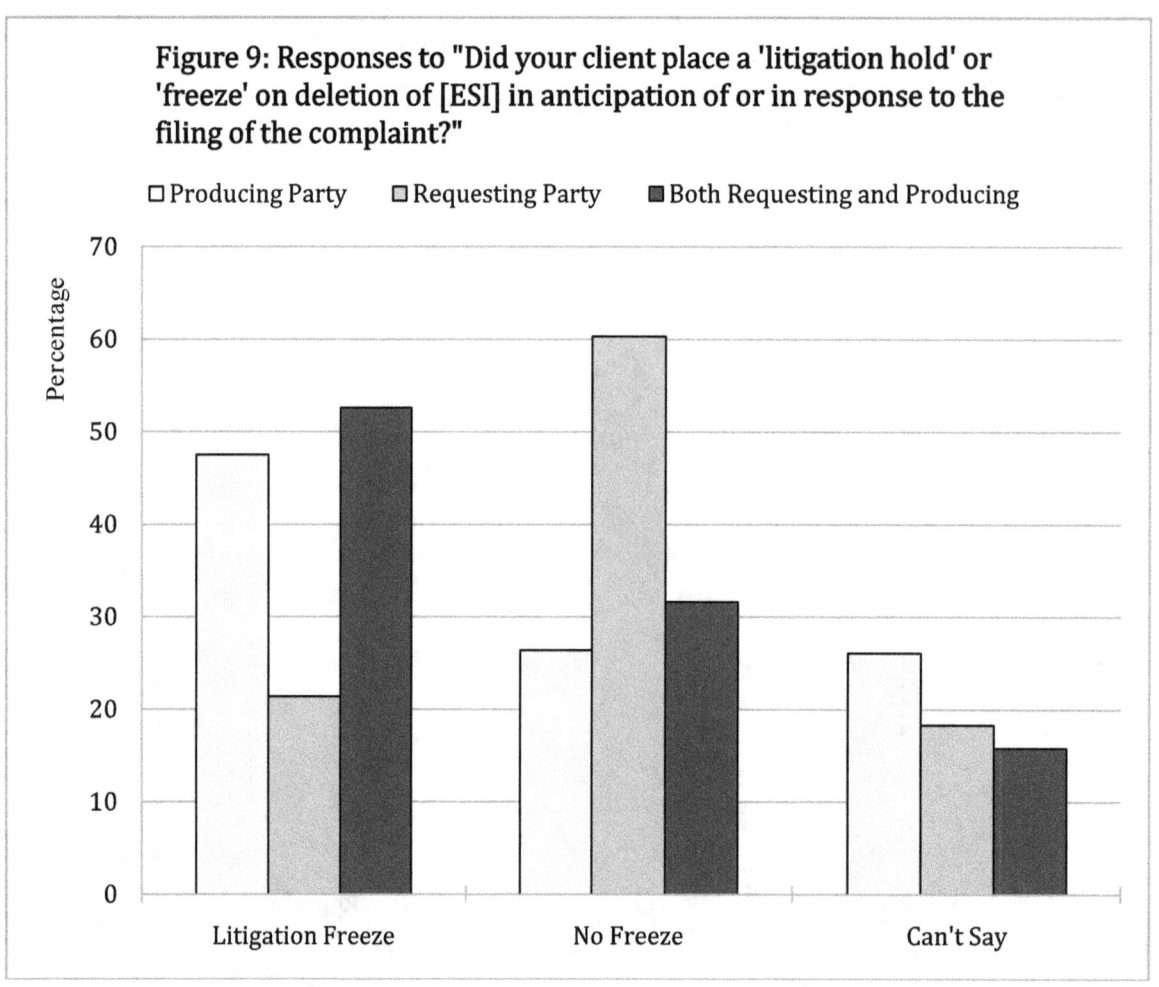

Figure 9: Responses to "Did your client place a 'litigation hold' or 'freeze' on deletion of [ESI] in anticipation of or in response to the filing of the complaint?"

Respondents were asked to estimate the percentage of the ESI collected on behalf of their clients that was reviewed for responsiveness and privilege prior to production. The median response for both plaintiff and defendant attorneys was 100 percent, although the mean responses for plaintiff and defendant attorneys were 63.3 and 64.9 percent, respectively. Respondents were then asked to estimate the percentage of ESI collected on their clients' behalf that was produced as responsive and non-privileged. The median response for plaintiff attorneys was 65.0 percent, and the mean was 53.7 percent. The median response for defendant attorneys was 50.0 percent, and the mean was 51.5 percent.

Respondents were asked to identify resources used in collecting and producing ESI. The following figures represent the responses of producing parties only. The most common response for both plaintiff and defendant attorneys was information technology (IT) staff internal to the client—30.7 percent for plaintiff attorneys and 54.3 percent of defendant attorneys—followed by IT staff internal to the law firm—30.2 and 32.2 percent, respectively. Relatively few respondents, 15.3 and 14.5 percent, respectively, reported using an IT vendor (not internal to the law firm or the client). Similarly, relatively few respondents reported using contract attorneys to conduct responsiveness review—5.6 and 6.7 percent, respectively—or privilege review—5.0 and 6.4 percent, respectively. About 1 in 7 respondents declined to answer this question.

Respondents were asked whether, prior to the filing of the closed case, the client had implemented an enterprise content management system or other information system designed to facilitate the identification and production of ESI in litigation. (This question was only asked of producing parties.) Only 6.4 percent of plaintiff attorneys and 22.4 percent of defendant attorneys reported that their client had implemented such a system. Fully 74.5 percent of plaintiff attorneys and 39.5 percent of defendant attorneys reported that the client had not implemented such a system; 19.1 and 38.1 percent, respectively, declined to answer.

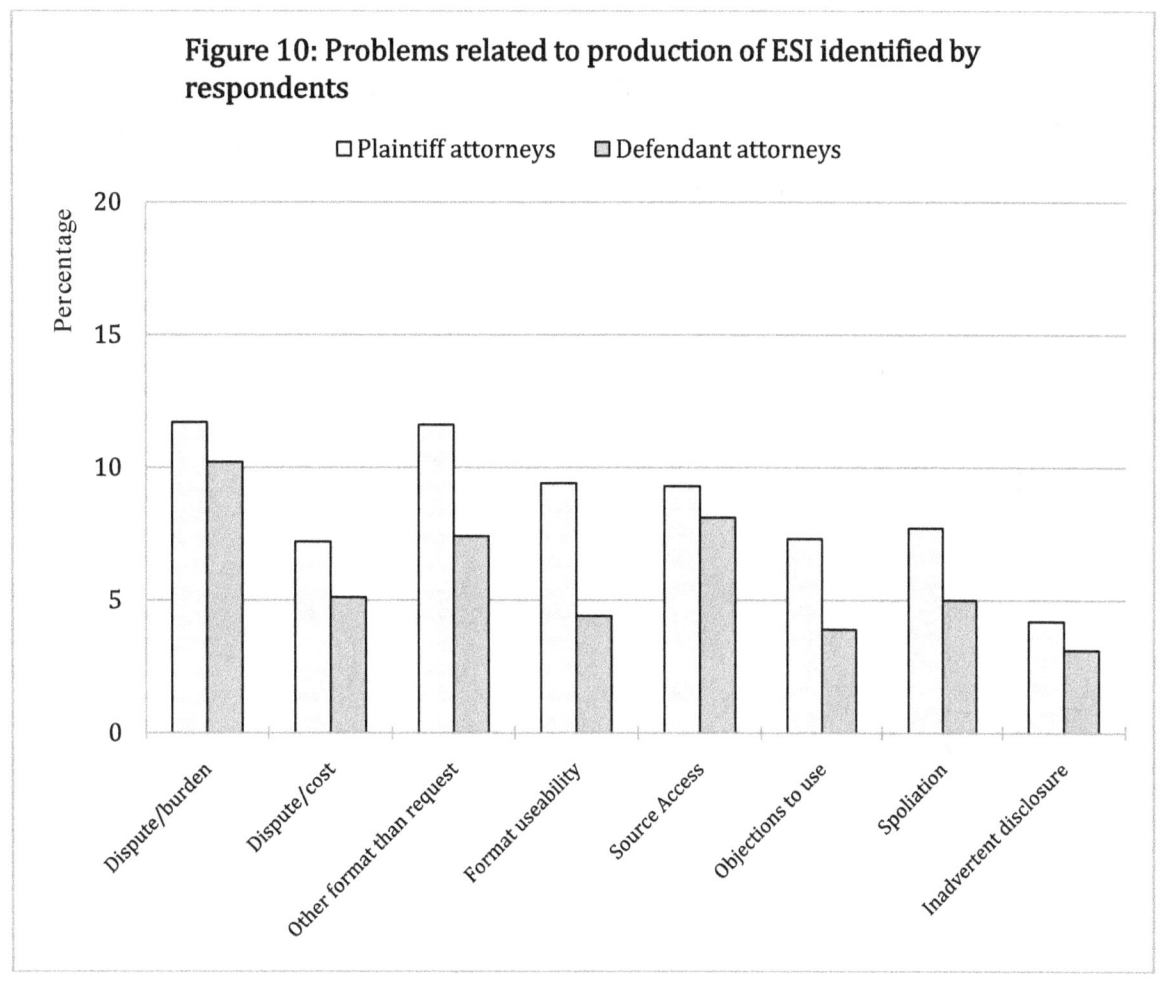

Respondents were asked, in question 18, about a number of possible problems or disputes that could arise over electronic discovery. The distribution of responses is displayed in Figure 10. The percentages shown are the percentages of respondents in electronic discovery cases. Plaintiff attorneys were more likely to report problems than defendant attorneys, which is probably related to their greater likelihood of being a requesting party.

The most commonly reported problem was a dispute over the burden of production of ESI that could not be resolved without court action, which plaintiff attorneys reported in 11.7 percent of ESI cases; defendant attorneys reported this dispute in 10.2 percent of ESI cases. The next most common problem was the production of ESI in a format other than that requested, which was reported by 11.6 percent of plaintiff attorneys and 7.4 percent of defendant attorneys. This was followed by the production of ESI that the requesting party asserted was not reasonably useable, reported by 9.4 percent of plaintiff attorneys but only 4.4 percent of defendant attorneys; requests to obtain ESI from a source the producing party contended was not reasonably accessible, reported by 9.3 and 8.1 percent, respectively; and claims of spoliation, reported by 7.7 and 5 percent, respectively. Other problems (disputes over cost, objections to use of ESI on grounds that it was not properly disclosed) were less common.

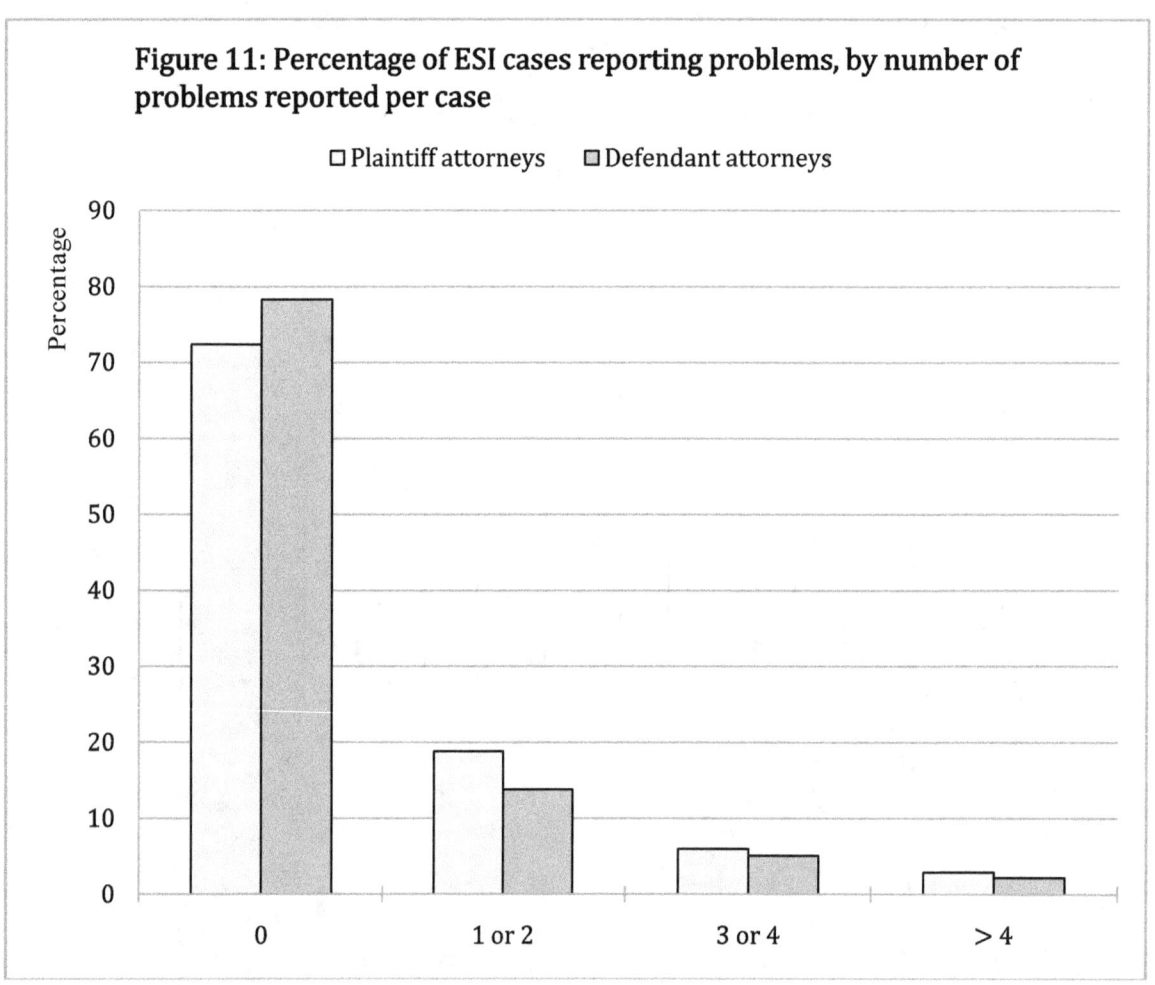

Figure 11: Percentage of ESI cases reporting problems, by number of problems reported per case

As the percentages shown in the previous figure suggest, ESI disputes were not very common in the sampled electronic discovery cases. The number of disputes over ESI per electronic discovery case is shown in Figure 11. The overwhelming majority of both plaintiff and defendant attorneys, 72.4 and 78.3 percent, respectively, reported that none of the disputes related to ESI included in question 18 had occurred in the closed case. In 18.8 and 14.3 percent, respectively, 1-2 disputes were reported; in 6.0 and 5.1 percent, respectively, 3-4 disputes were reported; and in 2.9 and 2.2 percent, respectively, more than 4 disputes were reported.

Finally, with respect to electronic discovery, specifically, respondents were asked how the ESI produced was used in the closed case. The distribution of responses is displayed in Figure 12.

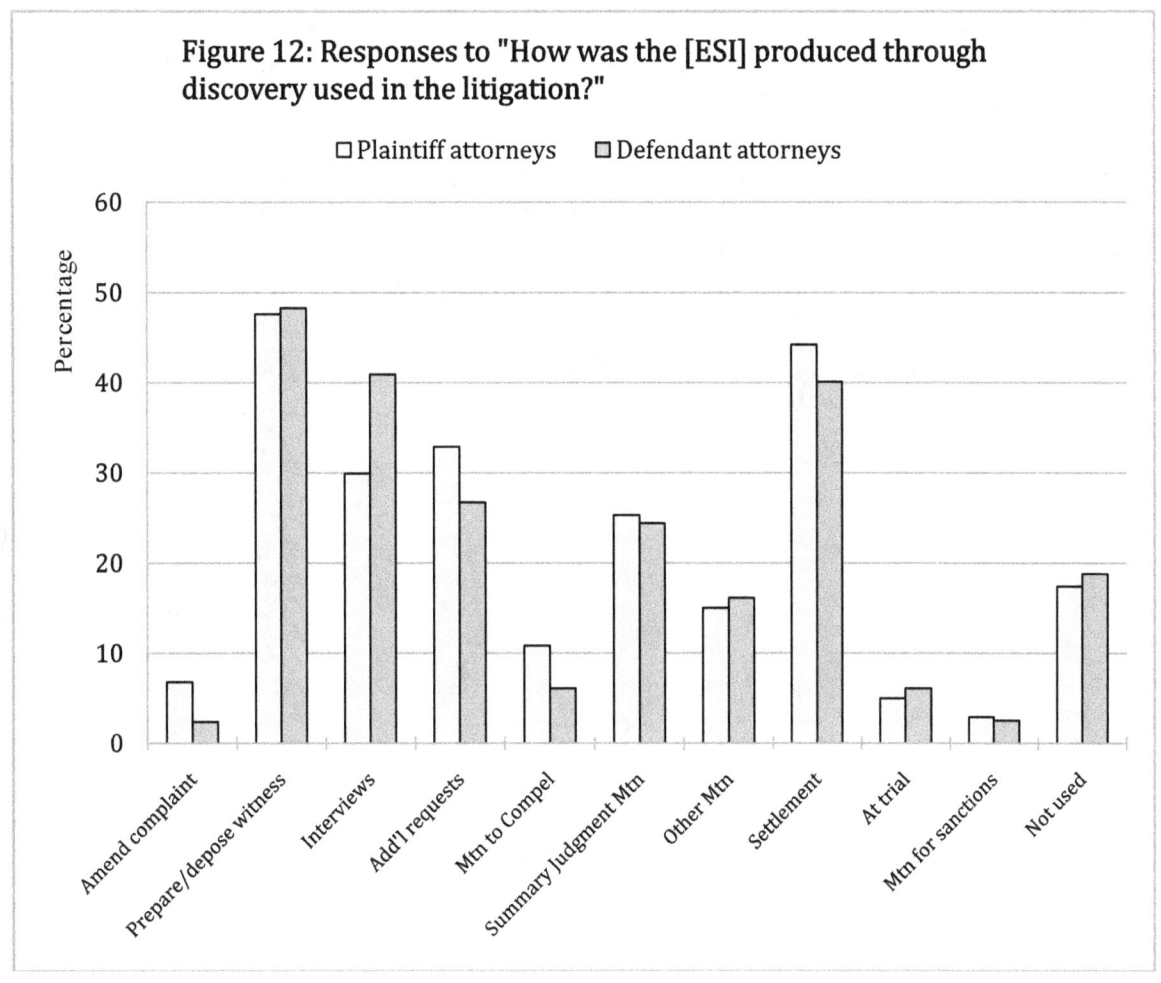

Fully 17.4 percent of plaintiff attorneys and 18.8 percent of defendant attorneys responded that the ESI produced in discovery was not used at all in the closed case. The most common use of ESI was in preparing or deposing a witness—reported by 47.6 percent of plaintiff attorneys and 48.3 percent of defendant attorneys—followed by facilitating a settlement—44.2 and 40.1 percent, respectively—and in interviews with clients or clients' employees, 29.9 and 40.9 percent, respectively. Other relatively common responses included use in an additional discovery request—reported by 32.9 percent of plaintiff attorneys and 26.7 percent of defendant attorneys—and in a motion for summary judgment—reported by 25.3 and 24.4 percent, respectively.

Respondents were asked in question 51 to estimate, in general, what percentage of their practice is spent in electronic discovery-related activities. Given the findings already presented in this section, it is not surprising that the median response for both plaintiff and defendant attorneys was 5 percent. Those representing primarily plaintiffs gave a lower mean response, 6.4 percent, than either those representing plaintiffs and defendants about equally, 9.2 percent, or those primarily representing defendants, 9.0 percent. The 95th percentile for those representing primarily plaintiffs was 20 percent of their practice time spent in electronic discovery-related activities; for those representing both about equally, it was 30 percent; and for those representing primarily defendants, it was 25 percent. The 10th percentile response was 1 percent for those primarily representing defendants, 0.5 percent for those representing both about equally, and 0 (zero) for those representing primarily plaintiffs.

In sum, a party requested production of ESI in 30 to 40 percent of the sampled cases with one or more reported type of discovery—in other words, in less than a majority of cases with discovery. Moreover, no disputes over electronic discovery occurred in a large percentage of those cases. Half of attorneys in the closed cases with some discovery activity reported that they spend no more than 5 percent of their overall practice in electronic discovery-related activities.

The next report to the Committee will include information on the volume of ESI produced by parties in the electronic discovery cases.

IV. Attorneys' Evaluation of Discovery in the Closed Cases

Respondents were asked to rate the information generated by the parties in discovery in the closed case on a 7-point scale, with 1 being too little, 4 being just the right amount, and 7 being too much. The distribution of responses is displayed in Figure 13. Both plaintiff and defendant attorneys tended to answer "just the right amount"; 56.6 and 66.8 percent, respectively, gave that answer. As can be seen in the figure, plaintiff attorneys (36 percent) were more likely to rate the information generated as too little (in the range of 1-3) than defendant attorneys (22.4 percent), and defendant attorneys (10.9 percent) were slightly more likely to rate the information generated as too much (in the range of 5-7) than plaintiff attorneys (7.5 percent).

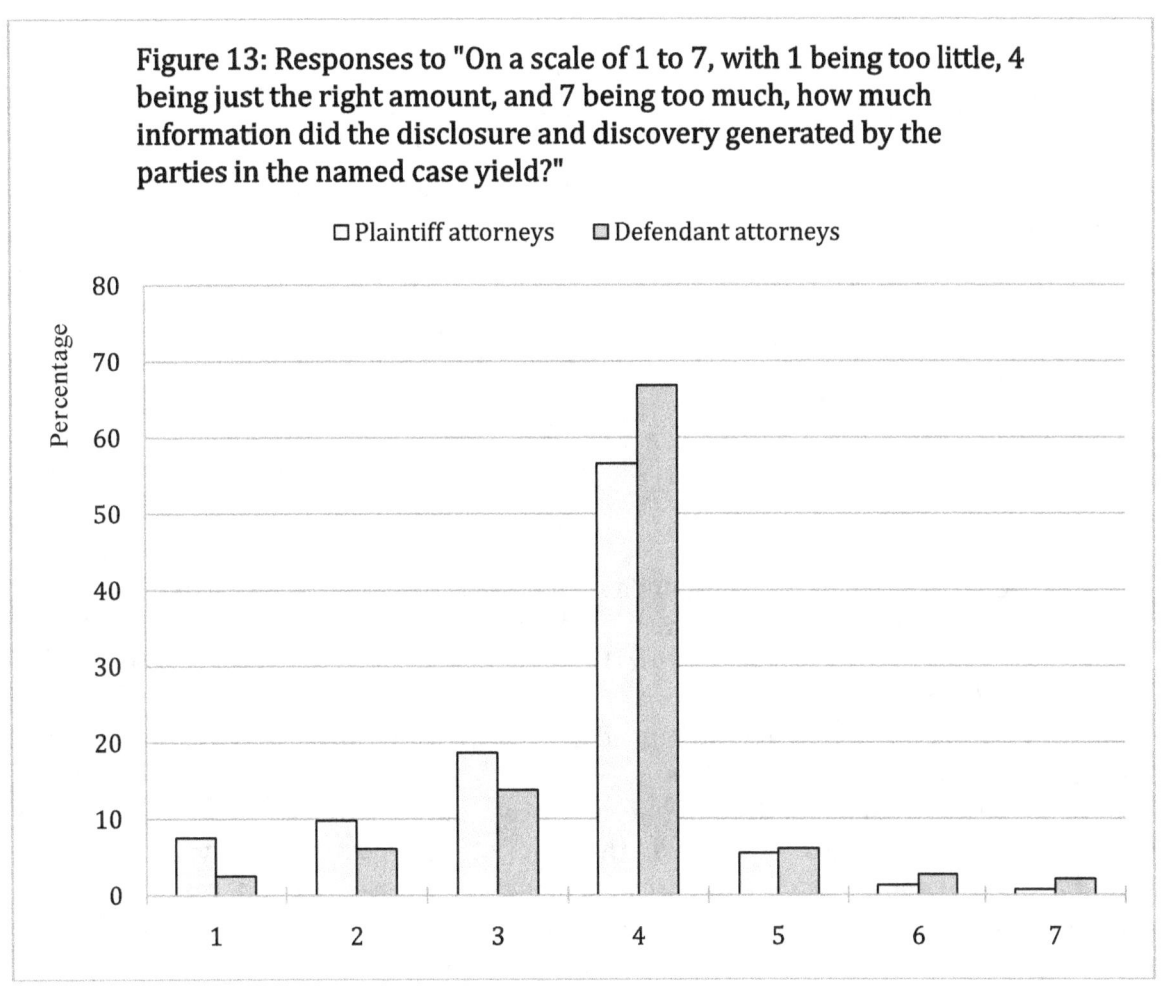

Figure 13: Responses to "On a scale of 1 to 7, with 1 being too little, 4 being just the right amount, and 7 being too much, how much information did the disclosure and discovery generated by the parties in the named case yield?"

Respondents were asked to compare the costs of discovery with their clients' stakes in the closed case on a 7-point scale, with 1 being too little, 4 being just the right amount, and 7 being too much. The distribution of responses is displayed in Figure 14. As with the previous question, both plaintiff and defendant attorneys tended to answer, "just the right amount"; 58.8 and 56.8 percent, respectively, gave that answer.

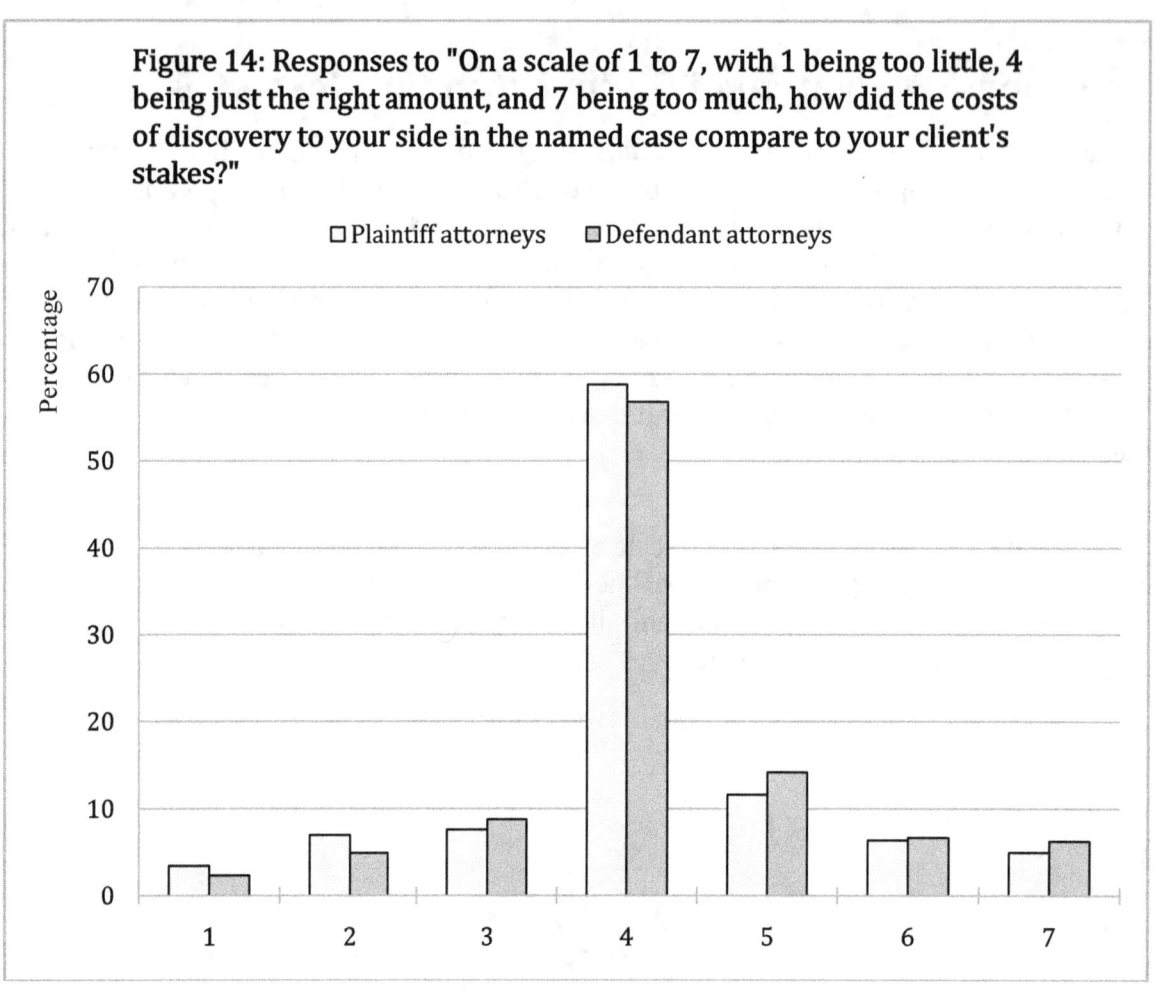

Figure 14: Responses to "On a scale of 1 to 7, with 1 being too little, 4 being just the right amount, and 7 being too much, how did the costs of discovery to your side in the named case compare to your client's stakes?"

Although more than half of respondents indicated that the costs of discovery were "just right" relative to their clients' stakes in the closed case, 27.2 percent of defendant attorneys and 23 percent of plaintiff attorneys indicated that the costs of discovery were too much relative to their client's stakes (in the range of 5-7). By comparison, 18 percent of defendant attorneys and 16 percent of plaintiff attorneys rated the cost comparison as "too little" (in the range of 1-3).

Respondents were asked a battery of questions about the effects of discovery in the closed case. The first such question was whether the potential costs of discovery to the producing party influenced the client's choice of forum. The distribution of responses is displayed in Figure 15. As one might expect, defendant attorneys tended to answer this question as "not applicable" (54.1 percent). Fully 46.5 percent of plaintiff attorneys disagreed or disagreed strongly with the statement. Only 7.2 percent of plaintiff attorneys and 6.3 percent of defendant attorneys agreed or strongly agreed with the statement.[8]

---

[8] *Cf.* Thomas E. Willging & Shannon R. Wheatman, An Empirical Examination of Attorneys' Choice of Forum in Class Action Litigation 18 & Table 2 (Federal Judicial Center 2005) (finding that the favorableness of discovery rules was a "secondary factor" affecting plaintiff attorneys' choice of forum, reported in 28 percent of state filings and 16 percent of federal filings).

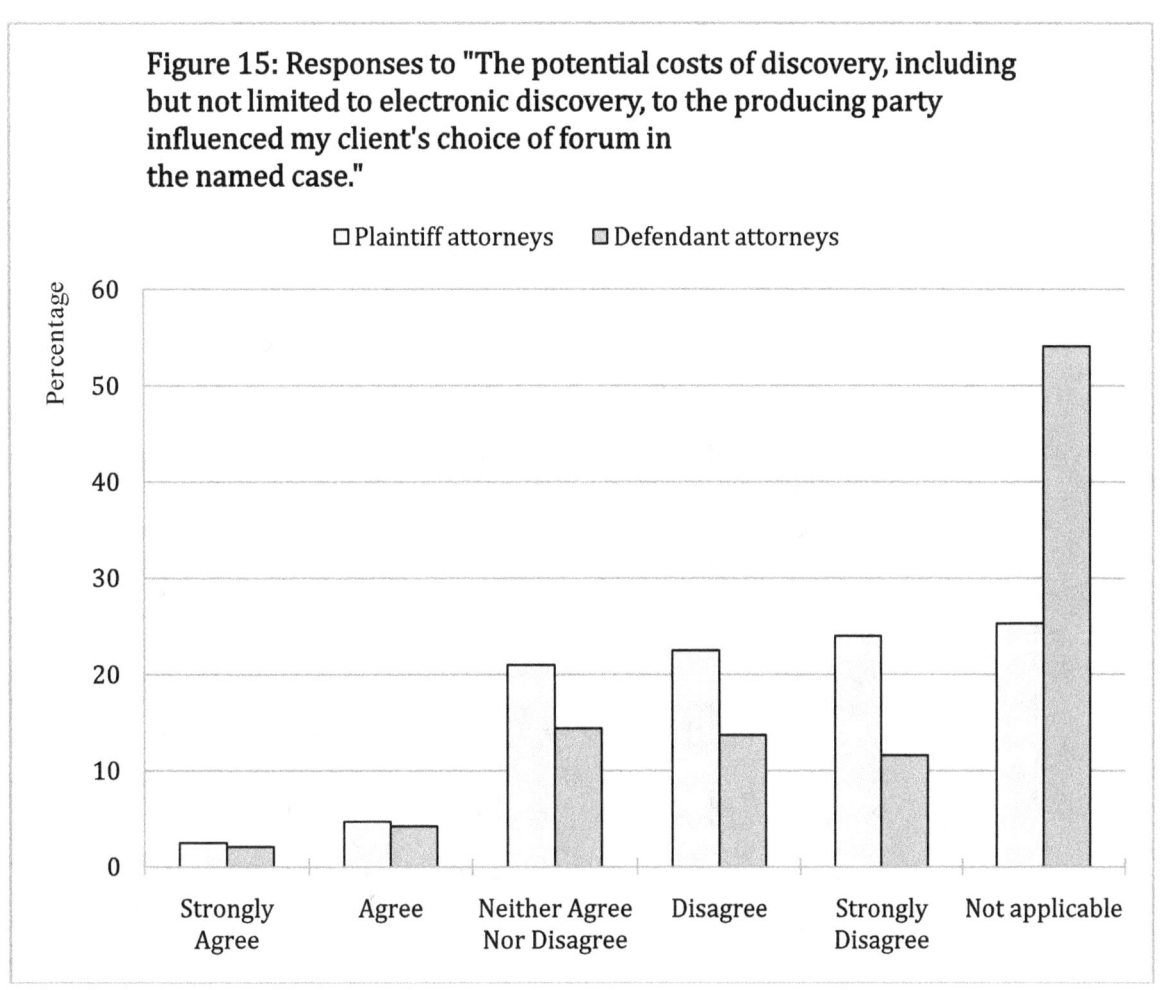

Figure 15: Responses to "The potential costs of discovery, including but not limited to electronic discovery, to the producing party influenced my client's choice of forum in the named case."

Next, respondents were asked whether the discovery produced in the closed case increased the fairness of the outcome. The distribution of responses is displayed in Figure 16. Fully 44.5 percent of plaintiff attorneys and 38.5 percent of defendant attorneys agreed or strongly agreed with the statement; only 12.4 percent of plaintiff attorneys and 14 percent of defendant attorneys disagreed or strongly disagreed with the statement. However, it is interesting that a large percentage of both groups refused to answer. About 1 respondent in 5 (19.7 and 19.8 percent, respectively) declined to answer, and almost 1 in 4 (23.4 and 27.7 percent) neither agreed nor disagreed. In other words, 43.1 percent of plaintiff attorneys and 47.5 percent of defendant attorneys—a plurality of defendant attorneys and a near plurality of plaintiff attorneys—did not express an opinion as to the effects of discovery on the fairness of the closed case's outcome.

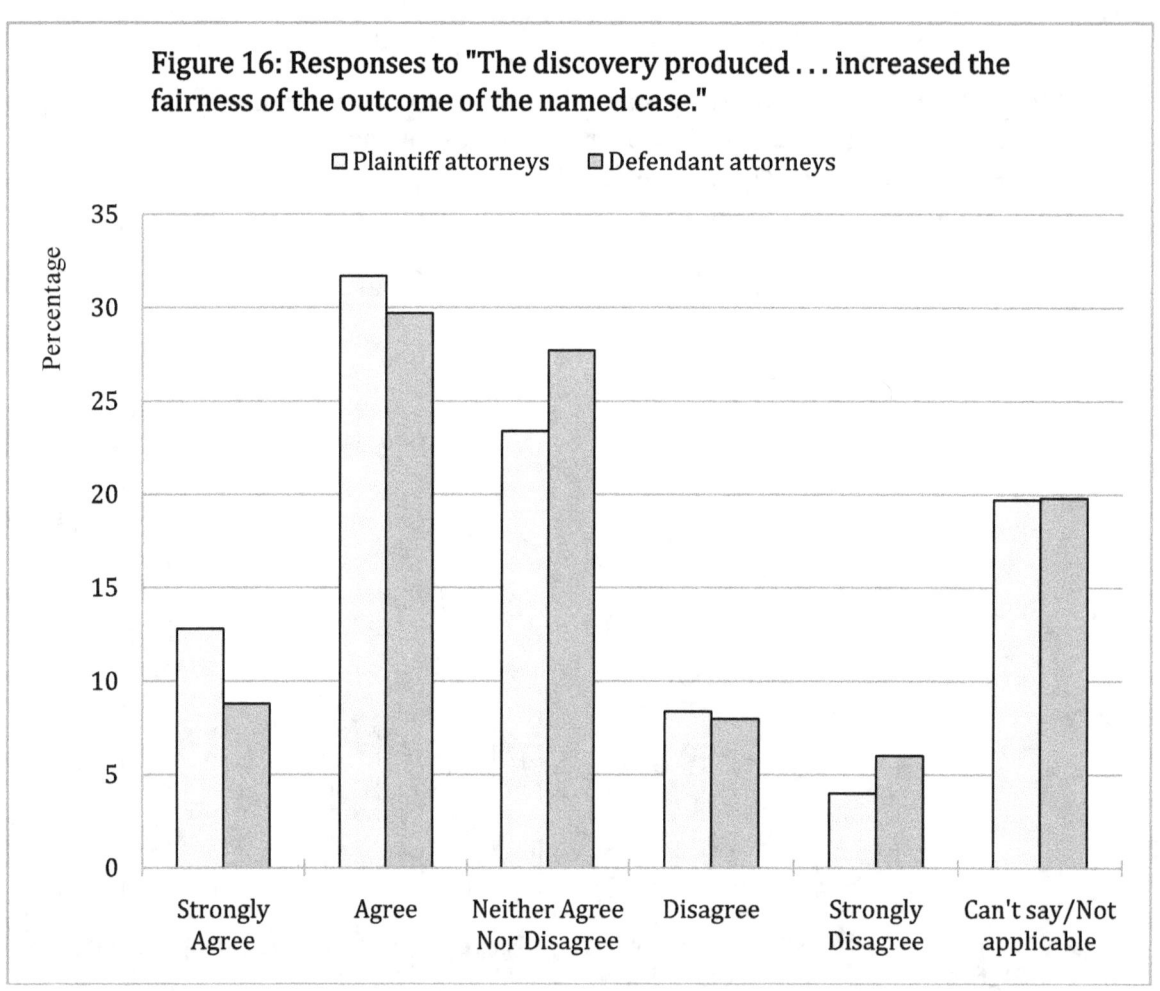

Figure 16: Responses to "The discovery produced... increased the fairness of the outcome of the named case."

The next two questions asked respondents about the parties' conduct with respect to discovery. First respondents were asked whether the parties were able to reduce the cost and burden of discovery through cooperation. The distribution of responses is displayed in Figure 17. As the figure clearly shows, respondents tended to agree or strongly agree with this statement; 63.8 percent of plaintiff attorneys and 61 percent of defendant attorneys agreed or strongly agreed. Only 11.3 and 12.3 percent, respectively, disagreed or strongly disagreed. About 1 respondent in 4 either declined to answer or did not express an opinion.

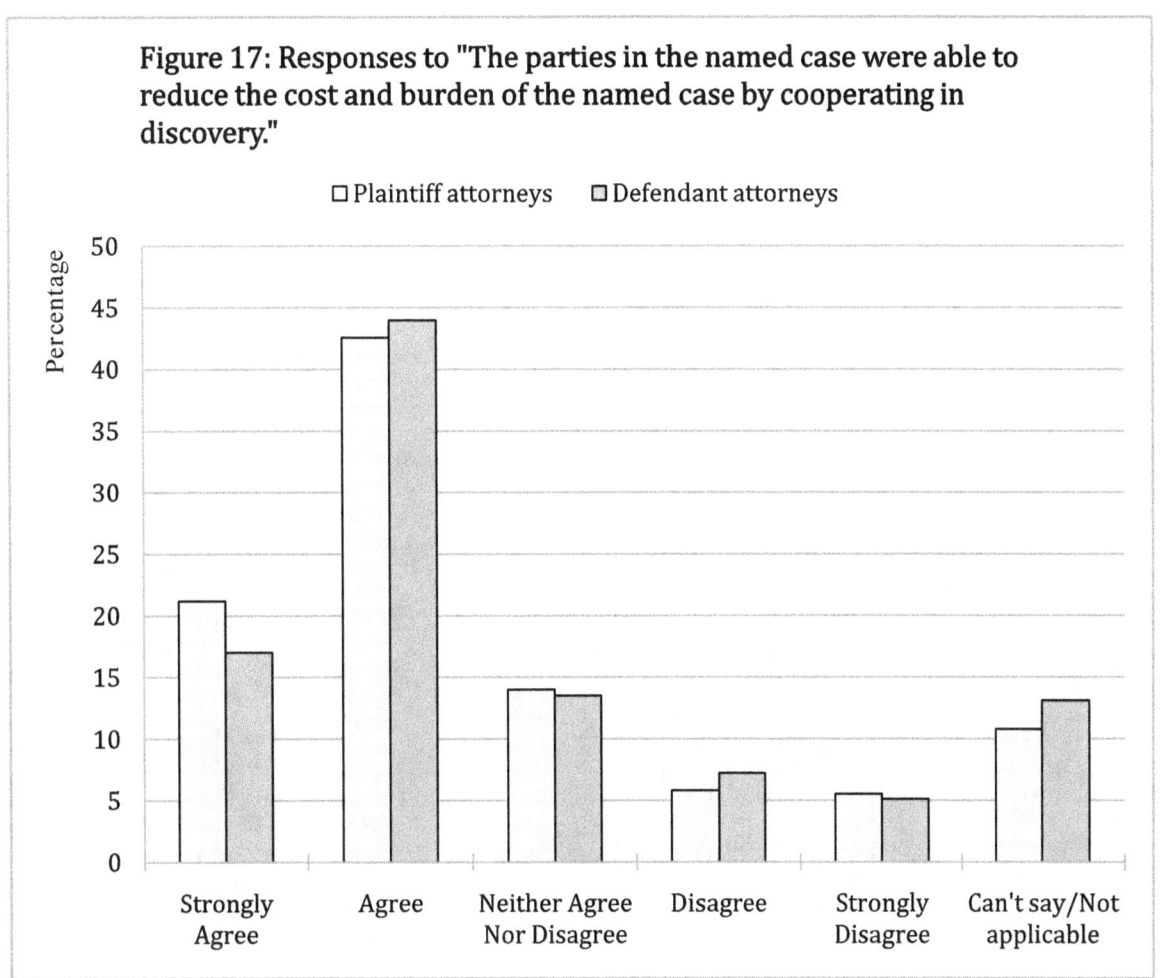

Figure 17: Responses to "The parties in the named case were able to reduce the cost and burden of the named case by cooperating in discovery."

The second question on the parties' conduct asked whether the parties *would have* saved significant time and money had they cooperated in discovery. The distribution of responses is displayed in Figure 18. Given the answers to the previous question, it is not surprising that many respondents found this question "Not applicable"—41.7 of plaintiff attorneys and 46.2 percent of defendant attorneys. These are, presumably, the respondents who indicated that the parties in fact reduced their costs by cooperating in discovery in the closed case. Still, 21.4 percent of plaintiff attorneys and 15.3 percent of defendant attorneys agreed or strongly agreed; and 13.9 and 14.5 percent, respectively, disagreed or disagreed strongly.

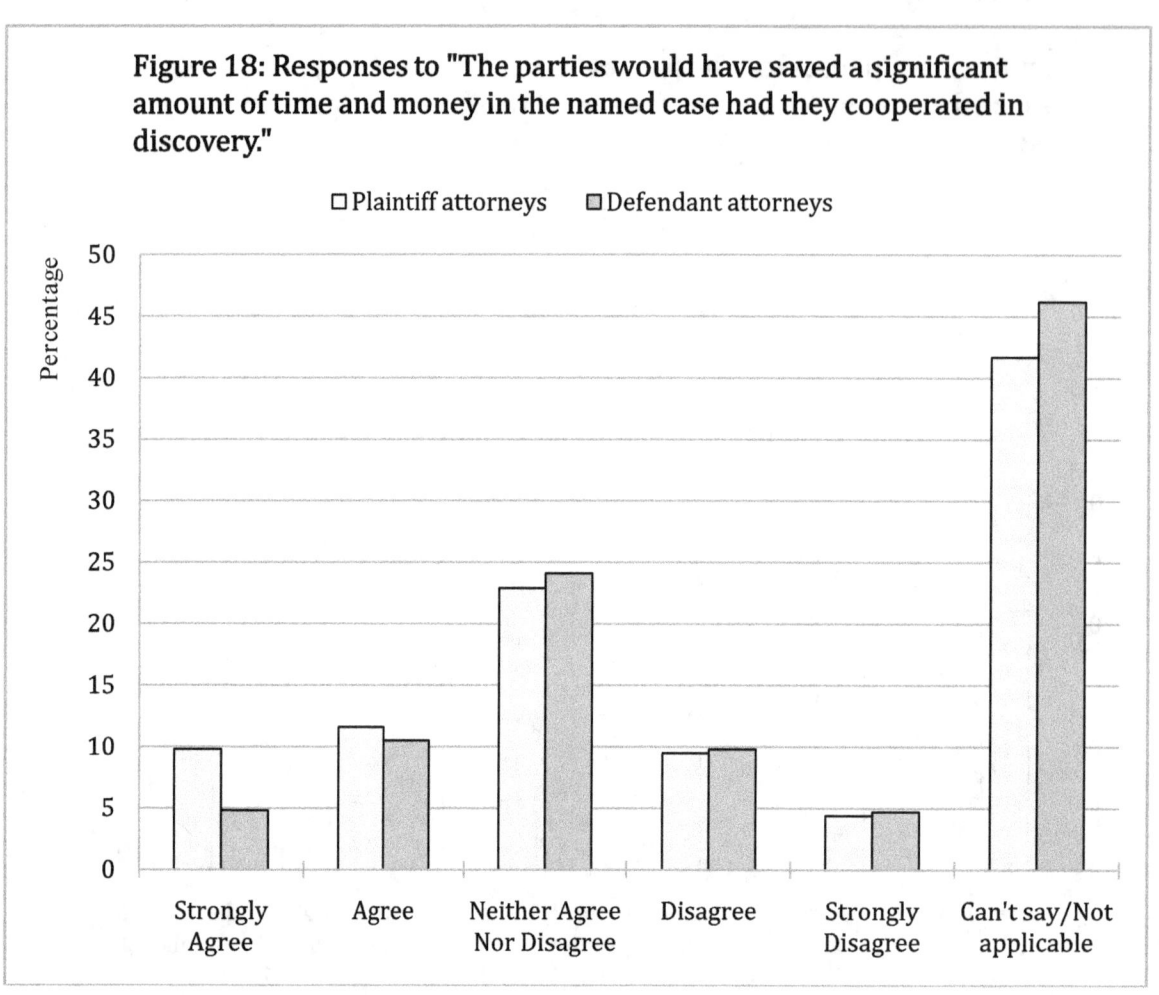

Respondents were next asked how the costs of discovery, including electronic discovery, affected the likelihood of the case settling. Figure 19 shows plaintiff and defendant attorney responses to this question in all cases in which there was at least one reported discovery event; these responses include cases that did not settle. By far, the largest response category for both plaintiff attorneys (49.8 percent) and defendant attorneys (52.6 percent) was "no effect." But 20.1 percent of plaintiff attorneys reported that the costs of discovery increased the likelihood of settlement, 5.3 percent reported that the costs greatly increased the likelihood of settlement, and 2 percent reported that the closed case "would not have settled but for the cost of discovery." Similarly, 21.7 percent of defendant attorneys reported that discovery costs increased the likelihood of settlement, 5.5 percent reported that the costs greatly increased the likelihood of settlement, and 2.8 percent reported that the closed case "would not have settled but for the costs of discovery." In sum, 27.4 percent of plaintiff attorneys and 30 percent of defendant attorneys indicated that the costs of discovery increased, to some extent, the likelihood of settlement in the closed case. Only 4.2 percent and 3.4 percent, respectively, indicated that the costs of discovery decreased or greatly decreased the likelihood of settlement.

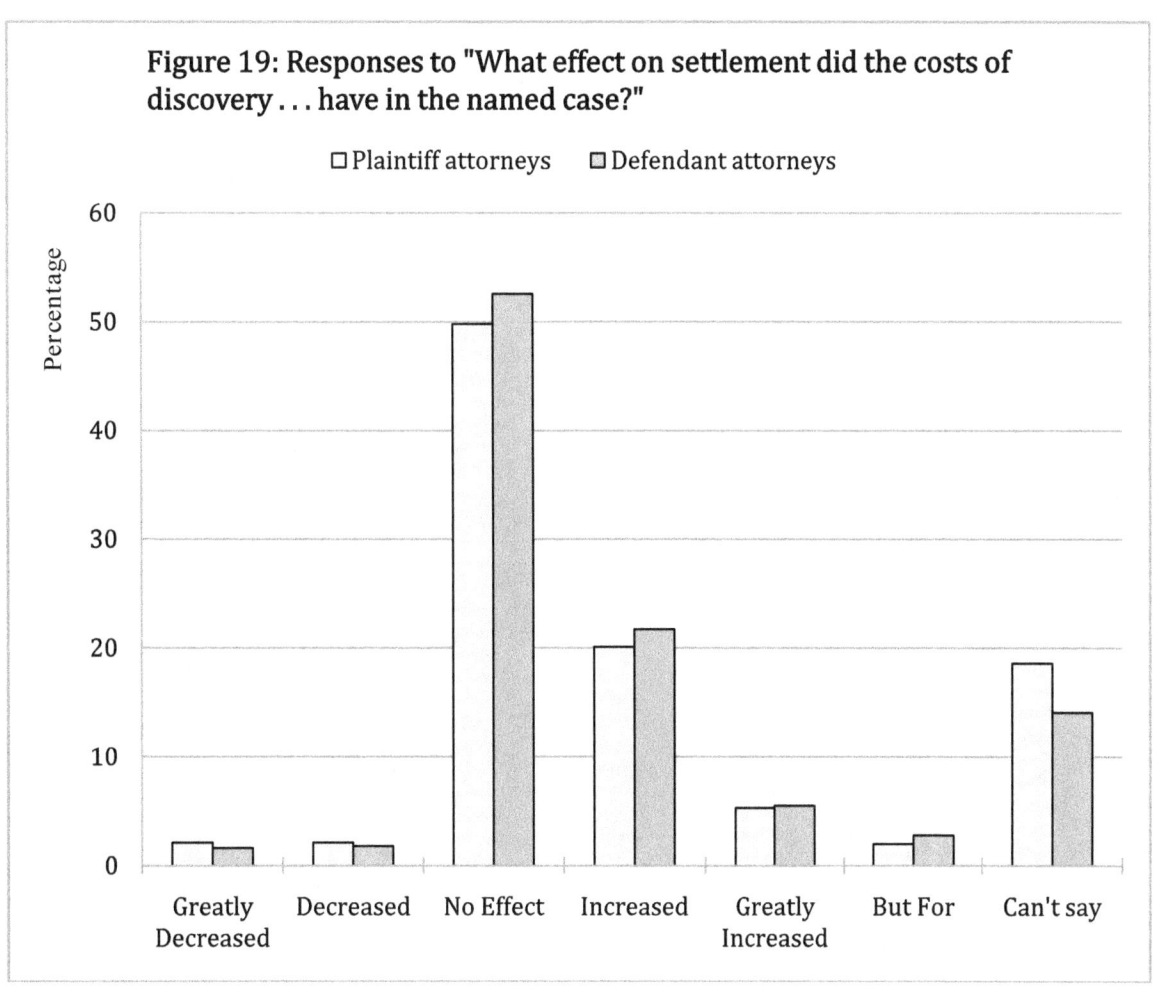

Do these findings change if we limit the analysis to cases that were reported as settled by respondents? If we restrict the analysis to cases reported as settled ($n = 1,304$), the percentage of cases in which respondents report that the costs of discovery increased the likelihood of settlement increases for both plaintiff attorneys and defendant attorneys. Fully 35.5 percent of plaintiff attorneys in settled cases reported that the costs of discovery increased or greatly increased the likelihood of settlement, or caused the case to settle; the comparable figure for defendant attorneys was 39.9 percent. However, even among settled cases, the most common response for both plaintiff attorneys (48.2 percent) and defendant attorneys (47.3 percent) is that the costs of discovery had no effect on the likelihood of settlement in the closed case.

V. Attorney Estimates of Costs in the Closed Cases

Respondents were asked, in question 27, to estimate the total litigation costs for their firms and/or clients in the closed case, including the costs of discovery and any hourly fees for attorneys or paralegals. If the case was handled on a contingency-fee basis, they were asked to estimate the total litigation costs to the firm. Table 4 first displays plaintiff attorneys' costs for all respondents providing cost information in cases with at least one type of discovery reported, then breaks down the costs into the following categories: no electronic discovery request in the closed case; any electronic discovery request in the closed case; electronic discovery case with the client as a producing party only; the client as a requesting party only; the client as both a producing and requesting party; five or fewer types of discovery reported in the closed case; and more than five types of discovery reported in the closed case.

Table 4: Plaintiff attorneys' reported costs, cases with at least one reported type of discovery

Category of Respondents		Reported Costs (in dollars)	N
All	Median	15,000	1,033
	10th percentile	1,600	
	95th percentile	280,000	
No electronic discovery	Median	8,126	517
	10th percentile	1,000	
	95th percentile	95,000	
Any electronic discovery	Median	30,000	451
	10th percentile	3,000	
	95th percentile	500,000	
Producing party only	Median	40,000	23
	10th percentile	2,500	
	95th percentile	400,000	
Requesting party only	Median	20,000	245
	10th percentile	3,000	
	95th percentile	280,000	
Producing and requesting party	Median	65,000	181
	10th percentile	5,000	
	95th percentile	850,000	
Five or fewer types of discovery reported	Median	10,000	489
	10th percentile	1,000	
	95th percentile	150,000	
More than five types of discovery reported	Median	20,000	544
	10th percentile	2,500	
	95th percentile	500,000	

The median cost reported by all plaintiff attorneys, in cases with at least one reported type of discovery, was $15,000. The 10th percentile was $1,600, and the 95th percentile was $280,000. The 1997 study found that the comparable figures were $10,000, $2,000, and $200,000, respectively.[9] Adjusted for inflation (2008 dollars), the comparable figures would be $13,363, $2,673, and $267,250, respectively. Although two studies, separated by twelve years, do not provide adequate information from which to establish a trend, comparing these cost estimates, the median estimate in 2009 exceeds the inflation-adjusted 1997 estimate by 12 percent, and the 95th percentile estimate exceeds the inflation-adjusted 1997 estimate by about 5 percent. The 10th percentile estimate is lower than the non-inflation-adjusted estimate from 1997.

As shown in Table 4, plaintiff attorneys reported that cases with electronic discovery requests were more expensive, at the median, than cases with no such requests. In cases without electronic discovery requests, the median reported cost was $8,126; the median reported cost, to the plaintiff, in cases with electronic discovery requests was $30,000. Among electronic discovery cases, the highest reported costs occurred in cases in which the plaintiff was both a producing and requesting party—$65,000 at the median. Costs were also higher in cases with more than five reported types of discovery—$20,000 at the median—than in cases with five or fewer reported types of discovery—$10,000.

Table 5 displays defendant attorneys' reports of costs, broken out in a similar fashion. The median cost reported by all defendant attorneys in cases with at least one reported type of discovery was $20,000. The 10th percentile was $5,000, and the 95th percentile was $300,000. The 1997 study found that the comparable figures were, at the median, $15,000, which when adjusted for inflation is about $20,043; the 10th percentile was $3,000, or $4,009 adjusted for inflation; and the 95th percentile was $150,000, or $200,438 adjusted for inflation. The median figure in Table 5, in short, is *slightly* lower than the 1997 median adjusted for inflation; the 10th and 95th percentiles, on the other hand, are larger by 25 and 50 percent, respectively.

Once again, cases in which an electronic discovery request was made were more expensive than those in which no such request was made—defendant attorneys reported median costs of $40,000 in electronic discovery cases, compared with $15,000 in cases without electronic discovery. Moreover, defendant attorneys reported the highest costs in electronic discovery cases when they were representing a party that both produced and requested electronic discovery—$60,000 at the median, compared with $25,000 at the median for producing parties only and $20,000 for requesting parties only. And, as in Table 4, cases with more than five reported discovery events were more costly than cases with five or fewer reported discovery events—$35,000 compared with $15,000.

---

[9] *Discovery and Disclosure, supra* note 3, at 15 (Table 3).

Table 5: Defendant attorneys' reported costs, cases with at least one reported type of discovery

Category of Respondents		Reported Costs (in dollars)	N
All	Median	20,000	945
	10th percentile	5,000	
	95th percentile	300,000	
No electronic discovery	Median	15,000	503
	10th percentile	5,000	
	95th percentile	200,000	
Any electronic discovery	Median	40,000	385
	10th percentile	6,214	
	95th percentile	600,000	
Producing party only	Median	25,000	136
	10th percentile	5,000	
	95th percentile	350,000	
Requesting party only	Median	20,000	51
	10th percentile	4,000	
	95th percentile	150,000	
Producing and requesting party	Median	60,000	197
	10th percentile	10,000	
	95th percentile	991,900	
Five or fewer types of discovery reported	Median	15,000	458
	10th percentile	4,000	
	95th percentile	250,000	
More than five types of discovery reported	Median	35,000	487
	10th percentile	7,500	
	95th percentile	400,000	

Respondents were also asked to estimate what percentage of the total litigation costs were incurred in requesting and/or producing disclosure and/or discovery, including but not limited to the discovery of electronically stored information (question 28). Plaintiff attorney responses in cases with at least one reported type of discovery are summarized in Table 6. The median response for all plaintiff attorneys providing such information was 20 percent; the 10th percentile was 0.1 percent, and the 95th percentile was 80 percent. It should be noted that almost 10 percent of plaintiff attorney respondents offering an estimate in response to this question answered 0 (zero). These figures are substantially lower than the comparable figures from the 1997 study, which found that the median for plaintiff attorneys was 50 percent.[10]

There is not much variation in the median percentage of total litigation costs associated with discovery among the subgroups shown in Table 6. In cases with an electronic

---

[10] *Id.* at 15 (Table 4).

discovery request, discovery accounts for 25 percent of total litigation costs, at the median, compared with 20 percent in a case without a request. Producing and requesting parties reported a higher median percentage (30 percent) than producing parties only (25 percent) or requesting parties only (25 percent), but again, the difference is 5 percentage points. Similarly, higher levels of discovery led to a 5 percentage point higher estimate of discovery costs as a share of total costs.

Table 6: Plaintiff attorneys' estimate of percentage of costs incurred in discovery, cases with at least one reported type of discovery

Category of Respondents		Estimate (%)	N
All	Median	20.0	1,031
	10th percentile	0.1	
	95th percentile	80.0	
No electronic discovery	Median	20.0	515
	10th percentile	0.0	
	95th percentile	80.0	
Any electronic discovery	Median	25.0	458
	10th percentile	5.0	
	95th percentile	80.0	
Producing party only	Median	25.0	22
	10th percentile	10.0	
	95th percentile	75.0	
Requesting party only	Median	25.0	247
	10th percentile	1.0	
	95th percentile	90.0	
Producing and requesting party	Median	30.0	188
	10th percentile	5.0	
	95th percentile	75.0	
Five or fewer types of discovery reported	Median	20.0	480
	10th percentile	0.0	
	95th percentile	80.0	
More than five types of discovery reported	Median	25.0	551
	10th percentile	3.0	
	95th percentile	80.0	

Defendant attorney responses to the same question are summarized in Table 7. Defendant attorneys estimated a higher median percentage of total litigation costs associated with discovery, 27 percent, than did plaintiff attorneys, 20 percent. The 10th percentile for defendant attorneys was 5 percent, and the 95th percentile was 80 percent. Almost 5 percent of respondents offering a response estimated the percentage of total costs associated with discovery at 0 (zero). Once again, these figures are substantially lower than the estimates in the 1997 study, which found that the median estimate for defendant attorneys was 50 percent of total litigation costs associated with discovery.

Table 7: Defendant attorneys' estimate of percentage of costs incurred in discovery, cases with at least one reported type of discovery

Category of Respondents		Estimate (%)	N
All	Median	27.0	989
	10th percentile	5.0	
	95th percentile	80.0	
No electronic discovery	Median	25.0	532
	10th percentile	3.0	
	95th percentile	80.0	
Any electronic discovery	Median	32.5	397
	10th percentile	10.0	
	95th percentile	80.0	
Producing party only	Median	40.0	140
	10th percentile	10.0	
	95th percentile	80.0	
Requesting party only	Median	40.0	53
	10th percentile	7.0	
	95th percentile	75.0	
Producing and requesting party	Median	30.0	204
	10th percentile	10.0	
	95th percentile	80.0	
Five or fewer types of discovery reported	Median	25.0	483
	10th percentile	2.0	
	95th percentile	75.0	
More than five types of discovery reported	Median	35.0	506
	10th percentile	10.0	
	95th percentile	80.0	

As with the plaintiff attorneys' estimates, electronic discovery in a case increased the median estimate of the percentage of total costs associated with discovery, but not substantially. For cases without a reported electronic discovery request, the median estimate was 25 percent of total costs incurred in discovery; for cases with such a request, the median estimate was 32.5 percent. Producing and requesting parties provided a lower median estimate (30 percent) than producing only or requesting only parties did (40 percent). Cases with more types of discovery produced higher estimates of the percentage of total costs associated with discovery, 35 percent compared with 25 percent.

To determine whether discovery costs in general are excessive, from the respondent's point of view, respondents were asked, in Question 78, to specify, in the typical case in federal court, the proper ratio of the costs of discovery to total litigation costs. The median response for plaintiff attorneys was 33 percent, and the median response for defendant attorneys was 40 percent. Surprisingly, the median estimates of discovery costs to total litigation costs provided by survey respondents were *lower* than the median responses to the normative question.

Respondents reporting an electronic discovery request in the closed case were asked to estimate the percentage of *discovery costs* that were incurred in producing or requesting electronic discovery. Table 8 summarizes this information for both plaintiff attorneys and defendant attorneys. The median estimate of electronic discovery costs as a percentage of discovery costs in cases with an electronic discovery request was 5 percent for plaintiff attorneys and 10 percent for defendant attorneys. In other words, in half of the cases with an electronic discovery request (and for which respondents provided an estimate), electronic discovery costs accounted for just 5 percent of plaintiff attorneys' discovery costs and 10 percent of defendant attorneys' discovery costs. In 5 percent of the cases, the electronic discovery costs exceeded 72.6 percent of plaintiff attorneys' discovery costs and 75 percent of defendant attorneys' discovery costs.

The medians for the break-out groups in Table 8 are remarkably similar. Plaintiff attorneys provided a higher estimate when they represented a party that was both a producing and requesting party (10 percent), as compared with a producing only party (5 percent) or a requesting only party (5 percent). Defendant attorneys representing a producing only party or a producing and requesting party provided very similar estimates of electronic discovery costs as a share of total discovery costs, 10 percent at the median; requesting parties reported a median of 4 percent.

Table 8: Attorneys' estimates of percentage of discovery costs incurred in electronic discovery; electronic discovery cases only

Category of Respondent		Estimate (%)	N
Plaintiff attorneys	Median	5.0	450
	10th percentile	0.0	
	95th percentile	72.6	
Defendant attorneys	Median	10.0	398
	10th percentile	1.0	
	95th percentile	75.0	
Plaintiff attorneys Producing party only	Median	5.0	22
	10th percentile	0.0	
	95th percentile	95.0	
Plaintiff attorneys Requesting party only	Median	5.0	243
	10th percentile	0.0	
	95th percentile	50.0	
Plaintiff attorneys Producing and requesting party	Median	10.0	183
	10th percentile	0.5	
	95th percentile	75.0	
Defendant attorneys Producing party only	Median	10.0	141
	10th percentile	1.0	
	95th percentile	75.0	
Defendant attorneys Requesting party only	Median	4.0	52
	10th percentile	0.0	
	95th percentile	37.5	
Defendant attorneys Producing and requesting party	Median	10.0	204
	10th percentile	1.0	
	95th percentile	80.0	

To compare these cost measures with the amount at stake in the underlying litigation, respondents were asked to estimate the best and worst "likely" outcomes, from the point of view of their clients. The question was drafted to parallel a similar question asked in the 1997 study. A measure of stakes was then calculated as the spread between the best outcome the client might hope for (largest gain or smallest loss) and the worst outcome that the client might legitimately fear (largest loss or smallest gain). Table 9 summarizes estimated stakes in plaintiff attorneys' and defendant attorneys' closed cases.

Table 9: Attorneys' estimates of the stakes; cases with one or more reported discovery types

Category of Respondent		Estimated stakes (in dollars)	N
Plaintiff attorneys	Median	160,000	923
	10th percentile	14,590	
	95th percentile	3,983,000	
Defendant attorneys	Median	200,000	916
	10th percentile	15,000	
	95th percentile	5,000,000	

The median estimate of stakes for plaintiff attorneys was $160,000, the 10th percentile was $14,590, and the 95th percentile was almost $4 million. In the 1997 study, the comparable figures were $125,000, or $167,031 in 2008 dollars; $2,100, or about $2,800 in 2008 dollars; and $3 million, which would be more than $4 million in 2008 dollars.[11] Plaintiffs attorneys' estimates of the stakes are relatively close, at the median and the 95th percentile, to the inflation-adjusted estimates. At the 10th percentile, the current estimate is much larger than the comparable 1997 estimate.

The median estimate of stakes for defendant attorneys was $200,000, the 10th percentile was $15,000, and the 95th percentile was $5 million. The comparable figures from the 1997 study were $200,000, or $267,250 in 2008 dollars; $10,000, or $13,362 in 2008 dollars; and $5 million, which would be more than $7 million in 2008 dollars. The current estimates are substantially lower at the median and the 95th percentile than the inflation-adjusted 1997 estimates; the 10th percentile is slightly higher than the 1997 estimate.

Discovery costs can be expressed as a percentage of the stakes, as estimated by the respondent. The 1997 study found that the median ratio of discovery costs to stakes was 3 percent, for both plaintiff and defendant attorneys, and that the 95th percentile was 32 percent, for both plaintiff and defendant attorneys.[12] As shown in Table 10, plaintiff attorneys in the present study reported a median ratio of 1.6 percent in cases with at least one reported type of discovery, and defendant attorneys reported a median ratio of 3.3 percent. The 95th percentile was 25.0 percent for plaintiff attorneys and 30.5 percent for defendant attorneys.

---

[11] *Id.* at 16 (Table 5).
[12] *Id.* at 17 (Table 6).

Table 10: Ratio of attorneys' estimates of discovery costs to attorneys' estimates of the stakes; cases with one or more reported discovery types

Category of Respondent		Estimate (%)	N
Plaintiff attorneys	Median	1.6	829
	10th percentile	0.0	
	95th percentile	25.0	
Defendant attorneys	Median	3.3	916
	10th percentile	0.2	
	95th percentile	30.5	

In other words, in half of cases with some reported discovery, plaintiff attorneys reported that their clients' discovery costs represented no more than 1.6 percent of the clients' stakes in the case, and defendant attorneys reported that their clients' discovery costs represented no more than 3.3 percent of their clients' stakes. In less than 5 percent of cases with some reported discovery costs plaintiff attorneys reported discovery costs that exceeded 25 percent of the client's stakes. The comparable figure for defendant attorneys was higher—in 5 percent of cases, defendant attorneys reported discovery costs exceeding 30.5 percent of the client's stakes.

Question 42 asked respondents to compare the costs of discovery to the client's stakes in the closed case, on a 7-point scale.[13] Scores of 5-7 on that scale represented discovery costs that were perceived as "too much," scores of 1-3 were "too little," and a score of 4 was designated "just the right amount." For plaintiff attorneys responding "just the right amount," the median ratio of discovery costs to stakes was 1.2 ($n = 463$), and for defendant attorneys responding "just the right amount," the median ratio was 2.5 ($n = 415$). The median ratios for respondents answering "too little" were lower, for the most part, and the median ratios for respondents answering "too much" were higher. For defendant attorneys, the median ratio for responders answering 5 out of 7 ($n = 124$) was 5.7 percent; for 6 out of 7 ($n = 10.9$), 10.9 percent; and for 7 out of 7 ($n = 40$), 7.0 percent. For plaintiff attorneys, the median ratio for responders answering 5 out of 7 ($n = 101$) was 4.2 percent; for 6 out of 7 ($n = 52$), 5.2 percent; and for 7 out of 7 ($n = 47$), 3.4 percent.

Finally, respondents were asked to what extent their client was concerned about nonmonetary relief in the closed case or about possible consequences such as future litigation based on similar claims, legal precedent, or harm to reputation, among other things. The responses are summarized in Table 11, which presents the median cost, stakes, and ratio of discovery costs to stakes for each category of respondent.

---

[13] See Figure 14 and accompanying text, *supra*.

Table 11: Responses on the importance of nonmonetary relief or adverse consequences of litigation, with median costs and stakes

Category	Percentage	Median cost (in dollars)	Median stakes (in dollars)	Median Ratio Discovery: Stakes (%)
Plaintiff attorneys				
Dominant concern	11.0	40,000	150,000	2.3
Some concern	22.4	20,000	270,000	1.4
Little/no concern	59.3	10,000	150,000	1.5
Defendant attorneys				
Dominant concern	16.4	33,360	170,000	4.8
Some concern	35.9	25,000	221,000	3.0
Little/no concern	43.1	20,000	175,000	3.0

As Table 11 shows, defendant attorneys were more likely to report that nonmonetary relief and/or adverse consequences were of dominant or some concern to the client (52.3 percent) than were plaintiff attorneys (33.4 percent). Almost 6 in 10 plaintiff attorneys reported that nonmonetary relief and/or adverse consequences of the litigation were of little or no concern (59.3 percent). For both plaintiff attorneys and defendant attorneys, the highest median litigation costs were reported by respondents most concerned with nonmonetary relief and/or adverse consequences, and the lowest median litigation costs were reported by those least concerned. Those reporting that such concerns were dominant also reported the highest ratio of discovery costs to stakes—discovery costs equaled 2.3 percent of stakes at the median for plaintiff attorneys in this category and 4.8 percent of stakes at the median for defendant attorneys. The median stakes followed a different pattern, with the highest median stakes for both plaintiff attorneys and defendant attorneys reported for cases in which the client was somewhat concerned with nonmonetary relief and/or adverse consequences.

VI. Reform Proposals

Respondents were asked a series of questions on two relatively common reform proposals—fact pleading and simplified procedures.

Question 56 asked respondents at what point, if any, the disputed issues central to the dispute in the named case were adequately narrowed and framed for resolution. The distribution of responses for cases in which there was at least one reported type of discovery is displayed in Figure 20.

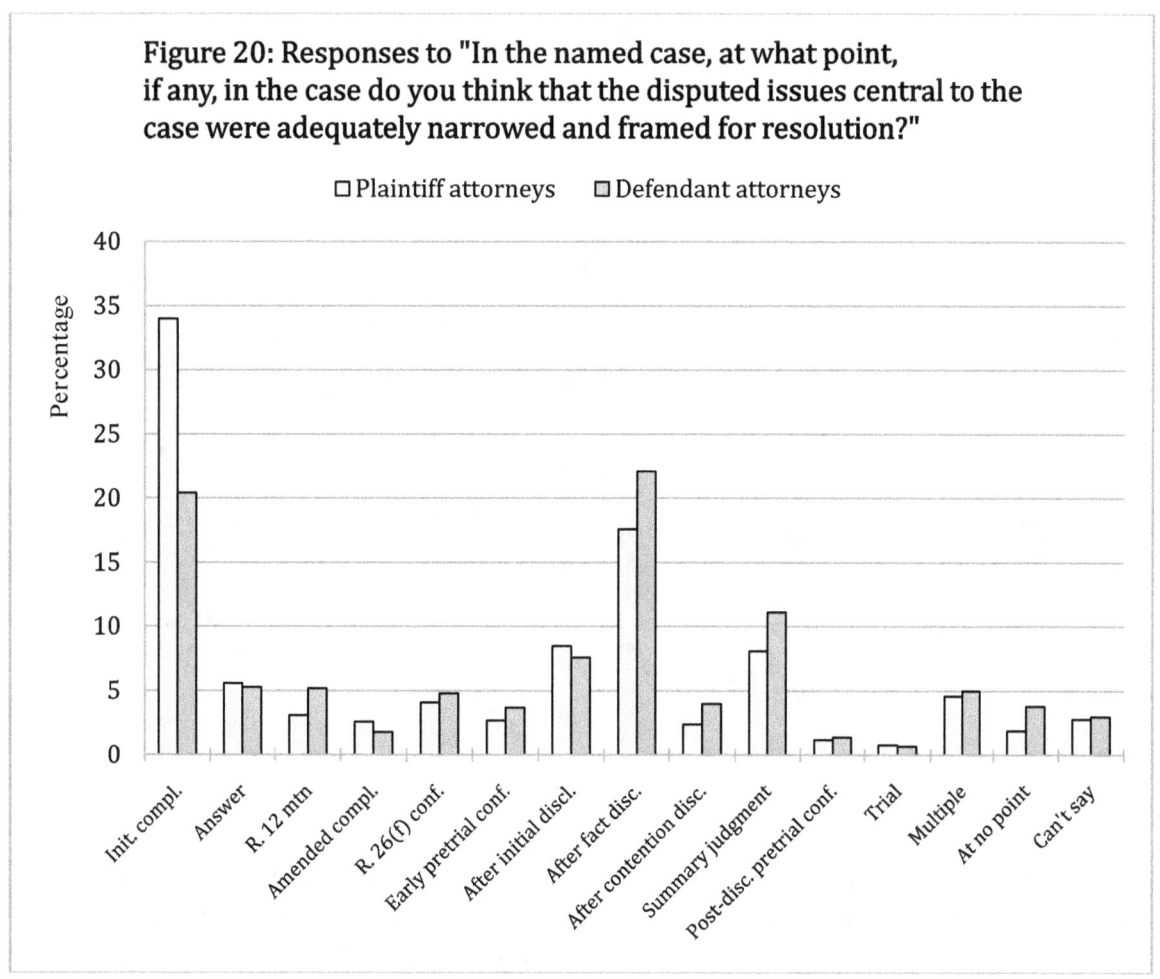

Figure 20: Responses to "In the named case, at what point, if any, in the case do you think that the disputed issues central to the case were adequately narrowed and framed for resolution?"

The most common response for plaintiff attorneys was the initial complaint, which was the response of 34 percent of this group. The next most common response for plaintiff attorneys was after fact discovery, at 17.6 percent. After fact discovery was the most common response for defendant attorneys, at 22.1 percent. Most surprising, however, is that the initial complaint was the next most common response among defendant attorneys, at 20.4 percent. Summary judgment (8.1 and 11.1 percent, respectively) and after initial disclosures (8.5 and 7.6 percent, respectively) were also relatively common responses.

Respondents were then asked (in question 57) at what point in the typical case, based on their experiences in federal court, are the disputed issues central to the case adequately narrowed and framed for resolution. The distribution of responses is displayed in Figure 21.

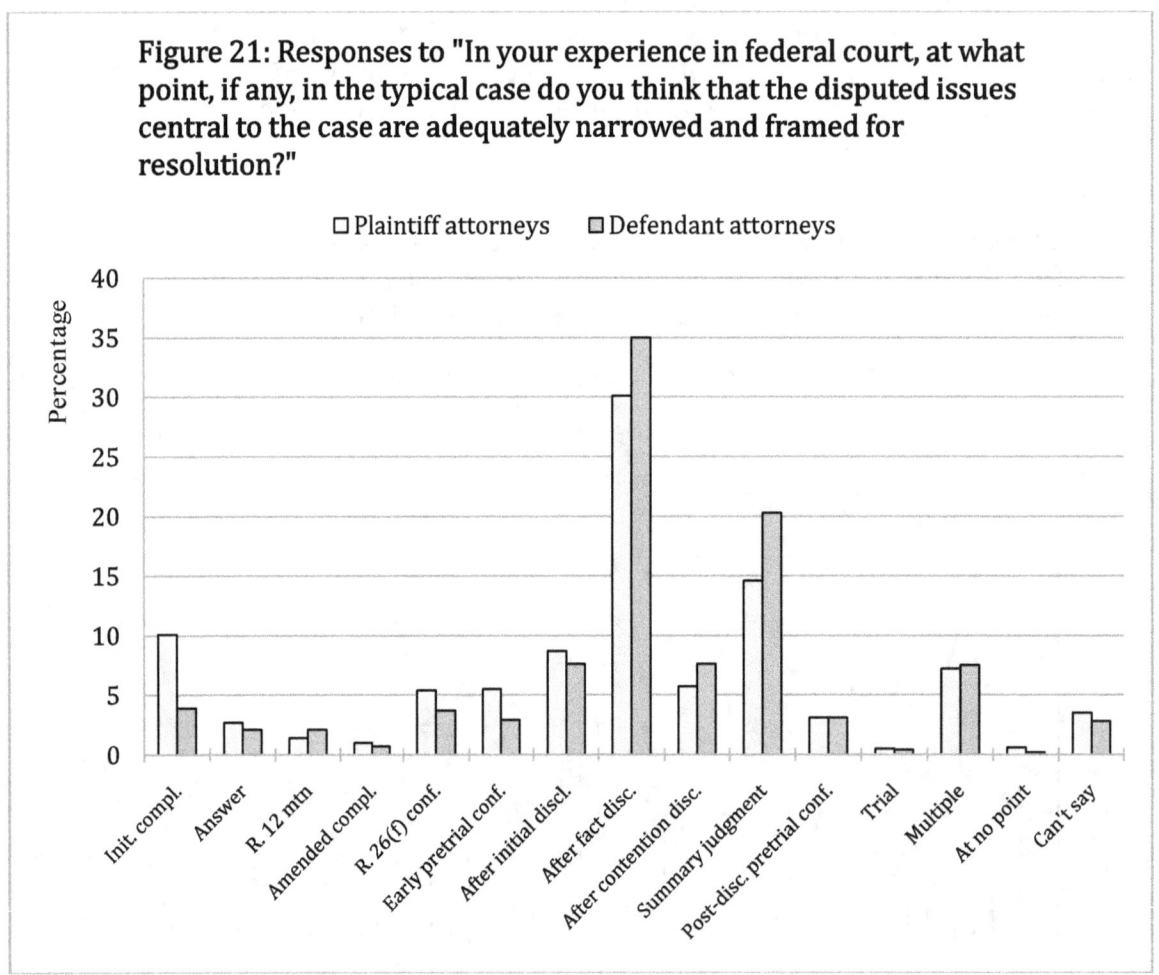

Figure 21: Responses to "In your experience in federal court, at what point, if any, in the typical case do you think that the disputed issues central to the case are adequately narrowed and framed for resolution?"

The responses for the typical case vary a great deal from those for the closed cases. The initial complaint was offered by only 10.1 percent of plaintiff attorneys and 3.9 percent of defendant attorneys—as opposed to 34 and 22.1 percent, respectively, in the previous figure. The most common response, for both groups, was after fact discovery, at 30.1 and 35 percent, respectively, followed by summary judgment, at 14.6 and 20.3 percent, respectively.

Figure 22 combines the information from the previous two figures, displaying the cumulative percentages of responses for plaintiff and defendant attorneys for the closed and typical case. Each line can be understood as the sum of responses (as percentages of all responses for that group) to that point on the horizontal axis. This figure illustrates at what point the issues central to resolving the cases have been adequately narrowed and framed for resolution.

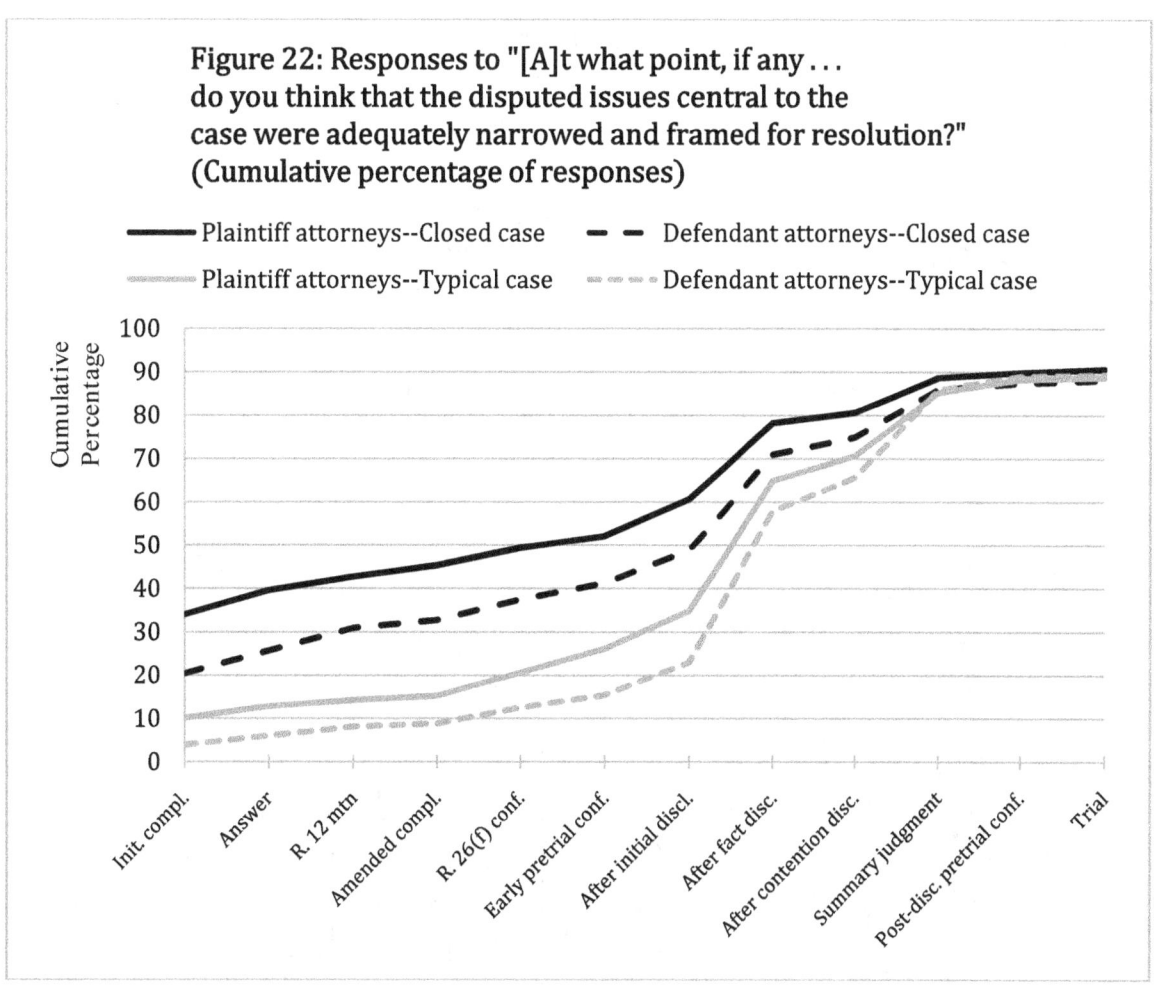

Figure 22: Responses to "[A]t what point, if any... do you think that the disputed issues central to the case were adequately narrowed and framed for resolution?" (Cumulative percentage of responses)

As shown in the previous figures, respondents reported that the issues central to the resolution of the closed case ("named case" in the survey) were adequately framed and narrowed much earlier than in the typical case in federal court. This figure also makes clear that plaintiff attorneys tend to perceive that the central issues are adequately framed and narrowed earlier in cases than do defendant attorneys. For example, by the time of initial disclosure of non-expert documents, more than 60 percent of plaintiff attorneys in the closed cases had reported that the issues had been adequately framed and narrowed, compared with about half of defendant attorneys. A similar gap exists between the two lines in the responses for the typical case.

In both the closed and typical cases, the lines for plaintiffs and defendants converge only late in the case—around summary judgment. By that time, for both the closed and typical case, 85 percent of respondents report that the central issues are adequately narrowed and framed for resolution. The biggest step increase in each line, however, occurs after fact discovery. As for the 10 percent of cases that are not included in the figure, these cases are those for which respondents declined to answer or chose "at no point" or "multiple points" as responses.

Question 58 then asked respondents whether the disputed issues would be identified at an earlier point in most cases if plaintiffs were required to plead more than "a short and plain statement of the claim showing that the pleader is entitled to relief." The distribution of responses is displayed in Figure 23.

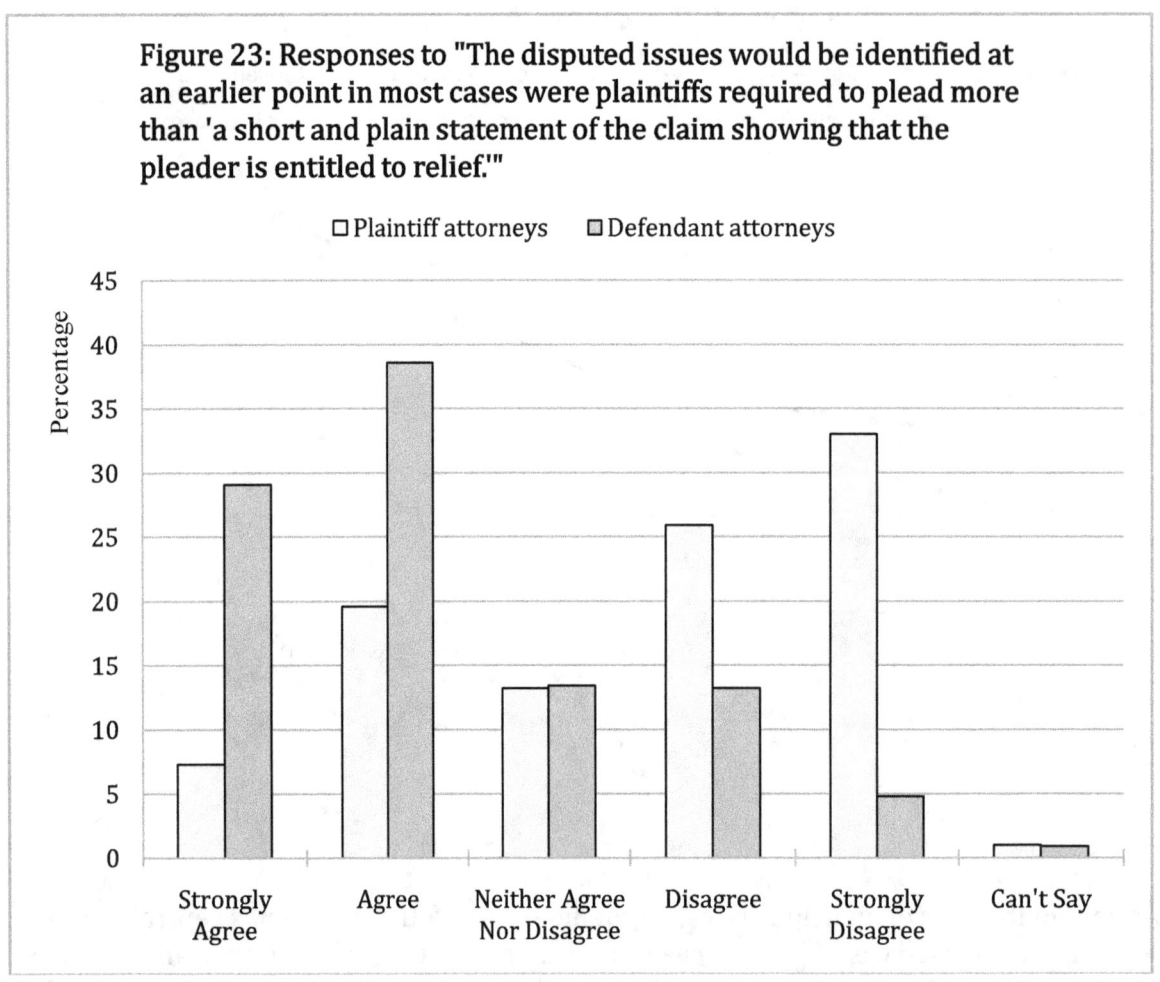

Figure 23: Responses to "The disputed issues would be identified at an earlier point in most cases were plaintiffs required to plead more than 'a short and plain statement of the claim showing that the pleader is entitled to relief.'"

As one would expect, plaintiff attorneys tended to disagree (25.9 percent) and strongly disagree (33 percent), while defendant attorneys tended to agree (38.6 percent) and strongly agree (29.1 percent).

Given the divergence of opinions on this question, it may be useful to classify respondents according to whether, in their overall practice, they primarily represent plaintiffs, primarily represent defendants, or represent both plaintiffs and defendants about equally, instead of according to their role in the closed case included in the sample. This distribution of responses is displayed in Figure 24.

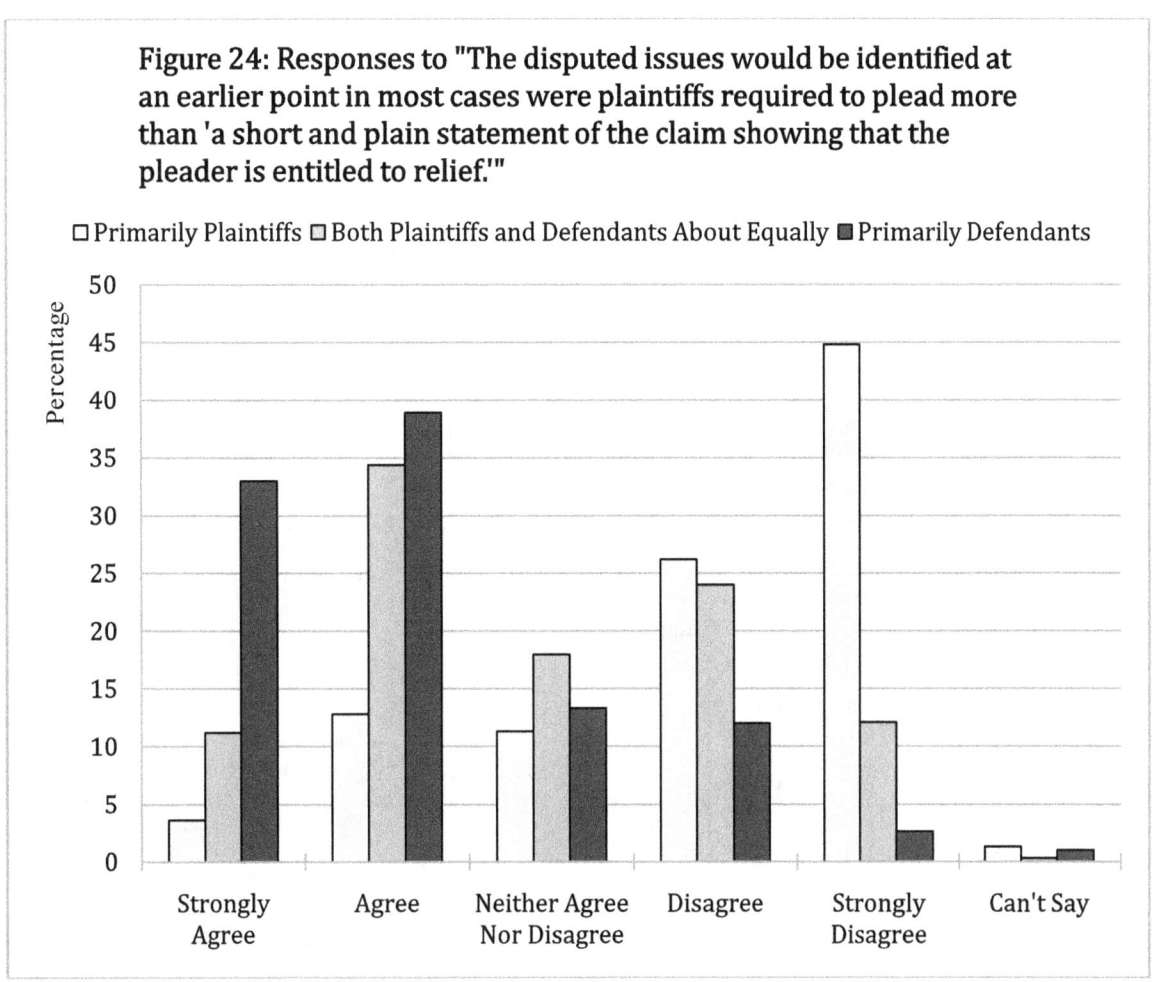

Figure 24: Responses to "The disputed issues would be identified at an earlier point in most cases were plaintiffs required to plead more than 'a short and plain statement of the claim showing that the pleader is entitled to relief.'"

Respondents who represent primarily plaintiffs disagreed (26.2 percent) and strongly disagreed (44.8 percent) with the statement; respondents who represent primarily defendants agreed (38.9 percent) and strongly agreed (33 percent). But the most interesting group is composed of attorneys who reported that they represent plaintiffs and defendants about equally. This group of attorneys agreed (34.4 percent) or strongly agreed (11.2 percent) with the statement 45.6 percent of the time and disagreed (24 percent) or strongly disagreed (12.1 percent) with the statement 36.1 percent of the time. Among attorneys who represent both plaintiffs and defendants about equally, in short, the plurality agrees that disputed issues would be identified earlier with fact pleading.

Respondents were then asked whether the added burdens for plaintiffs would outweigh any benefits, even if raising the pleading standards would help to identify and frame disputed issues at an earlier stage in litigation. The distribution of responses is displayed in Figure 25.

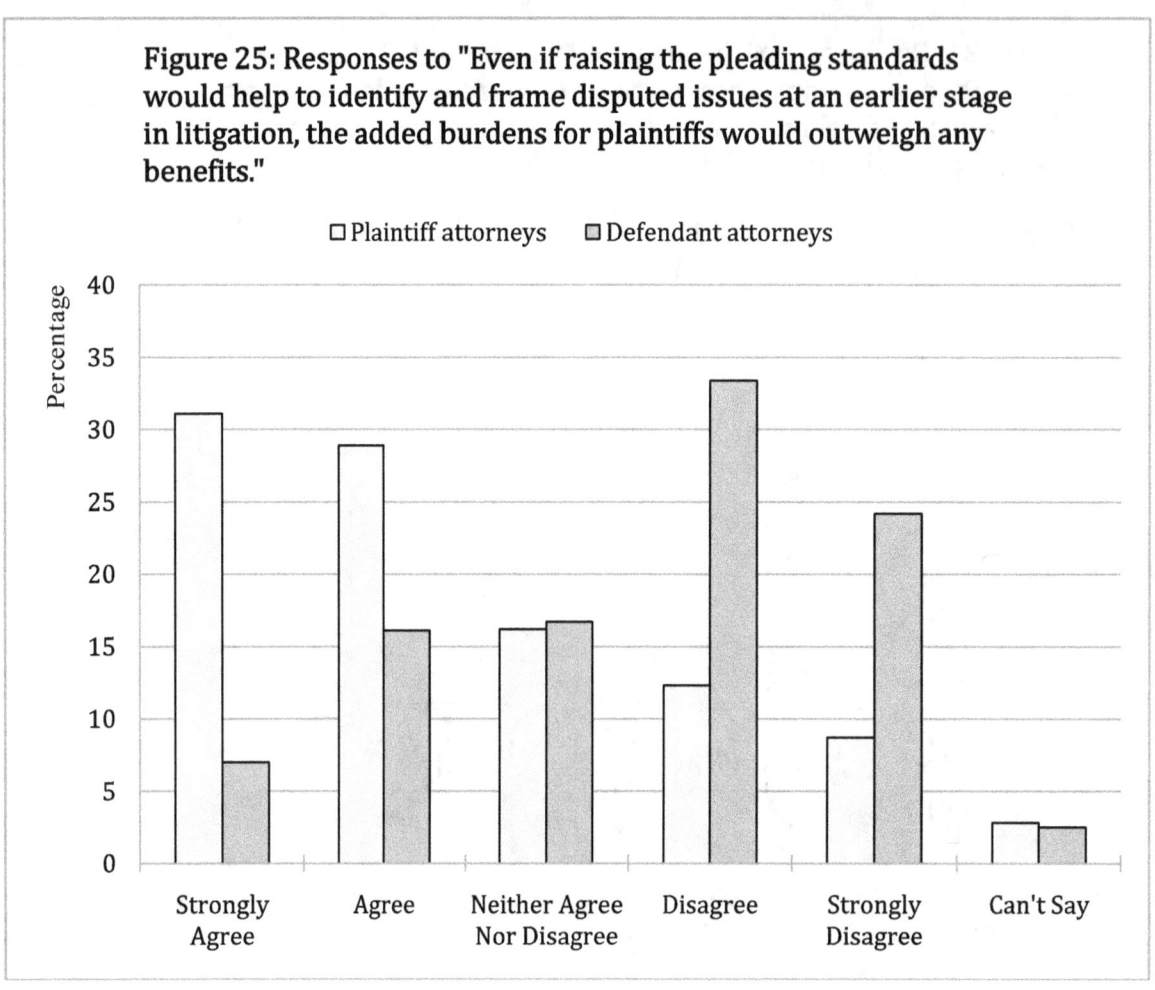

Figure 25: Responses to "Even if raising the pleading standards would help to identify and frame disputed issues at an earlier stage in litigation, the added burdens for plaintiffs would outweigh any benefits."

As in the previous figure, plaintiff and defendant attorneys expressed very different opinions regarding the potential burdens of fact pleading on plaintiffs. Plaintiff attorneys tended to agree (28.9 percent) or strongly agree (31.1 percent), while defendant attorneys tended to disagree (33.4 percent) or strongly disagree (24.2 percent).

Again, it may be useful to examine the opinions of attorneys who reported that they represent plaintiffs and defendants about equally. The distribution of responses is displayed in Figure 26. Respondents representing primarily plaintiffs agreed (28.8 percent) or strongly agreed (39.5 percent) with the statement 68.3 percent of the time. Respondents representing primarily defendants disagreed (34.1 percent) or strongly disagreed (27.7 percent) with the statement 61.8 percent of the time. Respondents representing both plaintiffs and defendants about equally agreed (32.7 percent) or strongly agreed (14.8 percent) with the statement 47.5 percent of the time and disagreed (21.5 percent) or strongly disagreed (10 percent) with the statement 31.5 percent of the time.

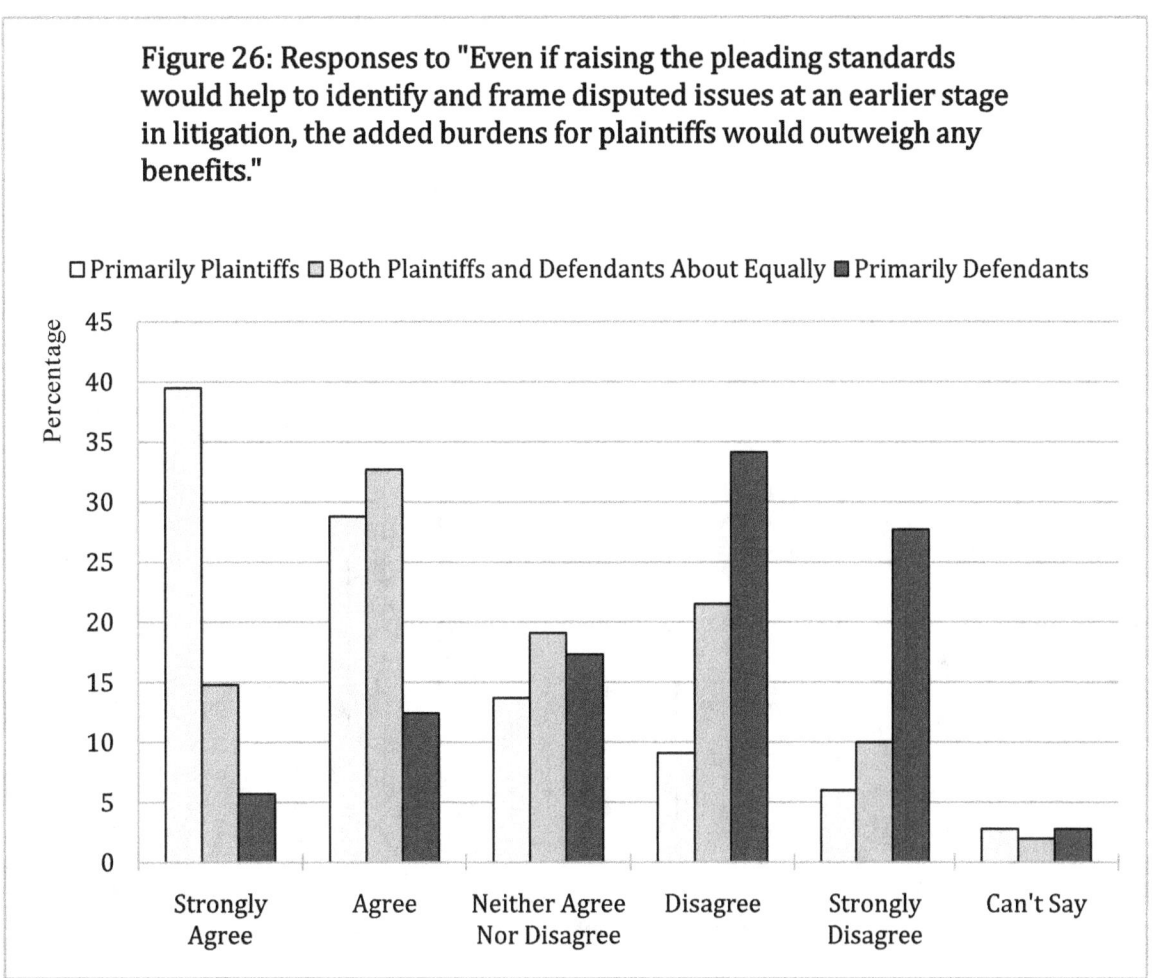

Figure 26: Responses to "Even if raising the pleading standards would help to identify and frame disputed issues at an earlier stage in litigation, the added burdens for plaintiffs would outweigh any benefits."

In short, while respondents who represent both plaintiffs and defendants about equally tend to agree that raising pleading standards would help to frame disputed issues earlier in litigation, they also tend to agree that the added burdens to plaintiffs would outweigh any benefits.

Respondents were then asked a series of questions about simplified procedures. The first such question, question 60, asked respondents whether the Rules' system of notice pleading and expansive discovery disproportionately increases the costs of litigating in federal court in relation to the system's benefits. For the rest of the simplified procedures questions, the report will continue to separate attorneys into three groups instead of two. The distribution of responses is displayed in Figure 27.

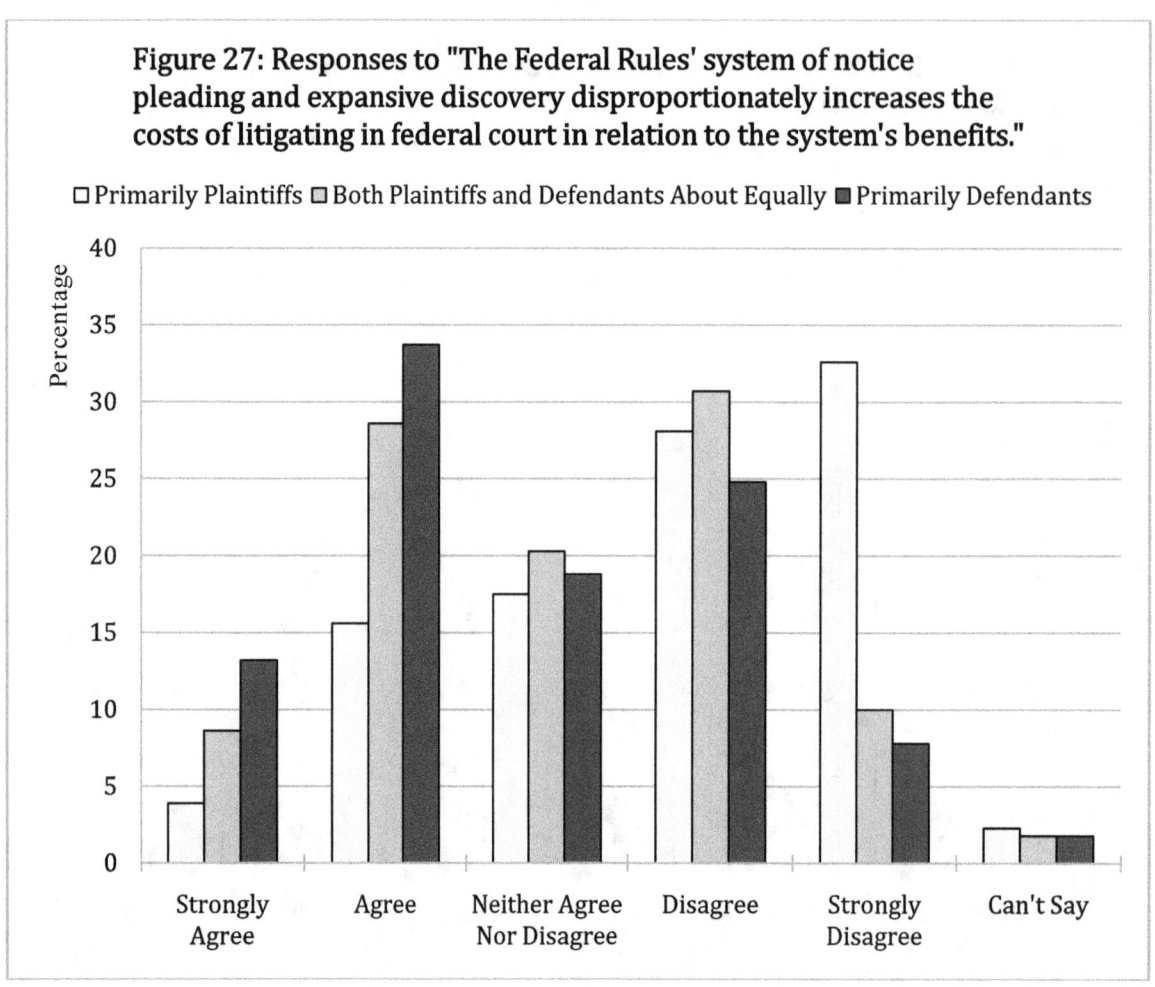

This question elicited mostly negative reactions from respondents representing primarily plaintiffs, relatively positive reactions from respondents representing primarily defendants, and decidedly mixed reactions from respondents representing both plaintiffs and defendants about equally. Respondents representing primarily plaintiffs disagreed or strongly disagreed with the statement 60.7 percent of the time, and agreed or strongly agreed just 19.5 percent. Respondents representing primarily defendants agreed or strongly agreed with the statement 46.9 percent of the time, and disagreed or strongly disagreed with the statement 32.6 percent of the time. Respondents representing both plaintiffs and defendants about equally agreed or strongly agreed with the statement 37.2 percent of the time and disagreed or strongly disagreed with the statement 40.7 percent of the time.

Respondents were next asked whether heightened pleading standards and restrictions on discovery would discourage litigants from filing cases in federal court. The distribution of responses is displayed in Figure 28.

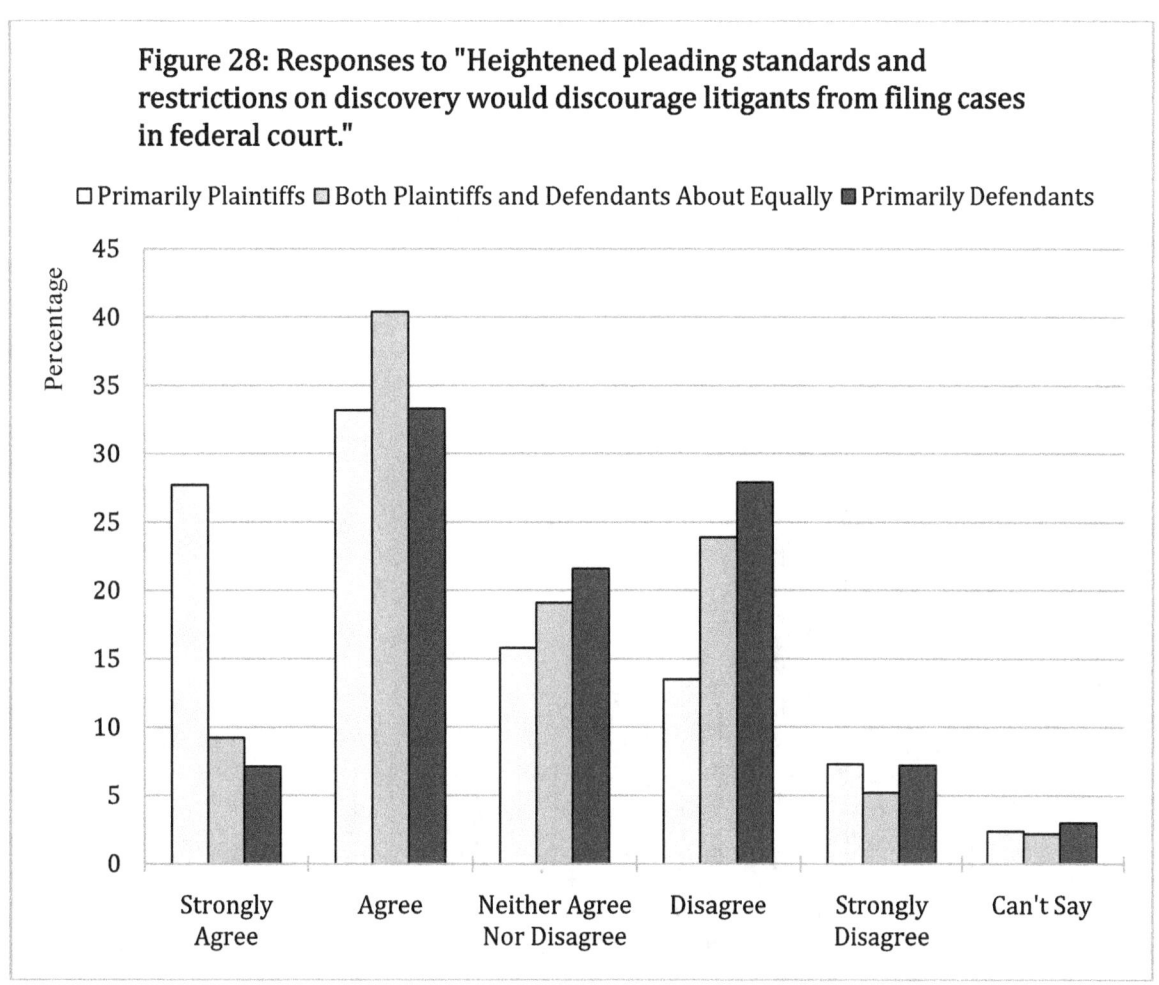

Figure 28: Responses to "Heightened pleading standards and restrictions on discovery would discourage litigants from filing cases in federal court."

This question elicited agreement from plaintiff attorneys and, to a lesser extent, from the other two groups, as well. Respondents representing primarily plaintiffs agreed or strongly agreed with the statement 60.9 percent of the time and disagreed or strongly disagreed 20.8 percent of the time. Respondents representing primarily defendants agreed or strongly agreed with the statement 40.4 percent of the time and disagreed or strongly disagreed with the statement 35.1 percent of the time; this group of respondents included 21.6 percent who expressed no opinion. Respondents representing both plaintiffs and defendants about equally agreed or strongly agreed with the statement 49.6 percent of the time and disagreed or strongly disagreed with the statement 29.1 percent of the time.

The next questions asked about potential "pilot" programs in the federal courts. Question 62 asked whether the federal courts should test simplified procedures, with all parties' consent, in a few select districts to determine whether such an idea is feasible. The distribution of responses is displayed in Figure 29.

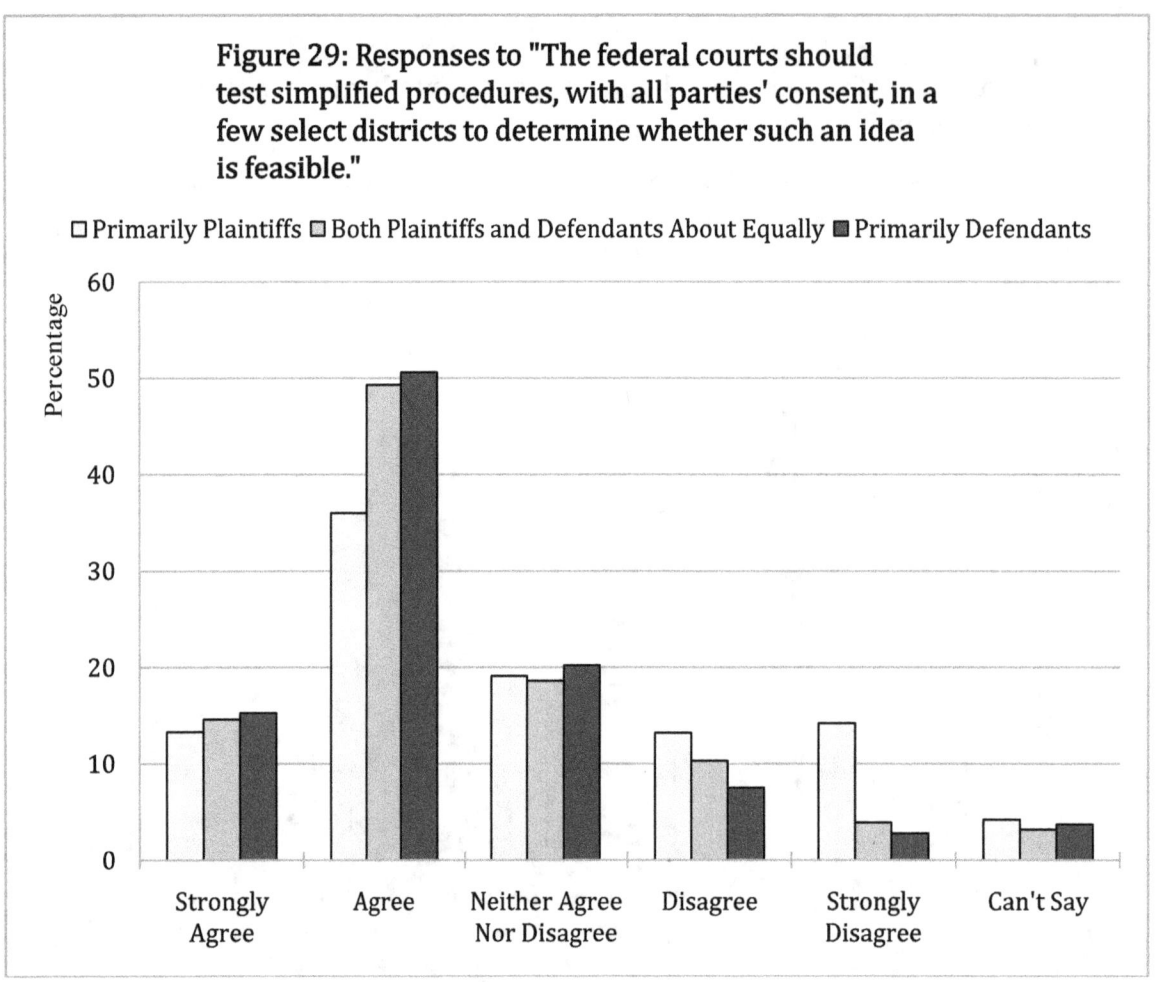

Figure 29: Responses to "The federal courts should test simplified procedures, with all parties' consent, in a few select districts to determine whether such an idea is feasible."

This question tended to elicit agreement, although more than a quarter of respondents representing primarily plaintiffs expressed disagreement. Respondents representing primarily plaintiffs agreed or strongly agreed with the statement 49.3 percent of the time; respondents representing both plaintiffs and defendants about equally agreed or strongly agreed 63.9 percent of the time; and respondents representing primarily defendants agreed or strongly agreed 65.9 percent of the time. About 1 in 5 respondents expressed no opinion.

Respondents were next asked, if such simplified procedures had been an available option as part of such a test program at the time the closed case was filed, would they have recommended that their clients choose them over the existing Rules. The distribution of responses is displayed in Figure 30.

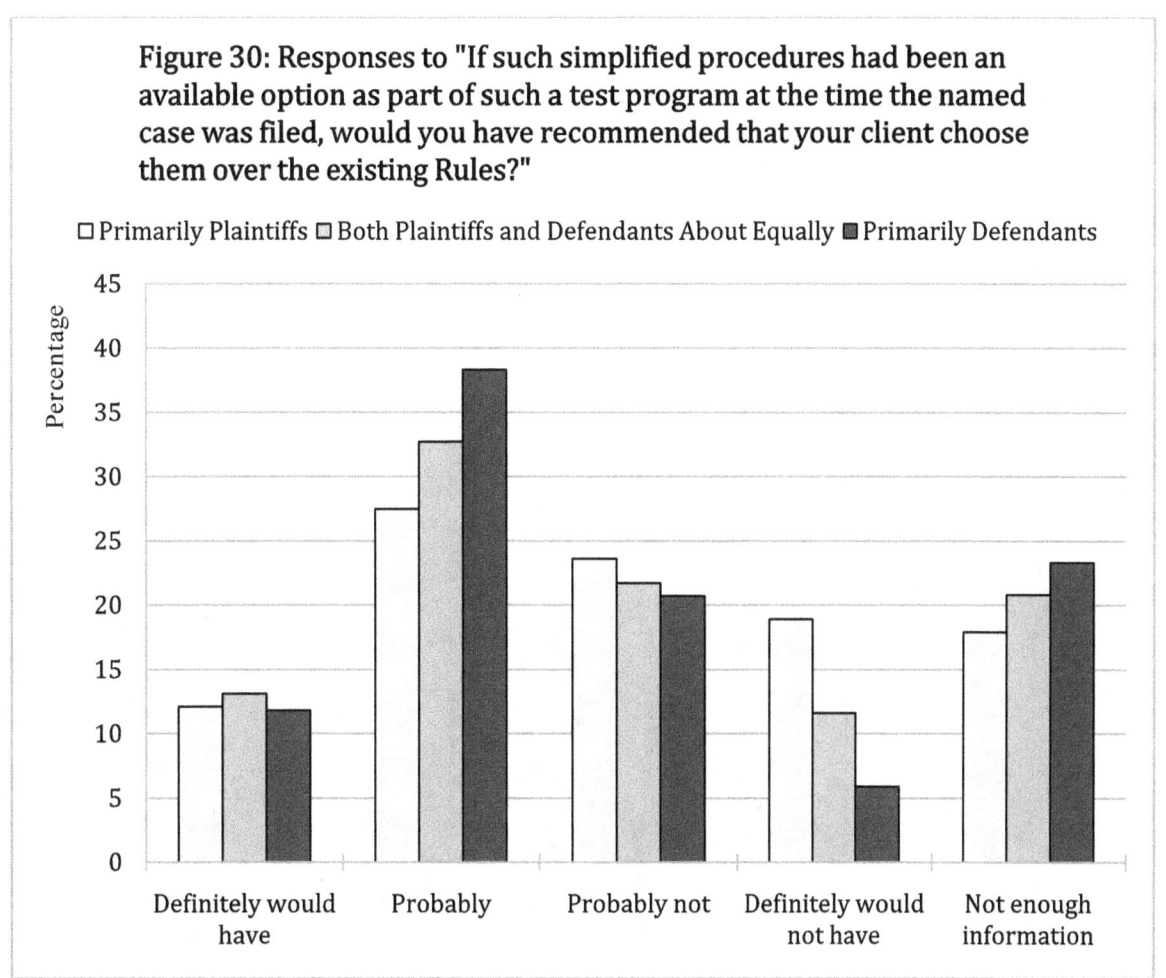

Figure 30: Responses to "If such simplified procedures had been an available option as part of such a test program at the time the named case was filed, would you have recommended that your client choose them over the existing Rules?"

As the figure illustrates, the most common response for all three groups of respondents was "probably, depending on circumstances." Fully 27.5 percent of those representing primarily plaintiffs, 32.7 percent of those representing both plaintiffs and defendants about equally, and 38.3 percent of those representing primarily defendants responded "probably." An additional 11.8 to 13.1 percent of each group responded "definitely." Respondents representing primarily plaintiffs expressed the most skepticism about the idea, responding "probably not" 23.6 percent of the time and "definitely would not have" 18.9 percent of the time. It should be noted that from 17.9 to 23.3 percent of each group responded that they did not have enough information to answer the question.

The final question in Section V asked whether respondents would recommend simplified procedures, if available, generally to their clients. The distribution of responses is displayed in Figure 31.

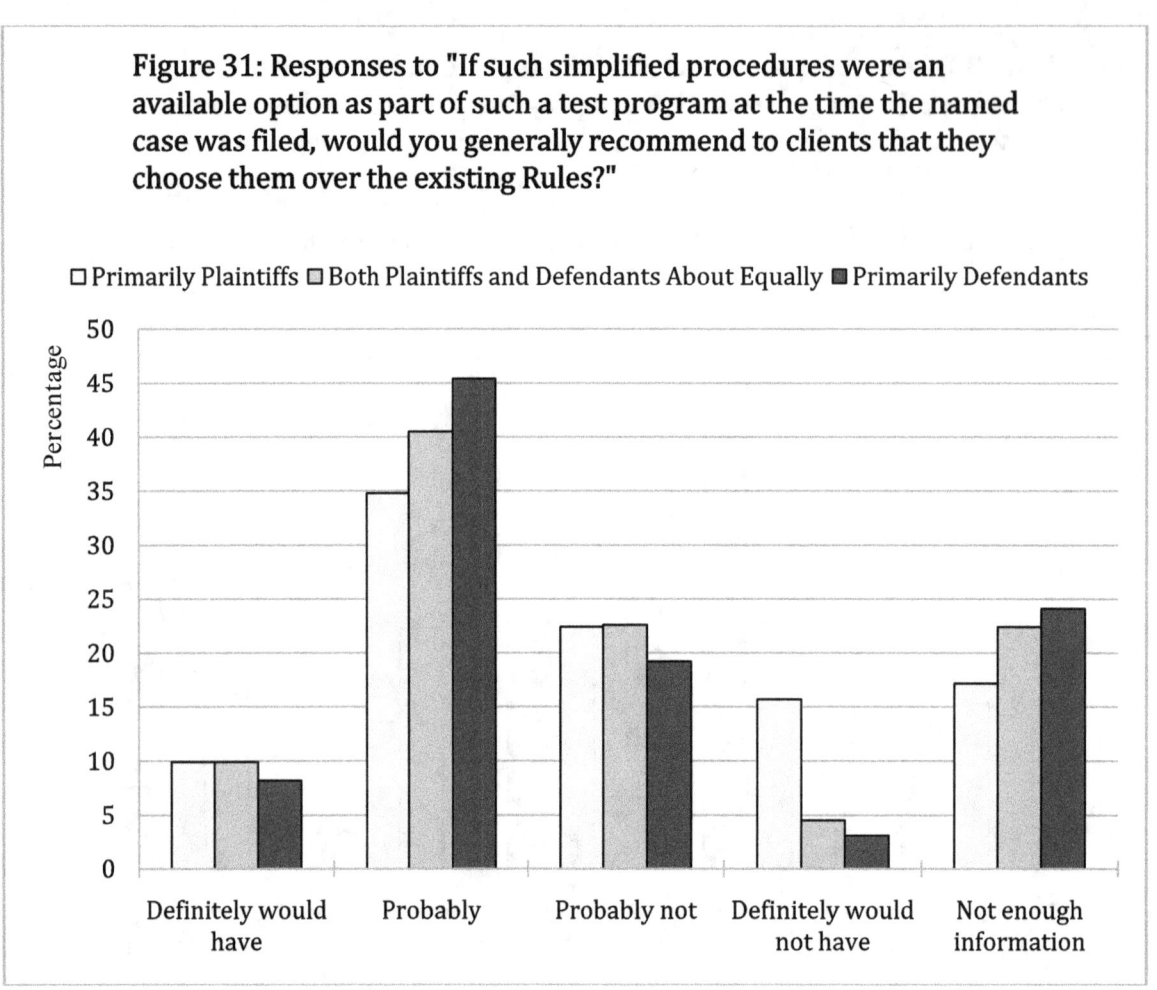

Figure 31: Responses to "If such simplified procedures were an available option as part of such a test program at the time the named case was filed, would you generally recommend to clients that they choose them over the existing Rules?"

Again, the most common response was "probably, depending on circumstances," which garnered 34.8, 40.5, and 45.4 percent, respectively, of the responses of the three groups. In short, respondents seemed somewhat more willing to consider participating in a test program in general than in the closed cases included in the sample. The percentage of respondents answering "definitely would," however, declined slightly, compared with the percentage for the closed case. Once again, those representing primarily plaintiffs were more likely to respond "definitely would not," and from 17.2 to 24.1 percent of respondents indicated that they did not have enough information to answer the question.

VII. The Federal Rules

The last section of the survey asked respondents a series of questions about the Rules based on their experiences in general. In this section, reported responses are not weighted; there is no reason to expect that the disposition or duration of a single case is related to attorney attitudes about the Federal Rules, in general. For this section, respondents are broken into three groups: those who represent primarily plaintiffs; those who indicated that they represent plaintiffs and defendants about equally; and those who primarily represent defendants. The analysis includes all respondents, including those not reporting any discovery in the closed case.

Respondents were first asked (in question 65) whether litigation in the federal courts is more expensive than litigation in the state courts in which they primarily practice. The distribution of responses is displayed in Figure 32.

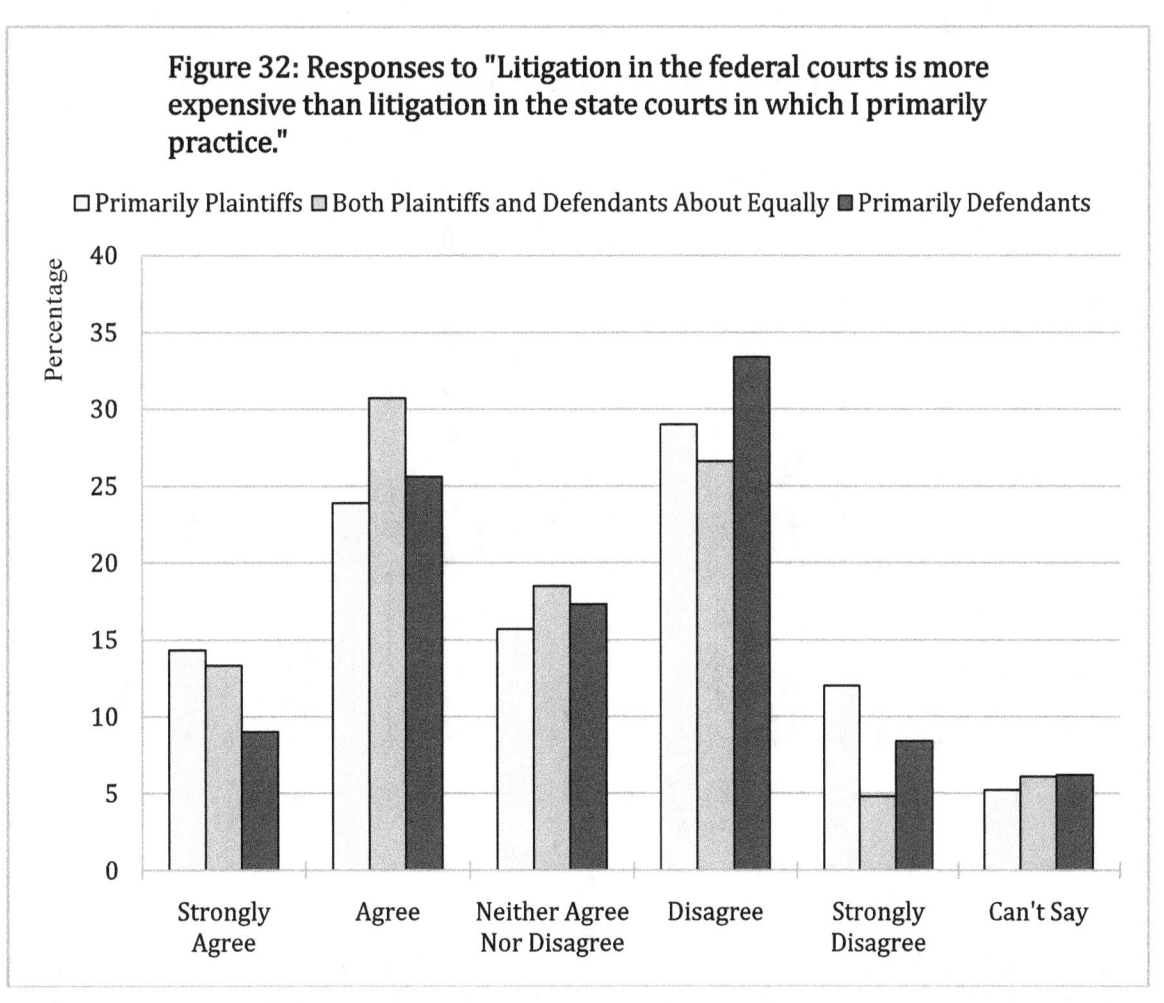

No group of attorneys agreed or disagreed with the statement a majority of the time. Those who primarily represent plaintiffs and those who primarily represent defendants disagreed or strongly disagreed 41.0 and 41.8 percent of the time, respectively, and agreed or strongly agreed 38.2 and 34.6 percent of the time, respectively. In short, these two groups were fairly evenly divided between agreeing and disagreeing, with the latter option taking a slight edge. In contrast, those who represent plaintiffs and defendants about equally were more likely to agree or strongly agree (44.0 percent of the time) than to disagree or strongly disagree (31.4 percent of the time).

Question 66 asked respondents to compare discovery costs in the federal courts with discovery in the state courts in which they primarily practice. The distribution of responses is displayed in Figure 33.

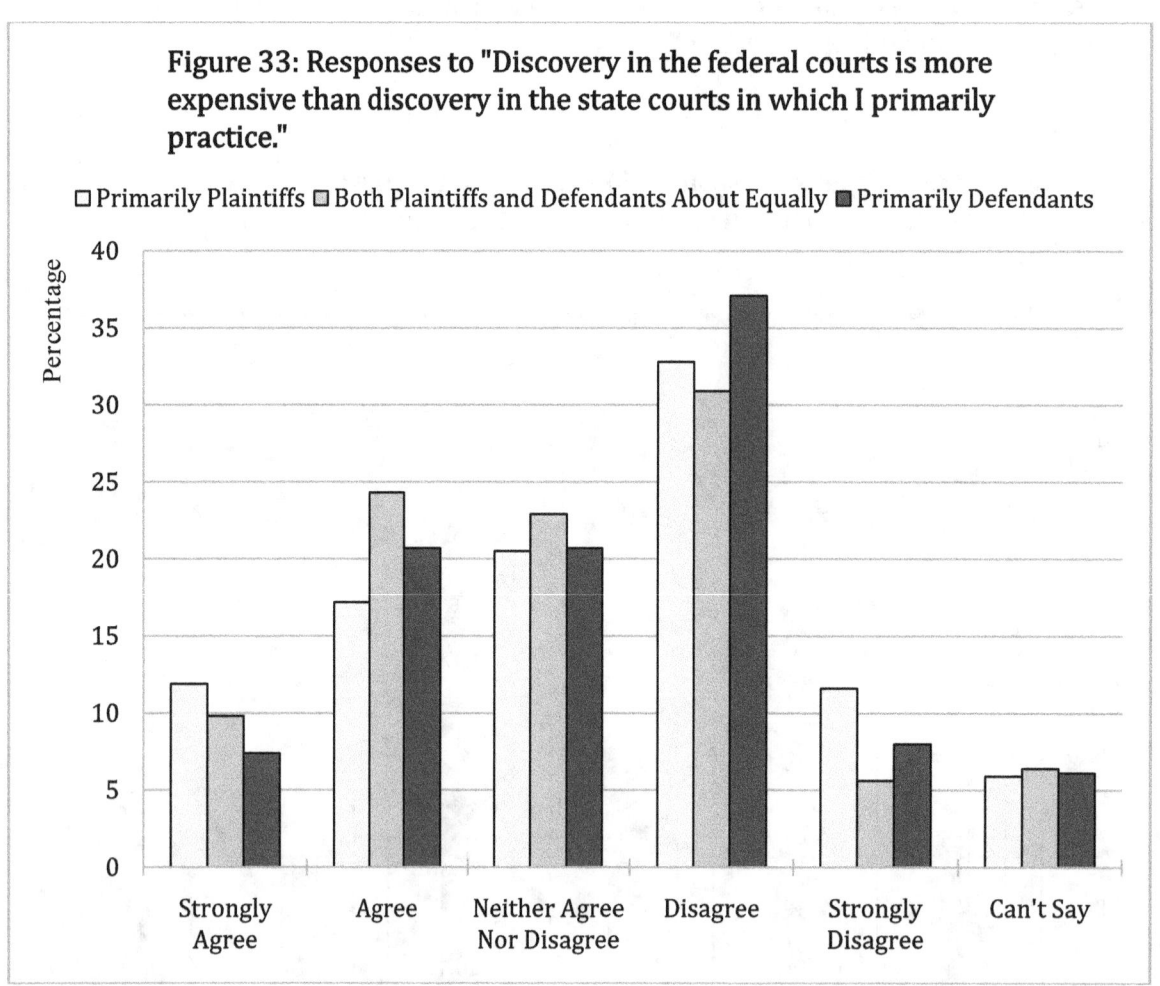

This question tended to elicit mixed reactions from respondents, with neither agreement nor disagreement representing a majority view for any group of respondents. For all three groups of respondents, the modal response was disagreement. In terms of agreement, 29.1 percent of respondents representing primarily plaintiffs agreed or strongly agreed with the statement, 34.1 percent of respondents representing plaintiffs and defendants about equally agreed or strongly agreed, and 28.1 percent of respondents primarily representing defendants agreed or strongly agreed. In terms of disagreement, 44.4 percent of respondents primarily representing plaintiffs disagreed or strongly disagreed, 36.5 percent of respondents representing plaintiffs and defendants about equally disagreed or strongly disagreed, and 45.1 percent of respondents primarily representing defendants disagreed or strongly disagreed. From 20 to 25 percent of respondents in each group neither agreed nor disagreed with the statement.

Question 67 asked respondents whether discovery in the federal courts leads to more reliable and predictable case outcomes than in courts with more restricted discovery. The distribution of responses is displayed in Figure 34.

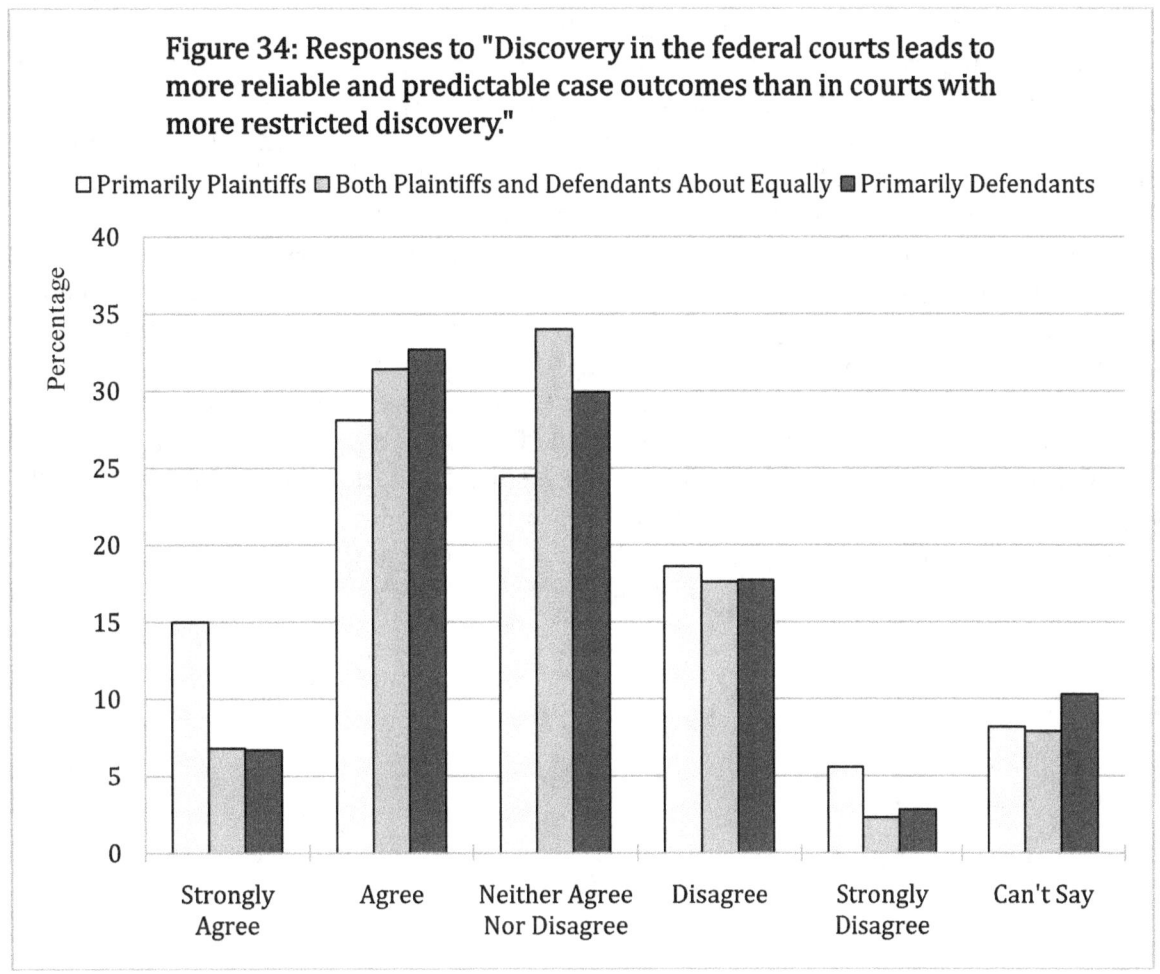

This question drew a large number of neutral responses. Almost 1 in 4 (24.5 percent) of those representing primarily plaintiffs neither agreed nor disagreed; 34 percent of those representing plaintiffs and defendants about equally neither agreed nor disagreed; and 29.9 percent of those primarily representing defendants neither agreed nor disagreed. In addition, about 10 percent of each group declined to answer. This level of neutrality to the statement may reflect a lack of experience in "courts with more restricted discovery" than in federal courts.

In terms of respondents taking a position on the question, agreement with the statement was around 20 percentage points higher in each group than disagreement. Respondents who primarily represent plaintiffs agreed or strongly agreed with the statement 43.1 percent of the time, and disagreed or strongly disagreed 24.2 percent of the time. Respondents who represent plaintiffs and defendants about equally agreed or strongly agreed with the statement 38.2 percent of the time, and disagreed or strongly disagreed 19.9 percent of the time. And respondents who primarily represent defendants agreed or strongly agreed with the statement 39.4 percent of the time, and disagreed or strongly disagreed 20.5 percent of the time. This level of agreement may simply reflect respondents' logical inference that less restricted discovery would give rise "to more reliable and predictable case outcomes," of course. It is still interesting that more than 1 respondent in 5 disagreed with the statement; the inference is that about 20 percent of respondents believe that more restricted discovery is not inconsistent with case outcomes at least as reliable and predictable as those in federal court.

Question 68 asked respondents whether the Rules should be revised to limit discovery in general. The distribution of responses is displayed in Figure 35. Unlike the previous question, this question did not draw a large number of neutral reactions. Respondents who primarily represent plaintiffs disagreed or strongly disagreed 70.7 percent of the time (37.7 percent strongly disagreed); this group agreed with the statement just 13.7 percent of the time. Somewhat surprisingly, respondents who primarily represent defendants disagreed or strongly disagreed with the statement 43.9 percent of the time, and agreed or strongly agreed 33.5 percent of the time. In other words, even those who primarily represent defendants were more likely to disagree than agree that discovery "in general" should be limited. A majority of respondents representing plaintiffs and defendants about equally disagreed or strongly disagreed with the statement (54.6 percent); this group agreed or strongly agreed with the statement about a quarter of the time (25.7 percent).

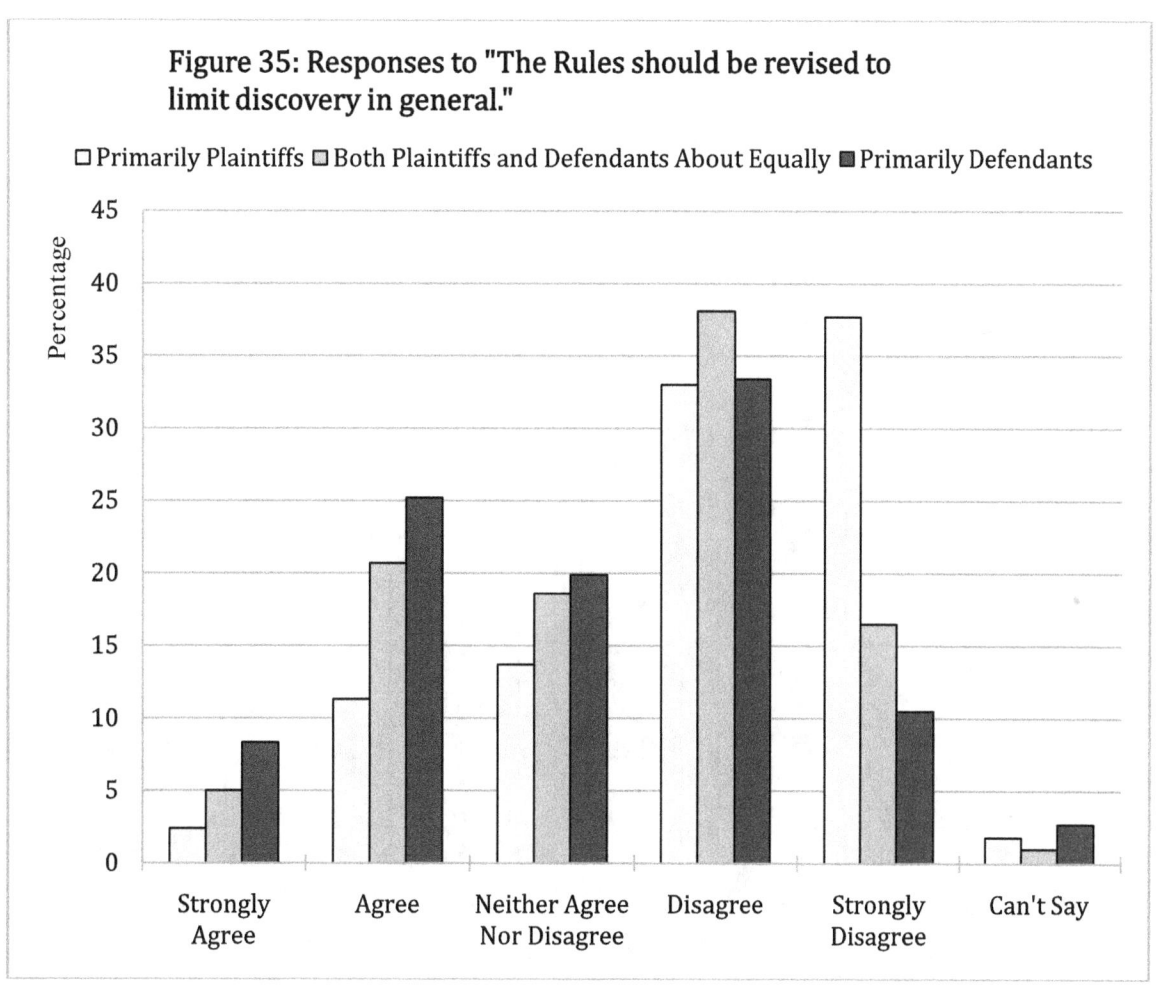

Figure 35: Responses to "The Rules should be revised to limit discovery in general."

Question 69 asked respondents whether the Rules should be revised to limit electronic discovery. The distribution of responses is displayed in Figure 36. The responses to this question were highly polarized. A majority of those primarily representing defendants agreed or strongly agreed that the Rules should be revised to limit electronic discovery—57.6 percent. A majority of those primarily representing plaintiffs disagreed—61.2 percent. Only 12.6 percent of those primarily representing plaintiffs agreed or strongly agreed, and 34.8 percent of those primarily representing defendants disagreed or strongly disagreed. Those representing plaintiffs and defendants about equally were about evenly split on this question—35.5 percent of this group agreed or strongly agreed that the Rules should be revised to limit electronic discovery, 39 percent disagreed or strongly disagreed, and 22.6 percent neither agreed nor disagreed.

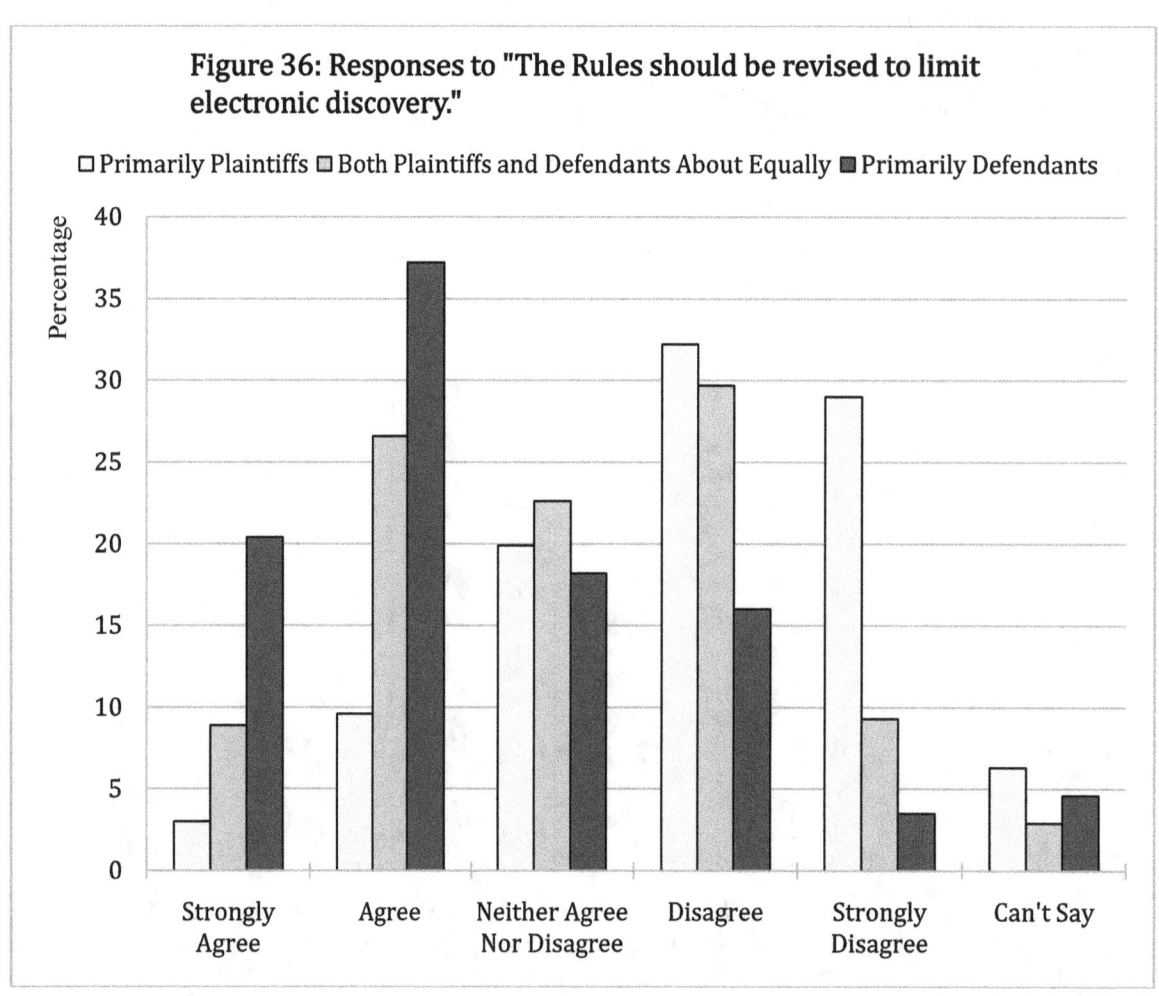

Figure 36: Responses to "The Rules should be revised to limit electronic discovery."

It is interesting that those representing primarily plaintiffs oppose limiting discovery in general 70.7 percent of the time but oppose limiting electronic discovery 61.2 percent of the time; the difference is almost certainly the larger number of respondents in that group taking a neutral or non-position with respect to electronic discovery. This probably reflects a lack of experience with electronic discovery issues—and thus less of a willingness to express a position on the issue—among this group of respondents. Those representing primarily defendants, on the other hand, are much more likely to support limited electronic discovery (57.6 percent) than to support limiting discovery in general (33.5 percent).

Question 70 asked respondents whether attorneys can cooperate in discovery while still being zealous advocates for their clients. The distribution of responses is displayed in Figure 37. There was little disagreement with this statement, and no substantive difference among the groups of respondents. Fully 93.1 percent of those representing primarily plaintiffs, 94.5 percent of those representing plaintiffs and defendants about equally, and 95.1 percent of those representing primarily defendants agreed or strongly agreed.

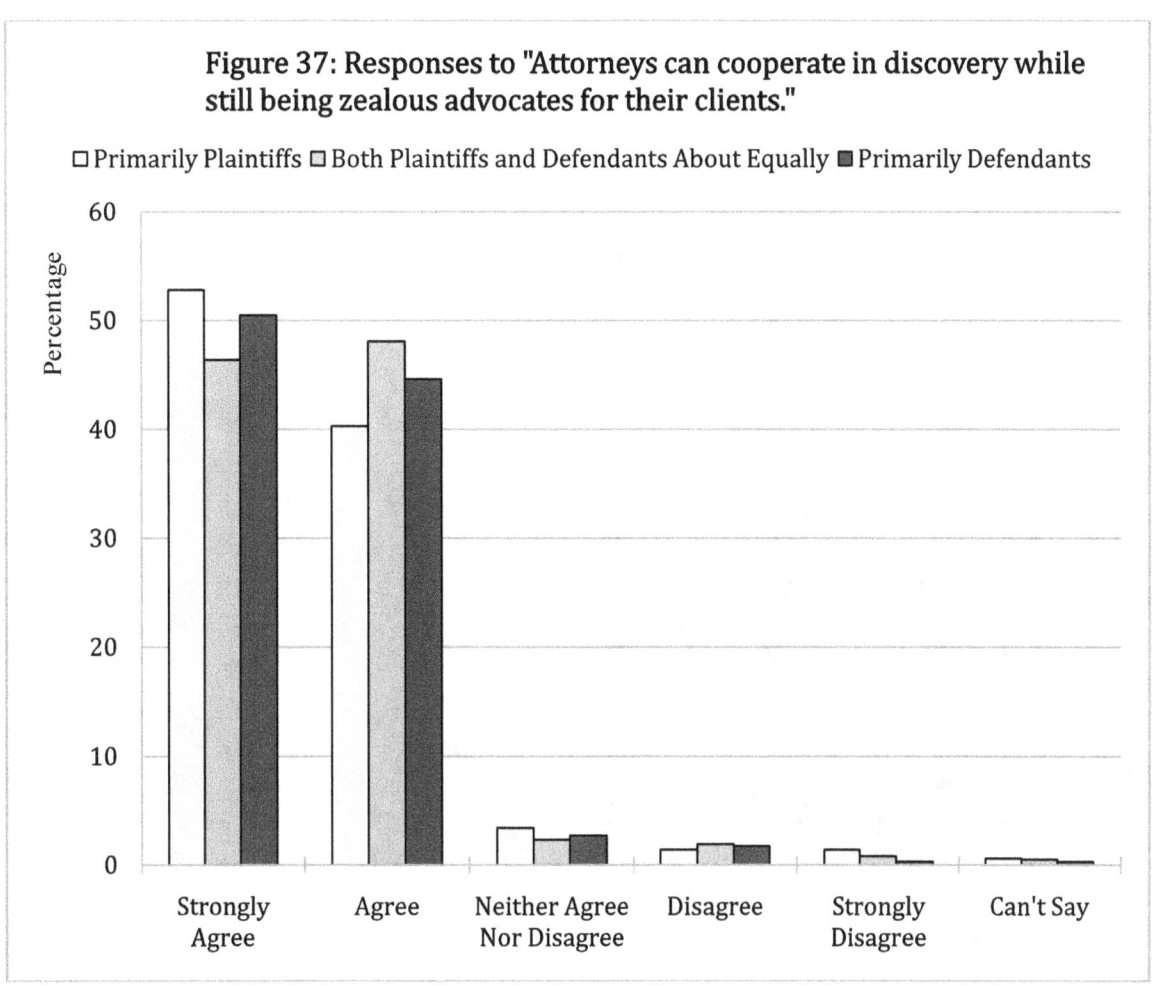

Figure 37: Responses to "Attorneys can cooperate in discovery while still being zealous advocates for their clients."

Question 71 asked respondents whether the Rules should be revised to enforce discovery obligations more effectively. The distribution of responses is displayed in Figure 38. This statement elicited agreement among all three groups. Those representing primarily plaintiffs agreed or strongly agreed 63.7 percent of the time, those representing plaintiffs and defendants about equally agreed or strongly agreed 61.8 percent of the time, and those primarily representing defendants agreed or strongly agreed 55.9 percent of the time. Disagreement with this statement was relatively uncommon—14 percent of those representing primarily defendants disagreed or strongly disagreed, and 13.5 percent of those representing primarily plaintiffs disagreed or strongly disagreed. Only 9 percent of those representing plaintiffs and defendants about equally disagreed or strongly disagreed.

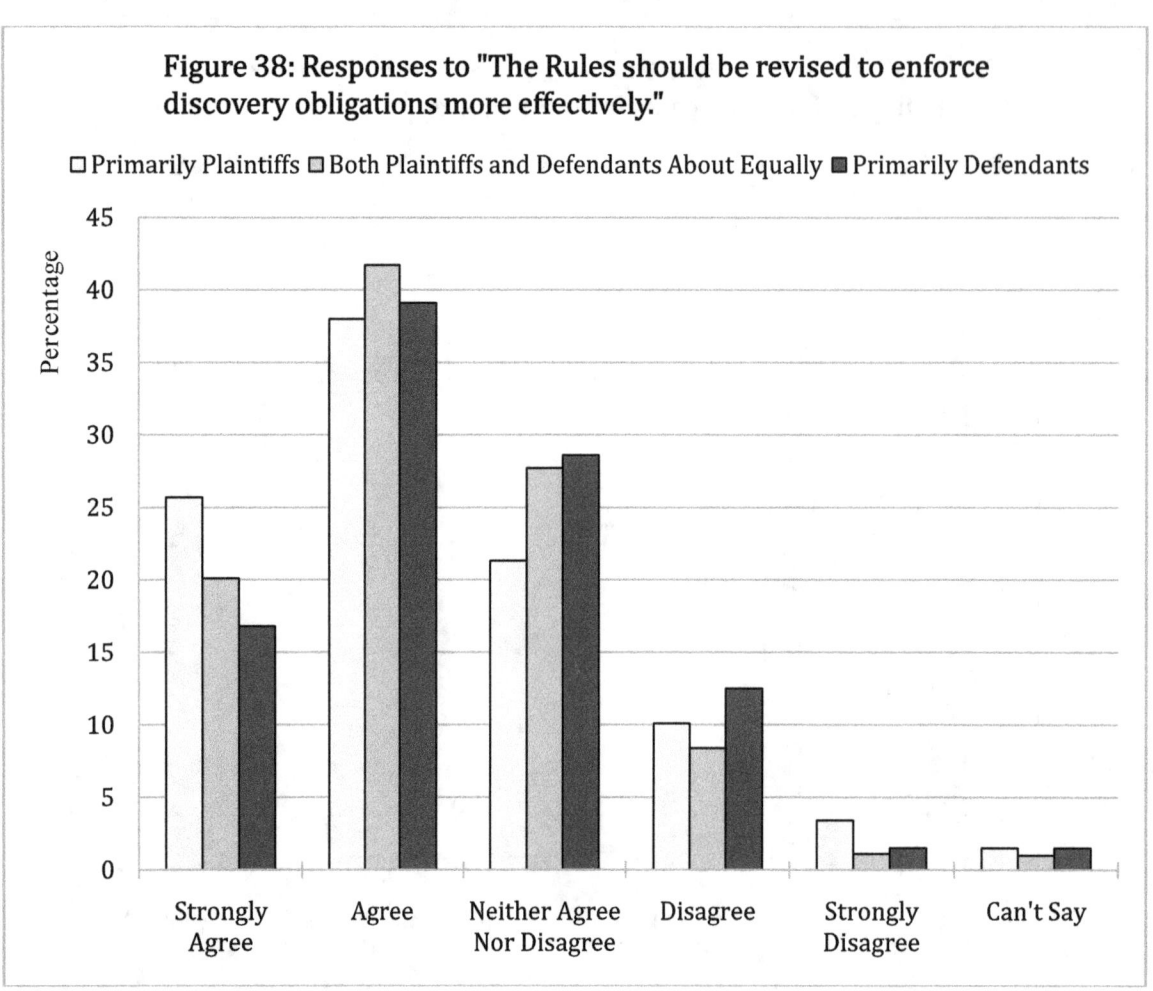

Figure 38: Responses to "The Rules should be revised to enforce discovery obligations more effectively."

Question 72 asked respondents whether the Rules should be revised to require additional mandatory disclosures. The distribution of responses is displayed in Figure 39. This statement elicited majority support from attorneys primarily representing plaintiffs; respondents primarily representing defendants were more likely to disagree than to agree, but respondents representing plaintiffs and defendants about equally were more likely to agree than to disagree. Respondents primarily representing plaintiffs agreed or strongly agreed with this statement 54.5 percent of the time; that group disagreed or strongly disagreed only 23.5 percent of the time, and neither agreed nor disagreed 20.1 percent of the time. Respondents representing plaintiffs and defendants about equally agreed or strongly agreed 42.2 percent of the time, disagreed or strongly disagreed 29.8 percent of the time, and neither agreed nor disagreed 26.4 percent of the time. Respondents primarily representing defendants agreed or strongly agreed 32.6 percent of the time, disagreed or strongly disagreed 40.5 percent of the time, and neither agreed or disagreed 24.2 percent of the time.

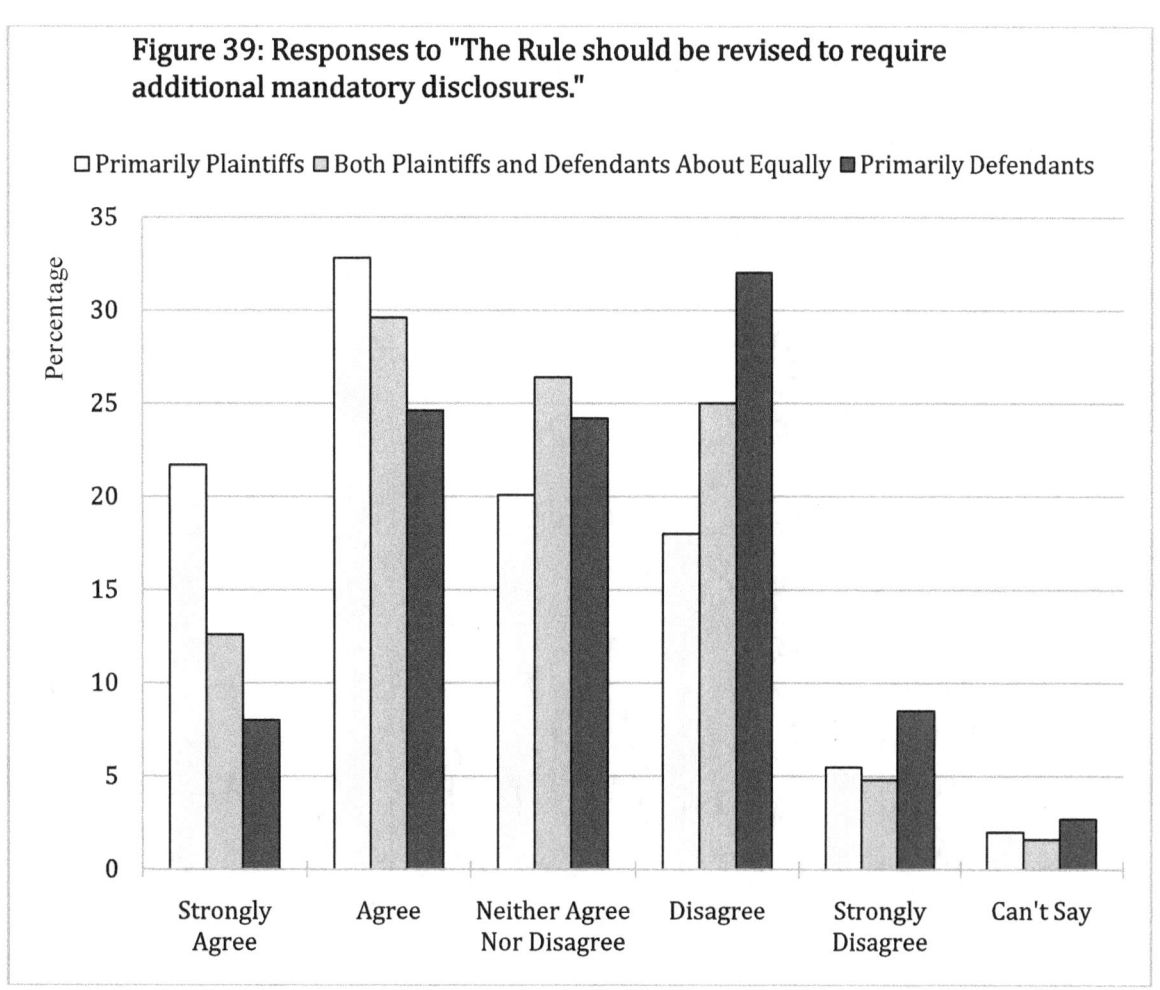

Figure 39: Responses to "The Rule should be revised to require additional mandatory disclosures."

Question 73 asked respondents whether the Rules should be revised to provide for routine sharing of the costs of producing ESI when the burdens of production are not equal. The distribution of responses is displayed in Figure 40. The responses varied considerably by group. Respondents primarily representing defendants agreed or strongly agreed with this statement 63.9 percent of the time, disagreed or strongly disagreed 12 percent of the time, and neither agreed nor disagreed 20.2 percent of the time. Those representing primarily plaintiffs agreed or strongly agreed 29.4 percent of the time and disagreed or strongly disagreed 37 percent of the time; slightly more than a quarter of this group neither agreed nor disagreed with the statement (27.4 percent). Respondents representing plaintiffs and defendants about equally agreed or strongly agreed 48.7 percent of the time, disagreed or strongly disagreed 20.4 percent, and neither agreed nor disagreed 27.7 percent of the time.

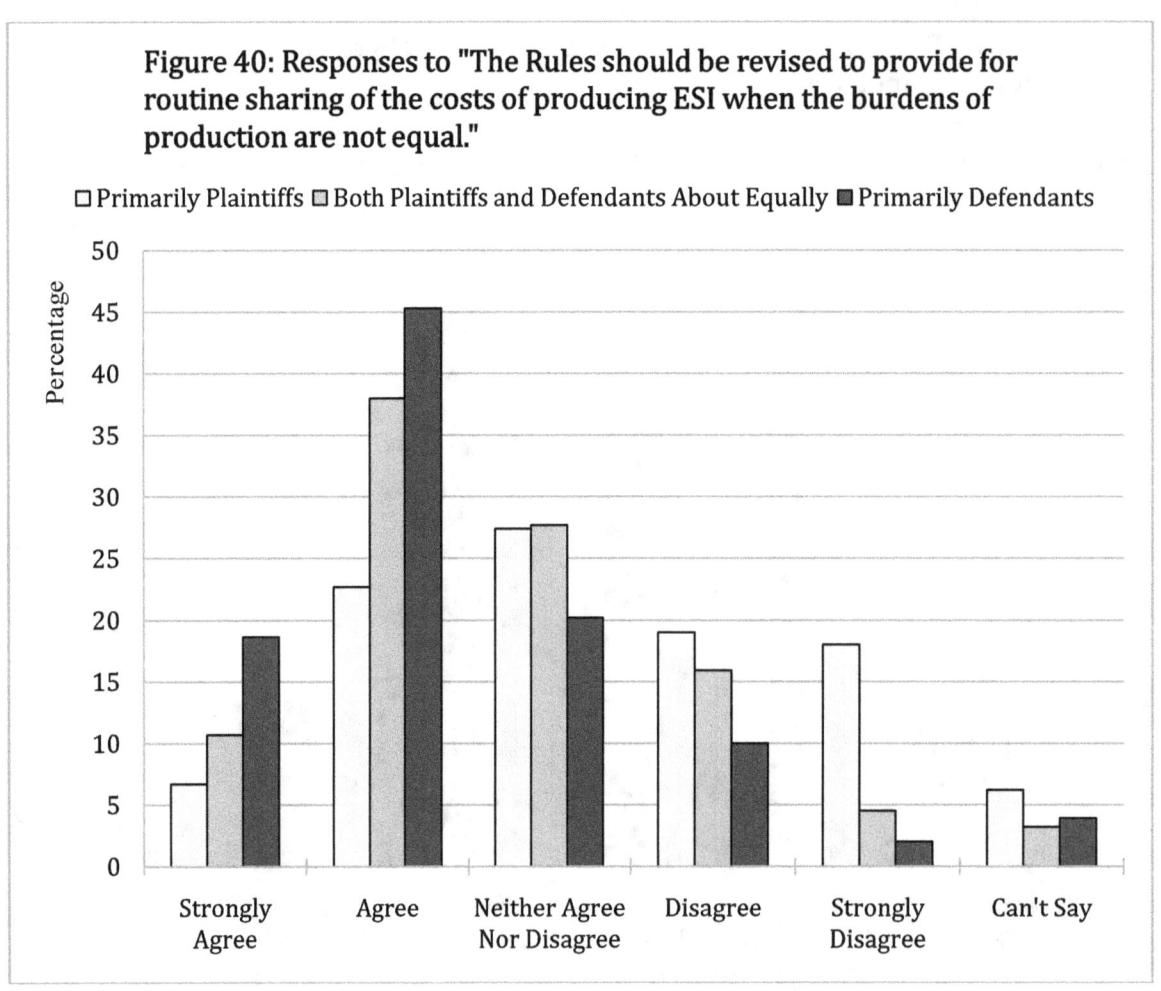

Figure 40: Responses to "The Rules should be revised to provide for routine sharing of the costs of producing ESI when the burdens of production are not equal."

Question 74 asked respondents whether the Rules should be revised to encourage more judicial case management. The distribution of responses is displayed in Figure 41. This statement did not elicit majority support from any of the groups. Respondents primarily representing plaintiffs agreed or strongly agreed 33.4 percent of the time, respondents representing both plaintiffs and defendants agreed or strongly agreed 42.6 percent of the time, and respondents representing primarily defendants agreed or strongly agreed 34.4 percent of the time. A substantial percentage of each group expressed no opinion in response to this statement: 28.9 percent of those representing primarily plaintiffs, 30.3 percent of those representing plaintiffs and defendants about equally, and 33.7 percent of those representing primarily defendants. Only those representing primarily plaintiffs were more likely to disagree or disagree strongly (34.7 percent) than to agree or agree strongly, and then only marginally so. Those representing plaintiffs and defendants about equally (25.8 percent) and those representing primarily defendants (29.9 percent) were less likely to disagree than to agree.

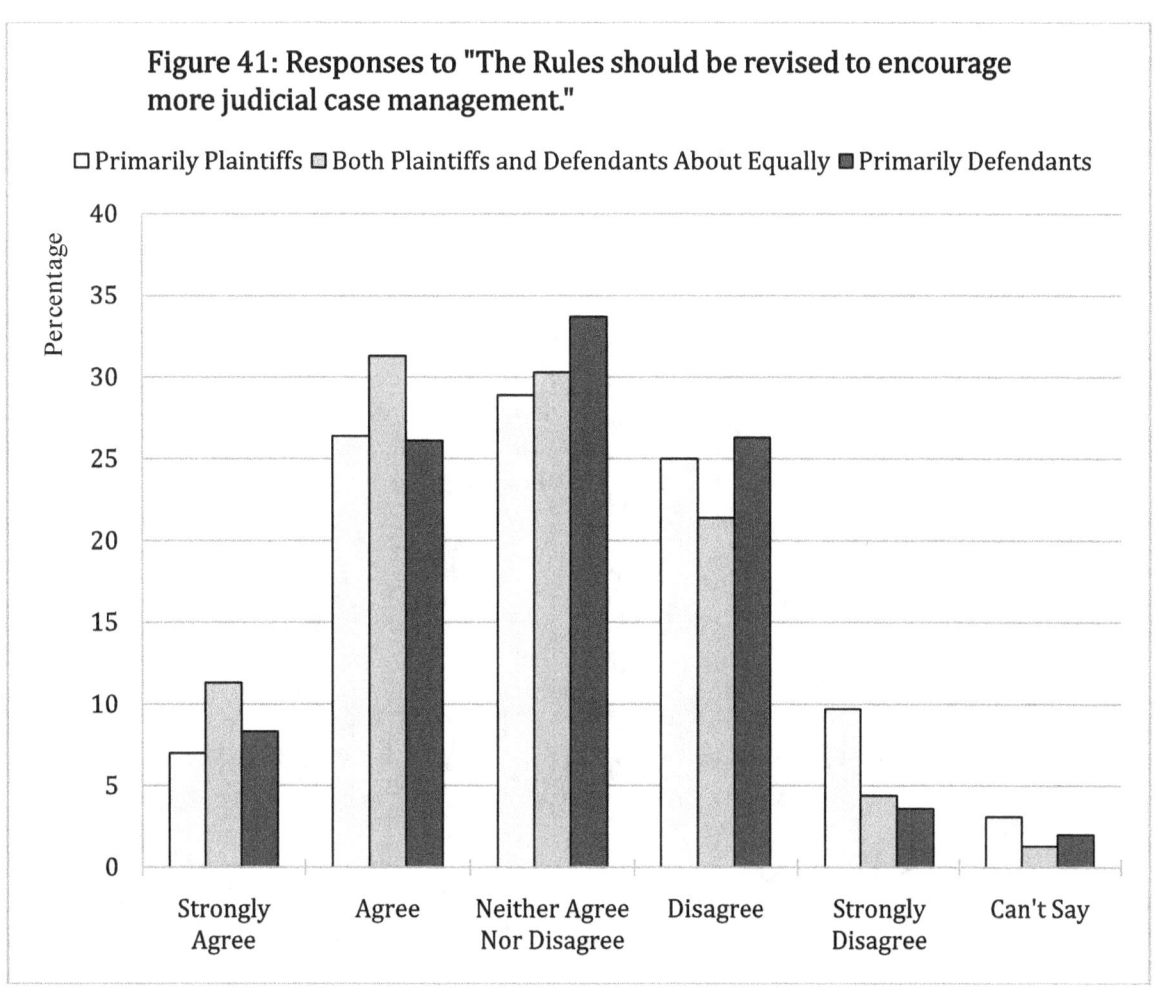

Question 75 asked respondents whether the Rules should be revised to discourage judicial case management. This statement tended to elicit neutral or negative reactions. The distribution of responses is displayed in Figure 42. Those representing primarily plaintiffs disagreed or disagreed strongly 46.2 percent of the time, those representing plaintiffs and defendants about equally disagreed or disagreed strongly 53.3 percent of the time, and those primarily representing defendants disagreed or strongly disagreed 48.9 percent of the time. Substantial percentages of each group neither agreed nor disagreed: 32.9 percent of those primarily representing plaintiffs, 31.6 percent of those representing plaintiffs and defendants about equally, and 37.4 percent of those representing primarily defendants. As one could infer from the preceding figures, few respondents agreed with this statement. Respondents primarily representing plaintiffs agreed or strongly agreed 15.8 percent of the time, those representing plaintiffs and defendants about equally agreed or strongly agreed 11.2 percent of the time, and those representing primarily defendants agreed or strongly disagreed 10.7 percent of the time.

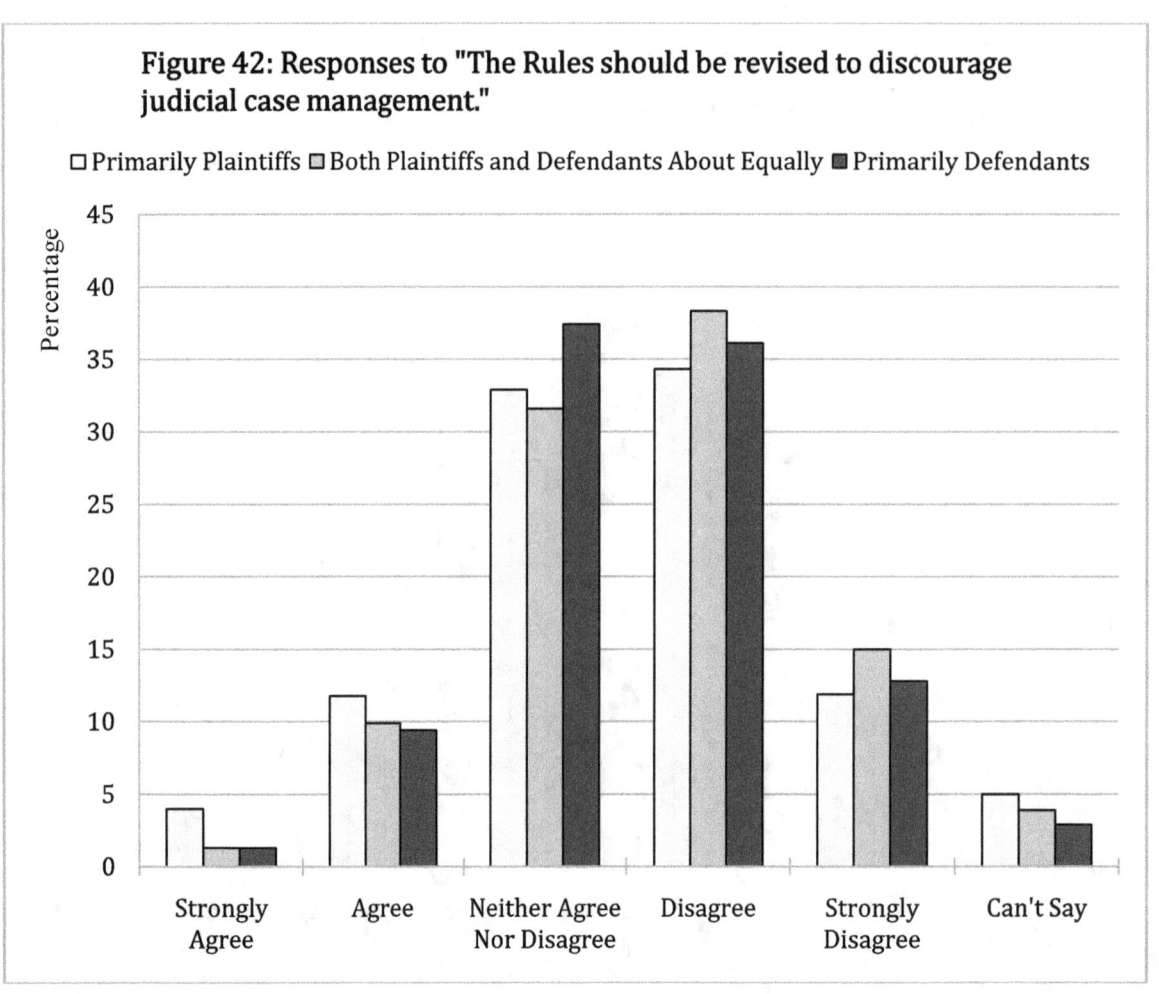

Taking questions 74 and 75 together, there appears to be some consensus that the Rules should not be revised to discourage case management by federal judges and that, moreover, the Rules should not be revised to encourage additional case management by those same judges.

Question 76 asked whether the outcome of cases in the federal system are generally fair. The distribution of responses is displayed in Figure 43. A majority of every group of attorneys agreed or strongly agreed with the statement. However, those primarily representing plaintiffs were less likely than the other two groups to agree or strongly agree. Those primarily representing defendants agreed (two-thirds of all respondents in this category agreed) or strongly agreed 80.3 percent of the time; those primarily representing plaintiffs agreed or strongly agreed 53.9 percent of the time. Attorneys representing both about equally agreed or strongly agreed 69.2 percent of the time. Fully 22.5 percent of those primarily representing plaintiffs disagreed or disagreed strongly, compared with 8.5 percent of respondents representing both about equally and 4.2 percent of those representing primarily defendants. Moreover, 20.3 percent of those representing primarily plaintiffs, 19.7 percent of those representing both about equally, and 13.7 percent of those representing primarily defendants expressed no opinion.

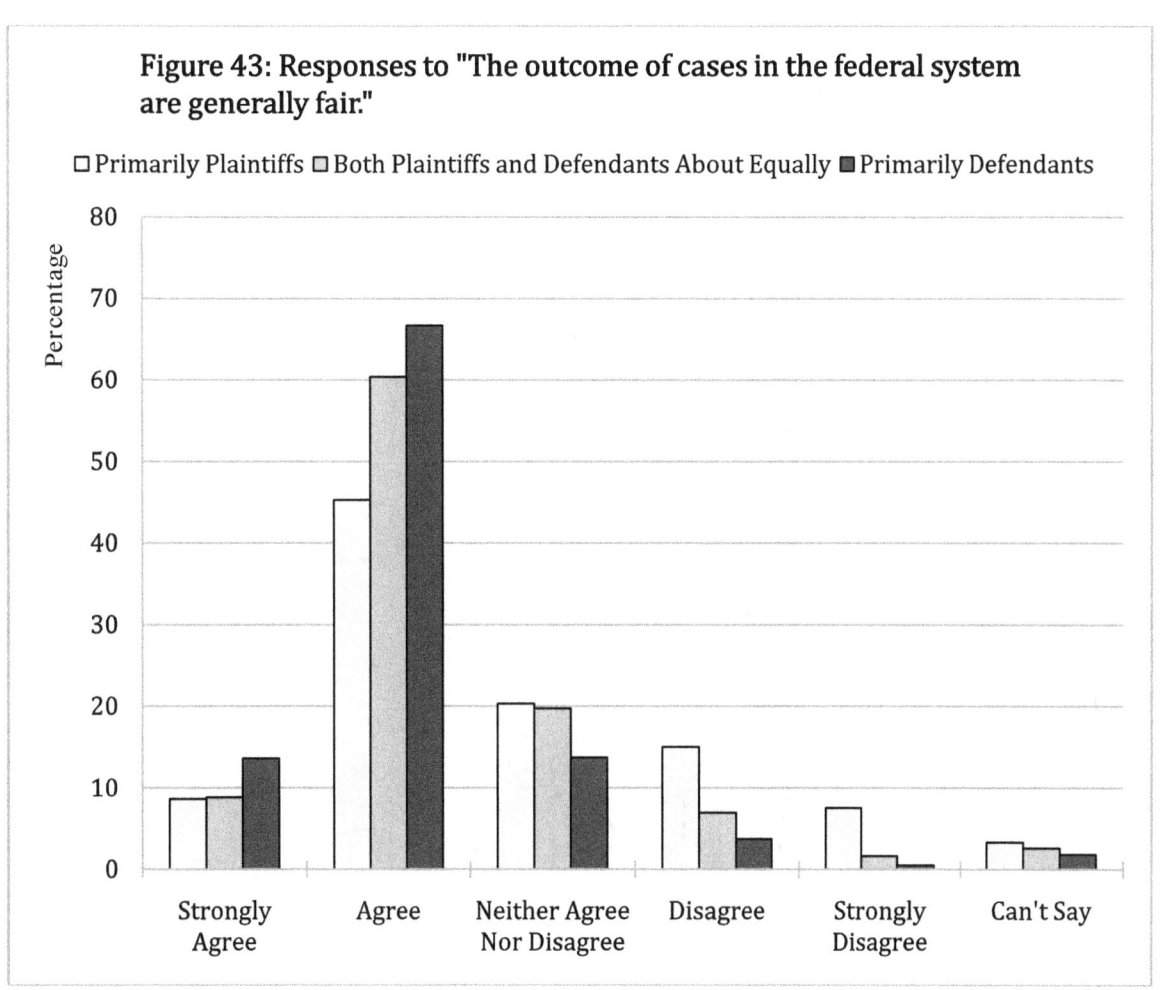

Figure 43: Responses to "The outcome of cases in the federal system are generally fair."

Question 77 asked whether the procedures employed in the federal courts are generally fair. The distribution of responses is displayed in Figure 44. All three groups agreed with this statement at least two-thirds of the time; however, those primarily representing defendants expressed the highest level of agreement with the statement. Those representing primarily plaintiffs agreed or strongly agreed 67.8 percent of the time, those representing both about equally agreed or strongly agreed 78.7 percent of the time, and those primarily representing defendants agreed or strongly agreed 85.5 percent of the time. Those primarily representing plaintiffs expressed no opinion 15.6 percent of the time, compared with 12.8 percent of those representing both about equally and 9 percent of those representing primarily defendants.

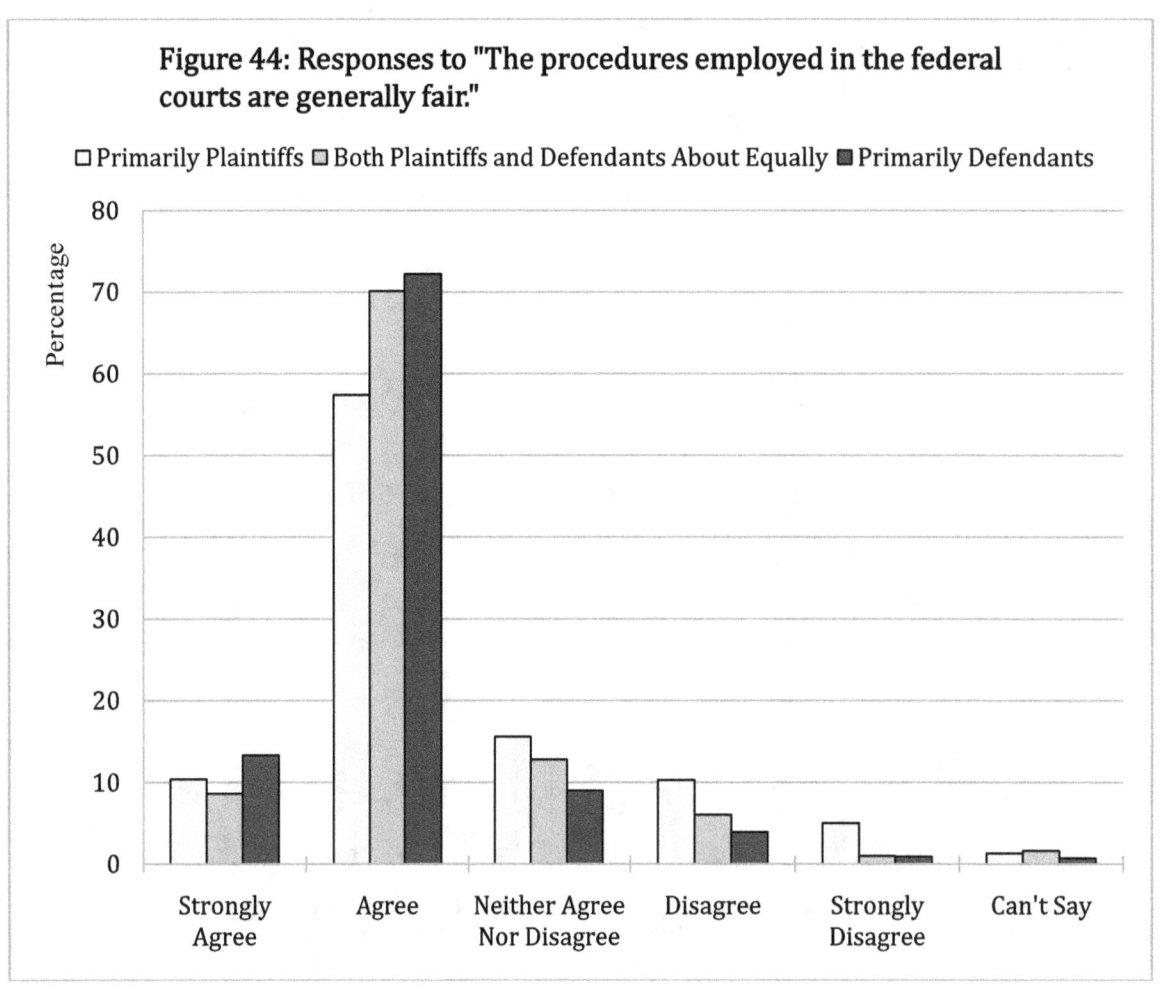

Figure 44: Responses to "The procedures employed in the federal courts are generally fair."

Question 79 asked whether discovery is abused in almost every case in federal court. The distribution of responses is displayed in Figure 45. This statement tended to draw negative responses. Those representing primarily plaintiffs disagreed or strongly disagreed 54.6 percent of the time, those representing both about equally disagreed or strongly disagreed 49.8 percent of the time, and those representing primarily defendants disagreed or strongly disagreed 60.6 percent of the time. By contrast, these groups agreed or strongly agreed 21, 22.8, and 16.3 percent of the time, respectively, and expressed no opinion 19.2, 24.7, and 20.1 percent of the time, respectively. Those representing primarily defendants had the most negative (and least positive) reaction to the statement.

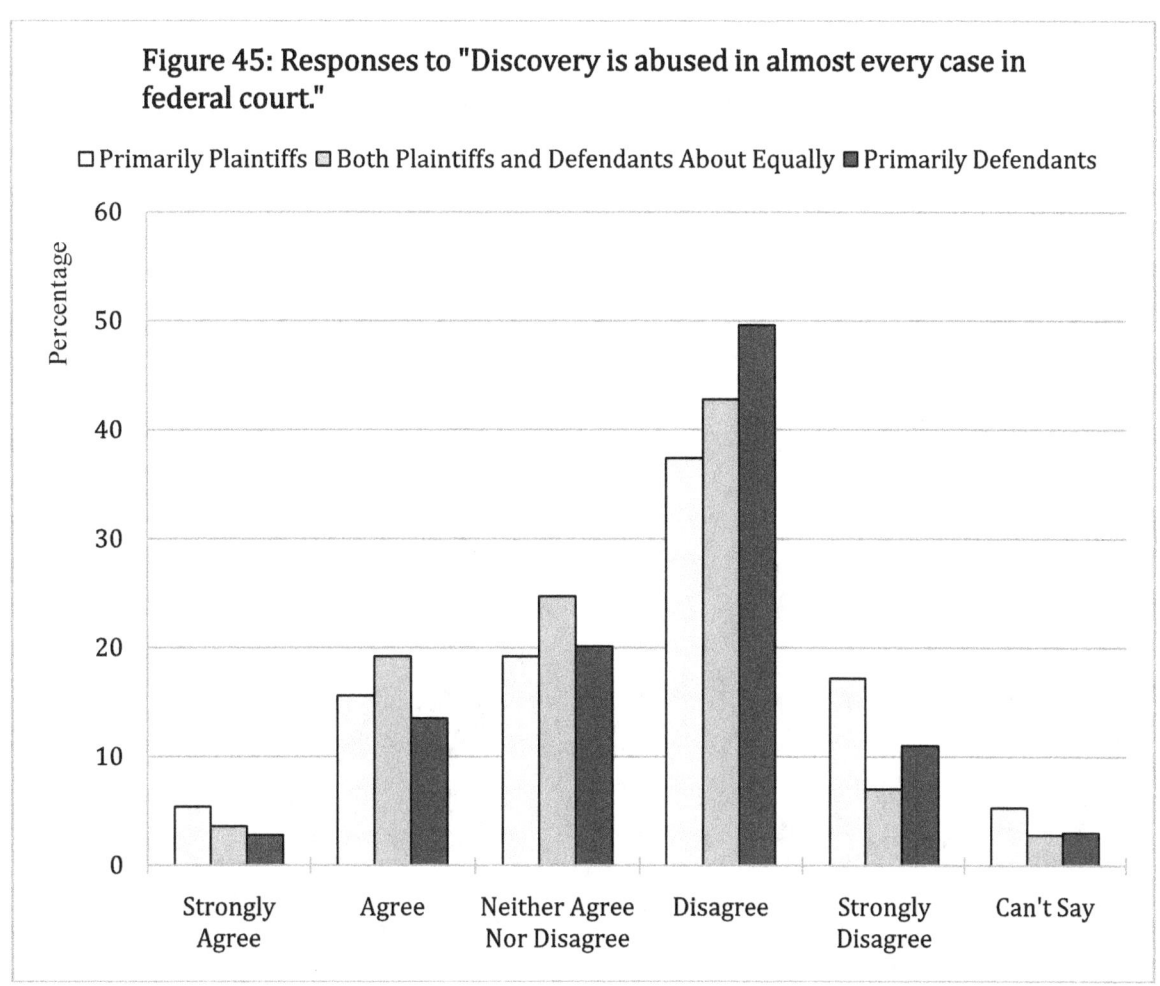

Figure 45: Responses to "Discovery is abused in almost every case in federal court."

Question 79 asked whether responding parties increase the cost and burden of discovery in federal court through delay and avoidance tactics. The distribution of responses is displayed in Figure 46. This question elicited an interesting set of responses. Those representing primarily plaintiffs tended to agree or strongly agree—63.9 percent of the time—as did those representing both plaintiffs and defendants about equally—52.9 percent of the time. Few respondents in these two groups—17.2 and 20.1 percent, respectively, disagreed or disagreed strongly. By contrast, those primarily representing defendants tended to disagree or strongly disagree (41.9 percent of the time), but this group also agreed or strongly agreed 32.5 percent of the time. Almost a quarter of both respondents primarily representing defendants (23.3 percent) and respondents representing both about equally (24.8 percent) expressed no opinion, as did 16.2 percent of those primarily representing plaintiffs.

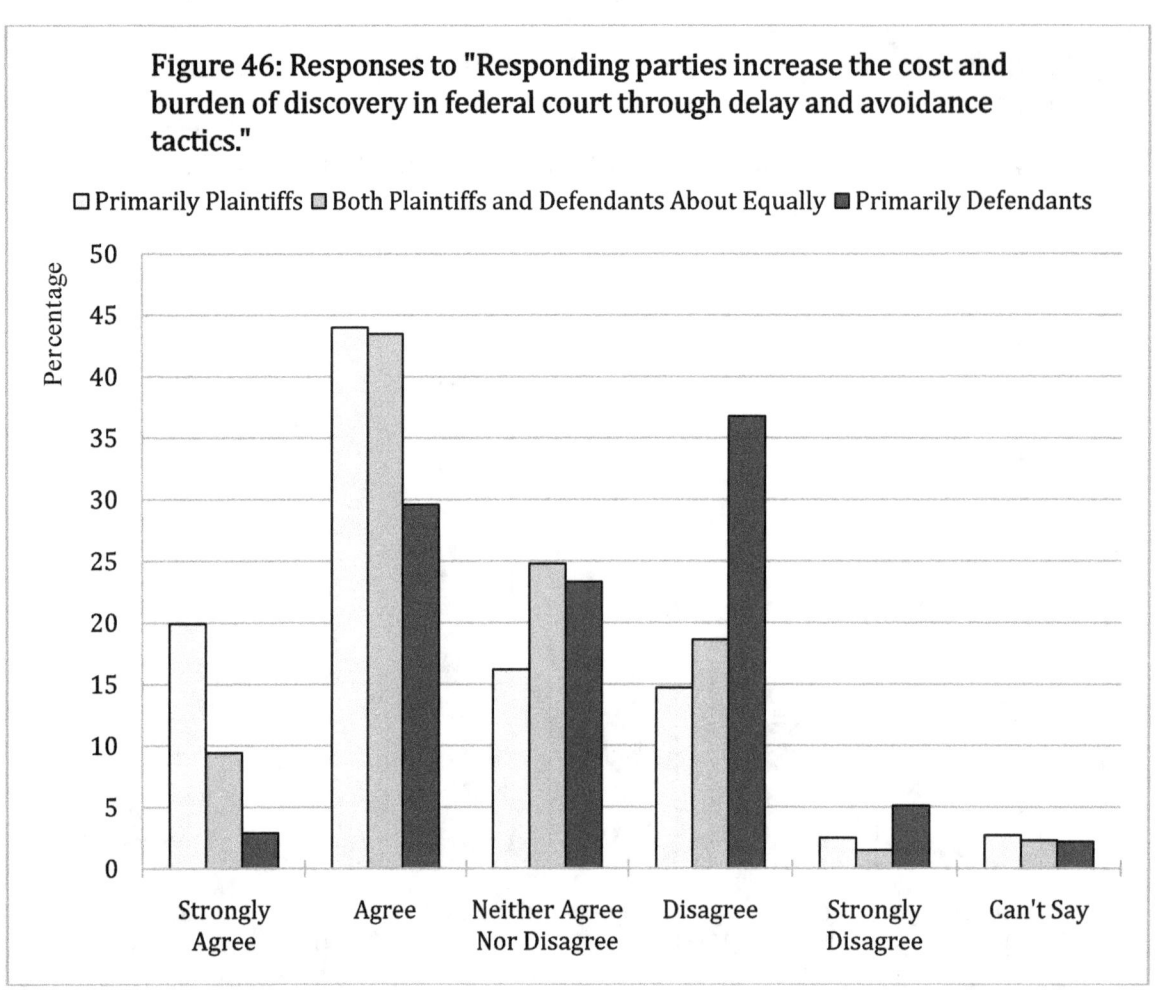

Figure 46: Responses to "Responding parties increase the cost and burden of discovery in federal court through delay and avoidance tactics."

Question 80 asked whether the cost of litigating in federal court, including the cost of discovery, had caused at least one client to settle a case that they would not have settled but for that cost. The distribution of responses is displayed in Figure 47. Those representing primarily defendants and those representing both about equally tended to agree, agreeing or strongly agreeing 58.2 and 57.8 percent of the time, respectively. Respondents in these groups disagreed or strongly disagreed 25.3 and 21.4 percent of the time, respectively. However, those representing primarily plaintiffs agreed or strongly agreed 38.6 percent of the time and disagreed or strongly disagreed 37.6 percent of the time.

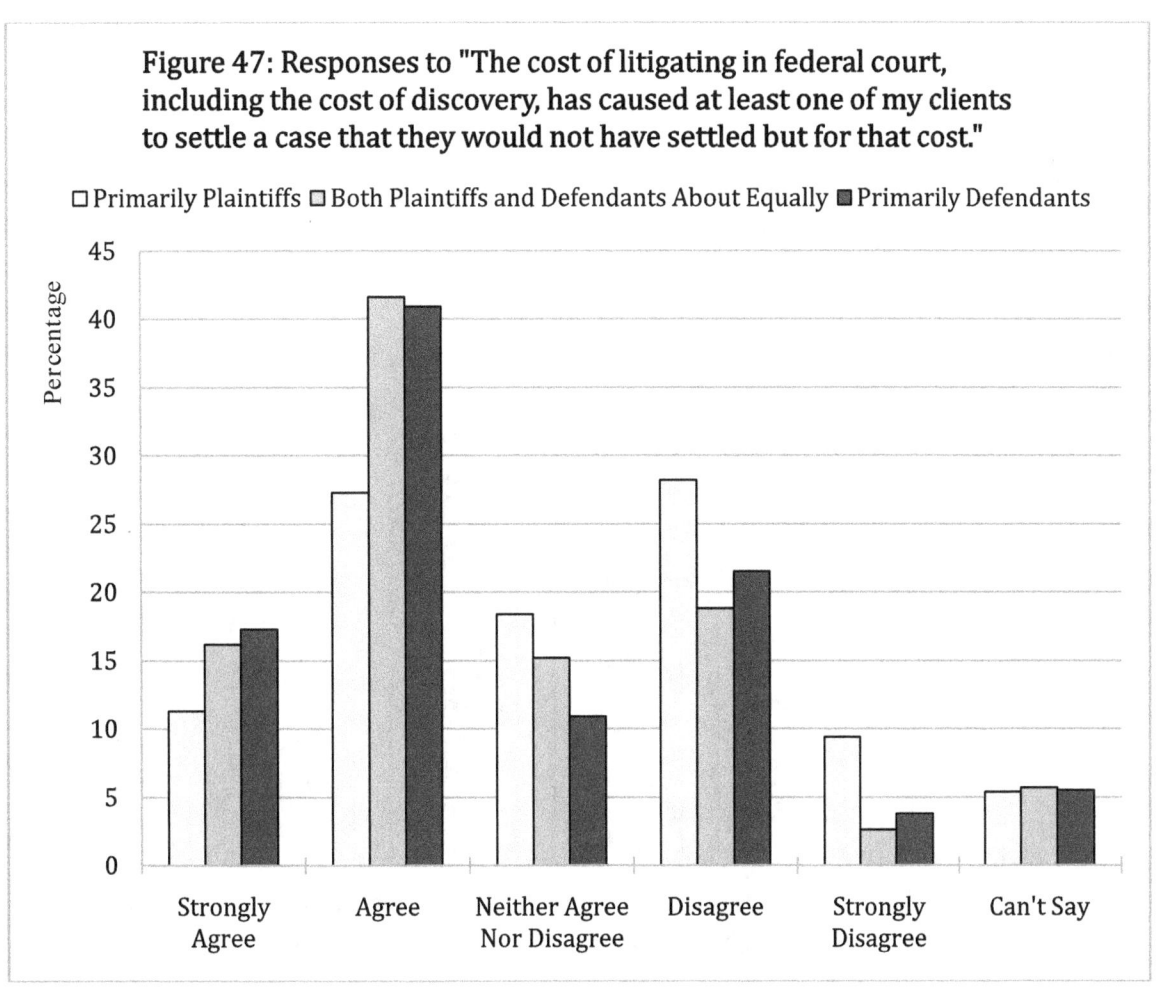

Figure 47: Responses to "The cost of litigating in federal court, including the cost of discovery, has caused at least one of my clients to settle a case that they would not have settled but for that cost."

Question 81 asked whether the cost of litigating in federal court, including the cost of discovery, had caused at least one client to abandon a claim that they would not have abandoned but for that cost. The distribution of responses is displayed in Figure 48. In none of the three groups did this statement yield a majority of positive responses. Those representing primarily plaintiffs were more likely to disagree with this statement than to agree, which is somewhat contrary to expectations. Fully 45.6 percent of this group disagreed or strongly disagreed with the statement, compared with 31.4 percent of the group who agreed or strongly agreed, and 17.3 percent who expressed no opinion. Those representing primarily defendants were also more likely to disagree than to agree. Of that group, 38.1 percent disagreed or strongly disagreed, compared with 21.5 percent who agreed or strongly agreed and 21.1 percent who expressed no opinion. A relatively large group of those representing primarily defendants (more than 1 in 5) declined to answer. The only group that was more likely to agree than to disagree was those representing both plaintiffs and defendants about equally. This group agreed or strongly agreed 42.6 percent of the time and disagreed or strongly disagreed 32.5 percent; they expressed no opinion 18.5 percent of the time.

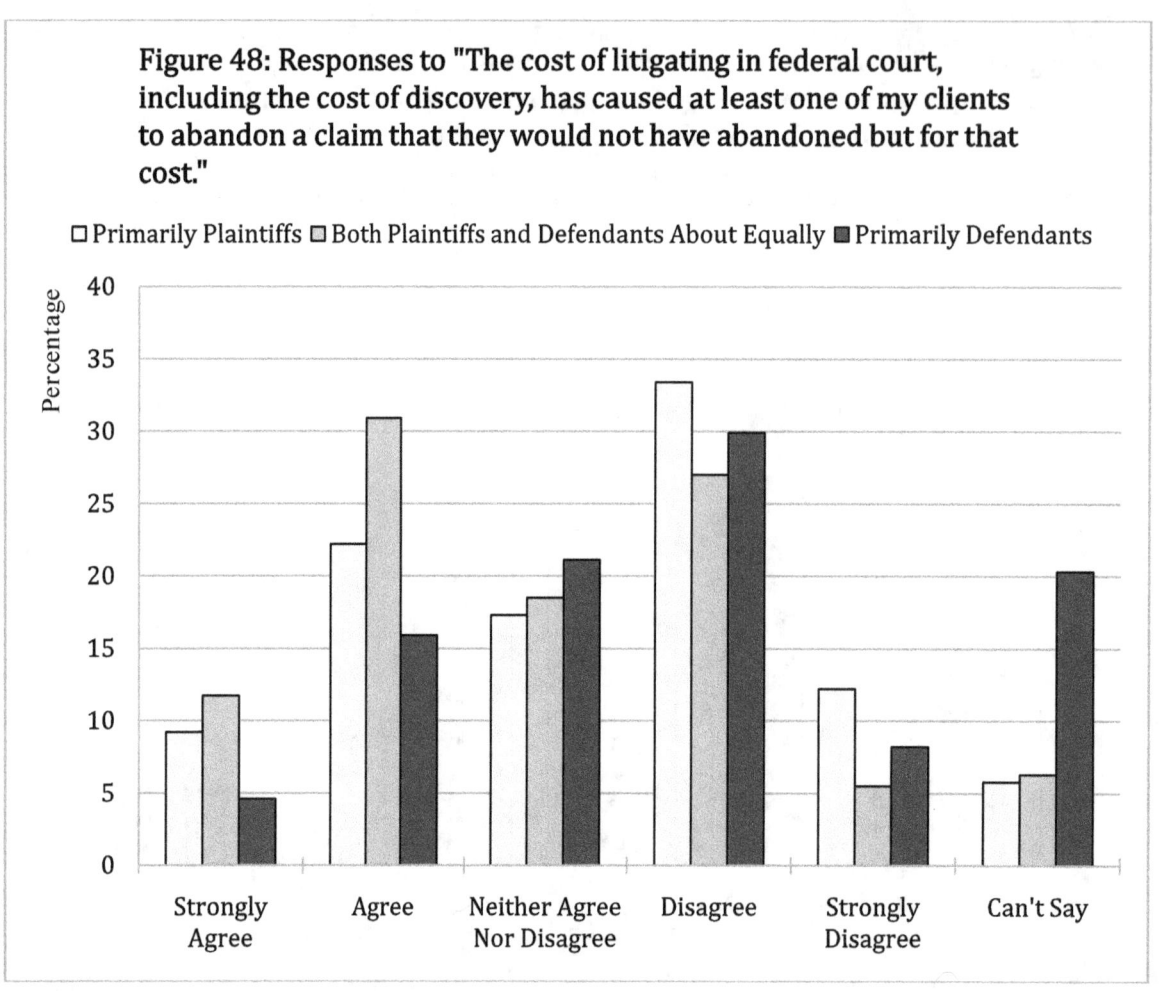

Figure 48: Responses to "The cost of litigating in federal court, including the cost of discovery, has caused at least one of my clients to abandon a claim that they would not have abandoned but for that cost."

Question 82, finally, asked respondents whether it would be better if more cases went to trial. The distribution of responses is displayed in Figure 49. This question elicited almost no differences among the groups of respondents, with the exception of the intensity of agreement among those primarily representing plaintiffs (who strongly agreed 17 percent of the time). The three groups agreed or strongly agreed 32.5, 30.5, and 32.2 percent of the time, respectively; expressed no opinion 27.1, 27.8, and 27.9 percent of the time, respectively; and disagreed or strongly disagreed 38.2, 39.4, and 37 percent of the time, respectively. In short, about 3 in 10 attorneys agree that it would be better if more cases went to trial; almost 3 in 10 have no opinion; and almost 4 in 10 disagree.

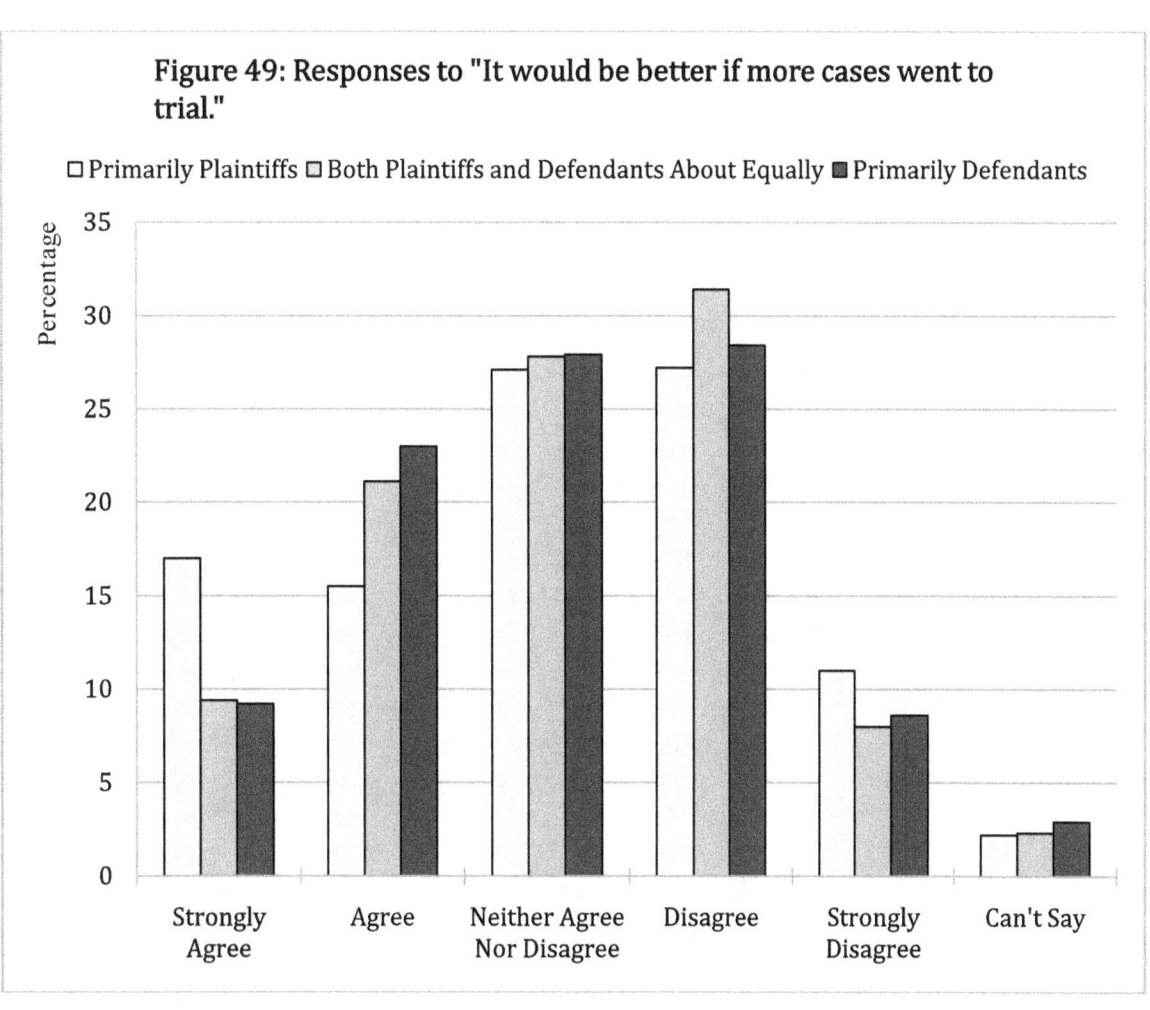
Figure 49: Responses to "It would be better if more cases went to trial."

Appendix A: Methods

The sampling frame for this study was constructed in a manner generally consistent with the approach of the 1997 study.[14] Using the Integrated Data Base (IDB), which the Center generates from data provided by the courts to the Administrative Office, we created a database of all civil case terminations in the last quarter of 2008. A number of general filters were applied to eliminate cases from the database in which discovery and discovery-related issues would be unlikely to occur. We excluded a number of nature of suit codes from the sampling frame, including prisoner civil rights and habeas cases (510, 530, 535, 540, 550, 555); Social Security and similar cases (860, 863, 864, 865); bankruptcy appeals (422, 423); student loan collection actions (152); land condemnation(210); forfeiture actions (625, 690); and asbestos products liability (368). We also excluded a number of disposition codes from the sampling frame, including interdistrict transfer, remand, and MDL transfer. Similarly, for origin codes, we omitted MDL transfers as well as remands from the courts of appeals, and first and subsequent reopens. As for MDL cases, our concern was that MDLs would present data quality issues; it was not clear that lawyers in MDL member cases would have experience with pretrial discovery in the overarching proceeding. Once the database of these cases was drawn from the IDB using the filters described, we deleted cases that terminated in less than 60 days.

The sampling frame was then divided into three parts. We decided to employ a stratified sample to ensure that we received adequate responses from two groups of respondents that would not be adequately sampled in a simple random draw: cases that terminated in district court by trial (jury or bench) and cases that terminated after having been open in district court for 4 years or longer. Any case that either terminated by trial (there were 529 such cases in the last quarter of 2008, once the general filters described above had been applied) or had been pending 4 years or longer when it terminated (there were 321 such cases) was included in the sample.

The largest stratum in the sample, however, is the random stratum. Choosing a sample size depends on a number of assumptions, including one's expected response rate. The most recent attorney survey conducted by the Center had obtained a response rate of 26 percent. Given this datum, we decided to err on the side of caution. From the 16,810 cases remaining in the sampling frame, we took approximately 16 percent at random, to arrive at an initial sample of 3,550 cases.

The next step was to obtain attorney e-mail addresses from the courts' Case Management/ Electronic Case Files (CM/ECF) system. After considering the available options, we decided simply to take the first listed attorney with an e-mail address from the plaintiff and defendant sides. From our sample of 3,550 cases, we obtained 5,685 attorney e-mail addresses from CM/ECF. That figure represents approximately 80 percent of the plaintiff and defendant attorneys ("sides") in the sampled cases. The missing sides in the sampled cases resulted from (1) no attorney listed on a side (pro se parties were excluded from the sample); (2) no attorney e-mail listed on a side; or (3) attorneys not designated plaintiff or defendant in a particular case (e.g., listed as respondents or petitioners in certain categories of cases). Moreover, in a somewhat laborious process, for attorneys

---

[14] *See Discovery and Disclosure*, supra note 3, at 57-58.

appearing in the sample more than one time (there were many), all but the lowest numbered closed case were eliminated from the sample.

From that sample of 5,685 unique attorneys with e-mail addresses, we obtained 2,690 responses—for a response rate of 47.3 percent. This calculation includes in the denominator attorney e-mail addresses that were no longer operative; if such e-mails were excluded from the calculation, the response rate would be slightly higher.

Attorneys in the sample were contacted by an e-mail message inviting them to complete the survey and providing a link to the on-line version of the survey. A small number of attorneys requested a paper version of the survey (reprinted herein as Appendix C), and a smaller number returned, either by mail or fax, the paper version for input. Two reminder e-mails were also sent to attorneys who had not yet responded to the survey.

In most of the analysis reported herein, responses were weighted to account for the stratified sampling design. In short, cases in the trial and long-pending strata of the sample must be given smaller weights than the cases in the random strata; otherwise, the reported results will give inordinate weight to types of cases that are overrepresented in the sample, compared with the underlying population. The design weights were calculated using the inverse of the probability of a case's inclusion in the sample. When reported in the text, tables, or footnotes, the number of observations presented is the actual number of respondents included in each analysis and not the weighted number of respondents.

This report does not, however, employ any post-stratification weights or weights designed to account for non-response bias. The primary reason for this decision is that we simply do not know enough about the attorneys in the overall sample, let alone the population, to have the confidence that we know how survey respondents differ from non-respondents.

Appendix B: Attorney Characteristics

This appendix provides information about the attorney respondents and their cases. The findings presented are unweighted and include all respondents with valid responses; in other words, this section is not limited to respondents reporting discovery in the closed case.

Table B-1 summarizes respondents' practice settings. As can be seen in the table, respondents representing primarily plaintiffs tend to work in relatively small private firms, either as sole practitioners (32.8 percent) or in firms of 2-10 attorneys (51.7 percent). An additional 7.7 percent of the plaintiff attorneys reported working in firms of 11-25 attorneys. In short, 92.2 percent of this category of respondents practices in a firm of 1-25 attorneys.

Table B-1: Respondents' practice settings

Practice Setting	Primarily Plaintiffs (%)	Both Plaintiffs and Defendants (%)	Primarily Defendants (%)
Sole practitioner	32.8	14.0	1.9
Private firm of 2-10 attorneys	51.7	36.3	17.9
Private firm of 11-25 attorneys	7.7	12.1	15.7
Private firm of 26-50 attorneys	1.6	7.9	10.8
Private firm of 51-100 attorneys	1.0	6.0	8.3
Private firm of 101-250 attorneys	1.3	7.6	9.5
Private firm of 251-500 attorneys	0.4	4.1	9.4
Private firm of > 500 attorneys	0.6	6.6	9.1
In-house for-profit	0.0	0.6	1.7
Legal staff, non-profit	1.2	0.6	0.3
Government	1.9	4.1	15.4
N	836	634	1,159

Respondents representing primarily defendants were infrequently sole practitioners—just 1.9 percent of respondents in this category practiced solo—and were also less likely to practice in firms of 2-10 attorneys—17.9 percent—than the other two groups of respondents. Compared with the other two categories, respondents representing primarily defendants were much more likely to work in firms of more than 250 attorneys. Fully 18.5 percent of the defendant attorneys in the sample worked in firms of more than 250 attorneys; the comparable figures for respondents representing plaintiffs and defendants about equally was 10.7 percent, and for those representing primarily plaintiffs, 1.0 percent.

Most of the respondents practicing as government attorneys reported that they are primarily in the role of the defendant. This group accounted for 15.4 percent of respondents representing primarily defendants.

The modal category for respondents representing plaintiffs and defendants about equally was a firm of 2-10 attorneys. This was also the modal category for plaintiff attorneys *and*, it bears emphasis, defendant attorneys. But respondents representing plaintiffs and defendants about equally are harder to characterize than the other two groups. Fully 14 percent of this group are sole practitioners, but an almost equal percentage, 13.6 percent, work in firms of 51-250 attorneys.

The median respondent representing primarily plaintiffs practices in a firm of 2-10 attorneys; the same median is obtained for those representing plaintiffs and defendants about equally. The median respondent representing primarily defendants, on the other hand, practices in a firm of 26-50 attorneys.

Respondents were also asked what their primary arrangement was with respect to fees. The findings are summarized in Table B-2. Not surprisingly, respondents representing primarily plaintiffs tended to work on a contingency-fee basis, 70.9 percent, and another 19.2 percent worked on an hourly-fee basis. Respondents representing primarily defendants reported working on an hourly-fee basis 74.5 percent of the time, and as salaried employees 13.6 percent of the time—those are the government lawyers shown in the previous table. The defendant attorneys reported working on a contingency-fee basis just 3.7 percent of the time. Those representing both plaintiffs and defendants about equally reported working on an hourly-fee basis 69 percent of the time, and on a contingency-fee basis 19.1 percent of the time—which is almost the reverse of those representing primarily plaintiffs.

Table B-2: Primary arrangement with client with respect to fees

Arrangement	Primarily Plaintiffs (%)	Both Plaintiffs and Defendants (%)	Primarily Defendants (%)
Hourly fees	19.2	69.0	74.5
Salaried employee	1.6	4.3	13.6
Contingent fee	70.9	19.1	3.7
Other	4.6	4.0	3.9
Can't say	3.7	3.7	4.2
N	833	629	1,158

Respondents were asked how many years they had practiced law. There would be little reason to expect, *ex ante*, that the categories would differ substantially in this regard, and they do not. The median and mean for all three groups are centered around 20-21 years, with slight differences. Half of respondents to the survey had practiced for 20 years or less; half, for 20 years or more. These findings are summarized in Table B-3.

Table B-3: Years of practice

	Primarily Plaintiffs *Median Mean*	Both Plaintiffs and Defendants *Median Mean*	Primarily Defendants *Median Mean*
Years practicing	20.0 21.3	20.5 21.3	20.0 20.4
N	827	621	1,143

Table B-4 summarizes the nature of suit (NOS) categories of the closed cases in the sample. The distribution of NOS categories for those representing primarily plaintiffs and those representing primarily defendants is similar, although the defendant attorneys were in more contract cases. For both plaintiff and defendant attorneys, the modal NOS category was civil rights.

Table B-4: Respondents' cases by nature of suit (NOS) category

NOS category	Primarily Plaintiffs (%)	Both Plaintiffs and Defendants (%)	Primarily Defendants (%)
Contract	12.9	32.9	20.6
Tort	21.5	8.0	19.2
Civil Rights	36.5	13.1	34.5
Consumer	4.0	4.3	3.1
Labor	12.3	8.3	8.9
Intellectual Property	2.6	17.8	2.4
Other	10.2	15.6	11.3
N	840	635	1,163

The distribution of respondents representing plaintiffs and defendants about equally is very different from those of the other two categories. Almost 1 in 5 of these respondents' closed cases was an intellectual property case. These attorneys were in more contract cases and in fewer civil rights cases.

Finally, Table B-5 summarizes the duration of the closed cases included in the sample. It should be kept in mind that the table includes cases included in the sample because they were especially long-pending, and thus, unweighted, these figures do not represent estimates of population parameters. Instead, they are intended as informational only. The medians are about 1.2 years; so half of the cases included in the sample took at least 1.2 years to close.

Table B-5: Respondents' cases by duration (in days)

	Primarily Plaintiffs *Median* *Mean*	Both Plaintiffs and Defendants *Median* *Mean*	Primarily Defendants *Median* *Mean*
Case duration	448.0 592.2	434.0 637.1	432.0 576.4
N	835	630	1,137

Appendix C: Survey Instrument

National Case-Based Survey of Counsel re Discovery, Electronic Discovery, Litigation Practices and the Costs of Civil Litigation

For the Advisory Committee on Civil Rules of the Judicial Conference of the United States

Designed and administered by the Federal Judicial Center

Introduction. You have been selected to receive this survey as part of a national random sample of attorneys in federal court cases terminating in the last quarter of 2008. The Federal Judicial Center ("FJC") designed the survey to aid the Judicial Conference Advisory Committee on Civil Rules in its current re-examination of the Federal Rules of Civil Procedure. The Advisory Committee is particularly interested in obtaining objective information relating to discovery and pleading practices. Information about your recent experiences in the federal courts will greatly assist the Advisory Committee in deciding whether any fundamental change in the Rules is needed.

Court records show that you represented a party in a recently terminated case identified in the <<insert caption, case number, and district information>> ("the named case"). The survey asks about that case. We ask that you complete the survey if you were one of the primary attorneys in the named case. If someone else was primarily responsible for the case, please forward the email containing the link to the survey to that person. The same survey is being sent to the primary attorneys for other parties in the named case.

Confidentiality. We recognize that much of this information is sensitive. Findings will be reported in the aggregate so that no individual party or case will be identifiable. Any information that might permit identification of the named case, the attorneys, or the parties will be treated as confidential.

Returning the survey. Please mail or FAX the completed survey to Emery Lee, Federal Judicial Center, One Columbus Circle, N.E., Washington, D.C. 20002 (FAX: 202-502-4199).

Results. Results of the survey will be published and available at www.fjc.gov.

Questions. If you have questions about the survey, please contact Emery Lee, elee@fjc.gov, (202) 502-4078, or Tom Willging, twillgin@fjc.gov, (202) 502-4049.

I. Discovery Activity in the Named Case

1. After the filing of the complaint and before the first pretrial conference, did you or any attorney for your client confer with opposing counsel—by telephone, correspondence, or in-person—to plan for discovery in the named case?
    ☐$_1$ Yes
    ☐$_2$ No --------------------→Go to Question 5
    ☐$_3$ I can't say -----------→Go to Question 5

2. If Yes, did the conference to plan for discovery include discussion of electronically stored information?
    ☐$_1$ Yes
    ☐$_2$ No --------------------→Go to Question 5
    ☐$_3$ I can't say -----------→Go to Question 5

3. If Yes, did the discussion of discovery of electronically stored information include any of the following topics related to collection (Check all that apply):

    ☐$_1$ Restricting the scope or avoiding altogether the discovery of electronically stored information
    ☐$_2$ The scope, cost, method, or duration of preserving electronically stored information
    ☐$_3$ The parties' practices with respect to retention of electronically stored information
    ☐$_4$ The potential cost or burden of collecting, reviewing, and producing electronically stored information
    ☐$_5$ The possibility of phased discovery of electronically stored information
    ☐$_6$ Whether potentially responsive information was stored on a device or in a format that a party considered "not reasonably accessible"
    ☐$_7$ The possibility of sampling electronically stored information from a particular source to determine if production was justified
    ☐$_8$ Issues relating to information contained in dynamic data bases
    ☐$_9$ Issues relating to Instant Messaging, Voicemail, VoiceoverIP and the like
    ☐$_{10}$ Use of culling techniques such as date ranges or file extensions
    ☐$_{11}$ Methods of searching for or reducing the scope of responsive documents by topic, including but not limited to the use of keyword search terms or deduplication for electronic documents
    ☐$_{12}$ Methods of searching for or reducing the scope of responsive documents by custodian or location regarding electronically stored information

4. Did the discussion of discovery of electronically stored information include any of the following topics related to production (Check all that apply):

☐$_1$ Format of production of electronically stored information (pdf, tiff, native format)
☐$_2$ The need for, or content of, accompanying load files (files used to import code or images into a database)
☐$_3$ Media on which the parties routinely maintain electronically stored information
☐$_4$ Media of production of electronically stored information (e.g., paper printouts, compact disks, hard drives)
☐$_5$ Document indexing or other method of organizing responsive electronic documents
☐$_6$ The production of metadata (metadata is information regarding the history or management of an electronic file usually not apparent to a reader viewing a hard copy or screen image)
☐$_7$ Methods of handling confidential or trade secret information, privileged communications, or information subject to work-product privilege
☐$_8$ Privilege log issues
☐$_9$ An agreement to permit a producing party to "claw back" or retract privileged material inadvertently produced
☐$_{10}$ An agreement to permit a requesting party to take a "quick peek" at documents prior to privilege review without the producing party's waiver of privilege

5. Did your client place a "litigation hold" or "freeze" on deletion of electronically stored information in anticipation of or in response to the filing of the complaint in the named case?
  ☐$_1$Yes
  ☐$_2$No
  ☐$_3$I can't say

6. Did the court adopt a discovery plan?
  ☐$_1$Yes
  ☐$_2$No ------------------- →Go to Question 8
  ☐$_3$I can't say -----------→Go to Question 8

7. If Yes, did the discovery plan include provisions related to electronically stored information?
  ☐$_1$Yes
  ☐$_2$No
  ☐$_3$I can't say

8. Before discovery began, did the parties agree how they would address the inadvertent disclosure of privileged materials through discovery?
 ☐₁ Yes
 ☐₂ No
 ☐₃ I can't say

9. What types of discovery occurred in the named case? Where indicated, please provide additional information.

Check all that apply	Type of discovery	Additional information
☐₁	Initial disclosure of non-expert documents, including but not limited to electronically stored documents	
☐₂	Informal exchange of documents, including but not limited to electronically stored documents	If _not_ used in the named case, did you discuss making an informal exchange with counsel for the other side? __ Yes __ No __ I Can't say
☐₃	Informal exchange of other materials	
☐₄	Interrogatories	
☐₅	Request for production of documents, including but not limited to electronically stored documents	
☐₆	Disclosure of expert reports	How many expert witnesses did each side identify? Your side: _____ The opposing side: _____

☐₇	Depositions of **experts**	How many **experts** did each side depose? Your side: _____ The opposing side: _____ How many expert depositions lasted more than seven hours?
☐₈	Depositions of **non-experts**	How many **non-experts** did each side depose? Your side: _____ The opposing side: _____ How many **non-expert** depositions lasted more than seven hours? ____
☐₉	Requests for admission	How many requests were propounded? Your side: _____ The opposing side: _____
☐₁₀	Physical or mental examination	
☐₁₁	Inspection of property, computer equipment or media, or designated objects	
☐₁₂	Third-party subpoena	How many third-party subpoenas were issued? Your side: _____ The opposing side: _____

10. Did any party in the named case request production of electronically stored information?
    ☐₁ Yes
    ☐₂ No ---------------------→Go to Question 20
    ☐₃ I can't say -------------→ Go to Question 20

11. If yes, **with respect to electronically stored information**, was your client
    ☐₁ A producing party
    ☐₂ A requesting party ---------------------→Go to Question 18
    ☐₃ Both a producing and requesting party

12. Please estimate, if possible, the percentage of the electronically stored information collected on behalf of your client (including by the client itself as well as any law firm(s))that was reviewed for responsiveness and privilege:

_____ %

13. Please estimate, if possible, the percentage of the electronically stored information collected on behalf of your client (including by the client itself as well as any law firm(s))that was produced as responsive and non-privileged: _____%

The next set of questions asks about the amount of electronically stored information produced to the requesting party. The amount of information may be estimated using bytes OR by using counts of the media of production (e.g., number of compact disks, number of hardcopy pages).

14. Please estimate, if possible, the amount of electronically stored information **produced** by your client in the named case **in bytes**. (Check one)

      ☐$_1$ Number of Terabytes (equivalent to about 500 million pages) _____
        $_2$ Number of Gigabytes (equivalent to about 500,000 pages) _____
        $_3$ Number of Megabytes (equivalent to about 500 pages) _____
        $_4$ I can't say

In answering the next question, please do not double count media. For example, if 1,000 hardcopy pages were produced in 5 boxes, please provide the number of hardcopy pages only.

15. Please estimate the amount of electronically stored information produced as
      ☐$_1$ Compact disks _____
      ☐$_2$ Hard drives or computers _____
      ☐$_3$ Hard copy pages _____
      ☐$_4$ Boxes of hard copy pages _____
      ☐$_5$ I can't say

16. What resources were used on behalf of your client (including by the client itself as well as any law firm(s)) in collecting and producing electronically stored information? (Check all that apply)
- $\Box_1$ Information technology vendor (not internal to the law firm or to client)
- $\Box_2$ Information technology staff internal to the law firm
- $\Box_3$ Information technology staff internal to the client
- $\Box_4$ Contract attorneys for responsiveness review
- $\Box_5$ Contract attorneys for privilege review
- $\Box_6$ Other (please specify) _____
- $\Box_7$ I can't say

17. Prior to the filing of the named case, had your client implemented an enterprise content management system or other information system designed to facilitate the identification and production of electronically stored information in litigation?
- $\Box_1$ Yes
- $\Box_2$ No
- $\Box_3$ I can't say

18. Did any of the following occur in the named case as a consequence of the requested or produced discovery of electronically stored information?(Check all that apply)
- $\Box_1$ Dispute over burden of production of electronically stored information that the parties could not resolve without court action
- $\Box_2$ Dispute over cost of production of electronically stored information that the parties could not resolve without court action
- $\Box_3$ Production of accessible electronically stored information in a format other than that requested
- $\Box_4$ Production of electronically stored information in a format requesting party asserted was not reasonably useable
- $\Box_5$ A request to obtain electronically stored information from a source (e.g., backup tapes) the producing party contended was not reasonably accessible due to burden or cost
- $\Box_6$ One or more objections to a party's use or anticipated use of electronically stored information on the grounds that it was not properly disclosed
- $\Box_7$ One or more claims of spoliation of electronically stored information
- $\Box_8$ Inadvertent disclosure through production of electronically stored information claimed to be privileged

19. How was the electronically stored information produced through discovery used in the litigation? Please check all that apply:

☐₁ In amending the complaint
☐₂ In preparing or deposing a witness
☐₃ In interviews with client representatives or non-parties
☐₄ In a request for additional discovery
☐₅ In a motion to compel discovery
☐₆ In a summary judgment motion
☐₇ In other pretrial motions
☐₈ In facilitating a settlement of the named case
☐₉ At trial
☐₁₀ In a motion for sanctions
☐₁₁ Not used in the case

20. Did a judicial officer, including a special master or other neutral, do any of the following in the named case **with respect to discovery in general**, including electronic discovery? (Check all that apply)

☐₁ Hold a conference (by telephone, correspondence, or in-person) to consider a plan involving discovery
☐₂ Hold a conference (by telephone, correspondence, or in-person) to address discovery issues not addressed in a discovery plan
☐₃ Limit the time for completion of discovery-----→ If so, how many months? _____
☐₄ Appoint a neutral to oversee discovery issues
☐₅ Refer any discovery issue to a magistrate judge
☐₆ Grant a motion for protective order limiting discovery
☐₇ Deny a motion for protective order limiting discovery
☐₈ Grant a motion to compel discovery
☐₉ Deny a motion to compel discovery
☐₁₀ Rule on any other discovery motion
☐₁₁ Impose sanctions related to discovery

21. Did the court rule on any of the following motions? (Check all that apply)
☐₁ Rule 12(b)(6) motion to dismiss for failure to state a claim
☐₂ Other Rule 12(b) motion to dismiss
☐₃ Rule 12(c) motion for judgment on the pleadings
☐₄ Rule 12(e) motion for a more definite statement
☐₅ Rule 56 motion for summary judgment
☐₆ I can't say

The Effects of Discovery in the Named Case

	Strongly Agree	Agree	Neither Agree nor Disagree	Disagree	Strongly Disagree	Can't Say/ Not Applicable
22. The potential costs of discovery, including but not limited to electronic discovery, to the producing party influenced my client's choice of forum in the named case.	☐₁	☐₂	☐₃	☐₄	☐₅	☐₆
23. The discovery produced, including but not limited to electronically stored information, increased the fairness of the outcome of the named case.	☐₁	☐₂	☐₃	☐₄	☐₅	☐₆
24. The parties in the named case were able to reduce the cost and burden of the named case by cooperating in discovery.	☐₁	☐₂	☐₃	☐₄	☐₅	☐₆
25. The parties would have saved a significant amount of time and money in the named case had they cooperated in discovery.	☐₁	☐₂	☐₃	☐₄	☐₅	☐₆

26. What effect on settlement did the costs of discovery, including but not limited to electronic discovery, have in the named case?
☐₁ The costs of discovery greatly decreased the likelihood of settlement.
☐₂ The costs of discovery decreased the likelihood of settlement.
☐₃ The costs of discovery had no effect on the likelihood of settlement.
☐₄ The costs of discovery increased the likelihood of settlement.
☐₅ The costs of discovery greatly increased the likelihood of settlement.
☐₆ The named case would not have settled but for the costs of discovery.
☐₇ I can't say

II. Litigation Costs

27. Please <u>estimate</u>, if possible, the total litigation costs for your firm and your client in the named case, including the costs of discovery and any hourly fees for attorneys or paralegals. If the case was handled on a contingency fee basis, please estimate the total litigation costs to your firm.

$ _____

28. Approximately what percentage of the total litigation costs in the named case was incurred in requesting and/or producing disclosure and/or discovery, **not** limited to the discovery of electronically stored information?

_____%

29. Of the costs of discovery in the named case, approximately what percentage was incurred in requesting and/or producing disclosure and/or discovery of electronically stored information, if any?

_____ %

30. Of the costs of discovery in the named case, approximately what percentage was incurred in preparing for and taking depositions?

_____ %

The next two pairs of questions attempt to measure how much was at stake for your client in the named case, aside from the costs of the litigation itself. If possible, please estimate and include the monetary value of any nonmonetary relief at stake.

31. If the named case had ended in the **worst** likely outcome, given the law and the facts, how would your client have stood at the end of the case with respect to damages, monetary relief, and quantifiable nonmonetary relief. (Check one)

    ☐$_1$My client would have lost money in the worst likely outcome.
    ☐$_2$My client still would have gained money, even in the worst likely outcome.
    ☐$_3$In the worst likely outcome, my client would have neither gained nor lost money.
    ☐$_4$I can't say

31a. Please estimate, in dollars, the gain or loss your client would have experienced in the worst likely outcome.

$ _____

32. If the named case had ended in the **best** likely outcome, given the law and the facts, how would your client have stood at the end of the case with respect to damages, monetary relief, and quantifiable nonmonetary relief. (Check one)

☐$_1$ My client would have still lost money, even in the best likely outcome.
☐$_2$ My client would have gained money in the best likely outcome.
☐$_3$ In the best likely outcome, my client would have neither gained nor lost money.
☐$_4$ I can't say

32a. Please estimate, in dollars, the gain or loss your client would have experienced in the best likely outcome.

$ _____

33. To what extent were you concerned in the named case about nonmonetary relief or about possible consequences to your client, beyond the relief sought, such as future litigation based on similar claims, legal precedent, harm to reputation, or a desire to maintain a business relationship with a party? (Check one)

☐$_1$ Such consequences were of dominant concern
☐$_2$ Such consequences were of some concern
☐$_3$ Such consequences were of little or no concern
☐$_4$ I can't say

34. Which of the following **best** describes your client? (Check one)

☐$_1$ Natural person (individual)
☐$_2$ Multinational corporation
☐$_3$ For-profit entity of national scope
☐$_4$ For-profit entity of regional scope
☐$_5$ For-profit entity of local scope
☐$_6$ Non-profit entity of national scope
☐$_7$ Non-profit entity of regional scope
☐$_8$ Non-profit entity of local scope
☐$_9$ Private educational institution
☐$_{10}$ Agency of the federal government
☐$_{11}$ Agency of a state or local government

35. Which of the following **best** describes the opposing party? (Check one)

  ☐₁ Natural person (individual)
  ☐₂ Multinational corporation
  ☐₃ For-profit entity of national scope
  ☐₄ For-profit entity of regional scope
  ☐₅ For-profit entity of local scope
  ☐₆ Non-profit entity of national scope
  ☐₇ Non-profit entity of regional scope
  ☐₈ Non-profit entity of local scope
  ☐₉ Private educational institution
  ☐₁₀ Agency of the federal government
  ☐₁₁ Agency of a state or local government

III. Case Characteristics

36. Did the plaintiff in the named case make class action allegations at any point?

  ☐₁ Yes
  ☐₂ No
  ☐₃ I don't know

37. On a scale of 1 to 7, with 1 being not complex at all, 4 being average complexity, and 7 being extremely complex, how complex were the **factual** issues in the named case? (Circle one)

Not complex at all			Average Complexity			Extremely complex
1	2	3	4	5	6	7

38. On a scale of 1 to 7, with 1 being not contentious at all, 4 being average contentiousness, and 7 being extremely contentious, how contentious was the relationship **between the parties** in the named case? (Circle one)

Not contentious at all			Average Contentiousness			Extremely contentious
1	2	3	4	5	6	7

39. On a scale of 1 to 7, with 1 being not contentious at all, 4 being average contentiousness, and 7 being extremely contentious, how contentious was the relationship **between the attorneys** in the named case? (Circle one)

Not contentious at all			Average Contentiousness			Extremely contentious
1	2	3	4	5	6	7

40. Before the filing of the complaint in the named case, had you ever (check all that apply):
  - ☐₁ Met in person any of the opposing attorneys
  - ☐₂ Opposed in another case any of the opposing attorneys
  - ☐₃ Opposed in another case the opposing party

41. On a scale of 1 to 7, with 1 being too little, 4 being just the right amount, and 7 being too much, how much information did the disclosure and discovery generated by the parties in the named case yield? (Circle one)

Too little			Just the right amount			Too much
1	2	3	4	5	6	7

42. On a scale of 1 to 7, with 1 being too little, 4 being just the right amount, and 7 being too much, how did the costs of discovery to your side in the named case compare to your client's stakes? (Circle one)

Too little			Just the right amount			Too much
1	2	3	4	5	6	7

43. How was the named case ultimately resolved in district court? (Check one)

    ☐₁ Dismissed on Rule 12 motion
    ☐₂ Summary judgment
    ☐₃ Settled by the parties
    ☐₄ Voluntarily dismissed without settlement
    ☐₅ Tried to jury verdict
    ☐₆ Resolved by bench trial
    ☐₇ Other → Please specify: _____

IV. Your Practice

44. What was your primary arrangement with your client regarding attorney fees in the named case? (Check one)
    ☐₁ Hourly fees
    ☐₂ Salaried employee of client (including government)
    ☐₃ Contingent fee (percentage of recovery or amount saved)
    ☐₄ Other arrangement not based on hours or case outcome
    ☐₅ I can't say

45. Was there a statutory provision for recovery of attorney fees applicable to any claim in the named case? (Check one)
    ☐₁ Yes
    ☐₂ No
    ☐₃ I don't know

46. Which of the following **best** describes your law practice setting? (Check one)
    ☐₁ Sole practitioner
    ☐₂ Private firm of 2-10 attorneys
    ☐₃ Private firm of 11-25 attorneys
    ☐₄ Private firm of 26-50 attorneys
    ☐₅ Private firm of 51-100 attorneys
    ☐₆ Private firm of 101-250 attorneys
    ☐₇ Private firm of 251-500 attorneys
    ☐₈ Private firm of more than 500 attorneys
    ☐₉ Legal staff of a for-profit entity
    ☐₁₀ Legal staff of a non-profit entity
    ☐₁₁ Government

47. How many years have you practiced law? _____ years

48. Please estimate the percentage of your work time during the past five years spent on civil litigation in the **federal courts**. If less than five years of practice, estimate the percentage of your work time during your years of practice dedicated to civil litigation in the federal courts.

_____ %

49. Please estimate: how many trials (in state and federal court) have you participated in as an attorney, including the named case (if applicable)?

_____ trials

50. Please estimate: what percentage of your practice is spent in discovery-related activities?

_____ %

51. Please estimate: what percentage of your practice is spent specifically on electronic discovery?

_____ %

52. Do you primarily represent plaintiffs, defendants, or both? (Check one)

☐₁ Primarily plaintiffs
☐₂ Both plaintiffs and defendants about equally
☐₃ Primarily defendants

53. In the named case, did you represent a (Check one)
☐₁ Plaintiff
☐₂ Defendant
☐₃ Other → Please specify: _____

54. Have any of your clients tried to reduce the costs of discovery, including but not limited to electronic discovery, by doing discovery-related work themselves or by contracting for discovery-related services?
☐₁ Yes
☐₂ No
☐₃ I can't say

55. Have any of your clients tried to reduce the costs of electronic discovery by implementing information management programs designed for that purpose?
    ☐$_1$ Yes
    ☐$_2$ No
    ☐$_3$ I can't say

V. Reform Proposals

Federal Rules of Civil Procedure 8 provides access to the court if a plaintiff presents "a short and plain statement of the claim showing that the pleader is entitled to relief." Some critics of Rule 8's notice pleading standard argue that the issues central to the resolution of most cases are not identified in the initial complaint and answer, but must be identified through subsequent motions practice and discovery.

56. In the named case, at what point, if any, in the case do you think that the disputed issues central to the case were adequately narrowed and framed for resolution? (Check one)
    ☐$_1$The initial complaint
    ☐$_2$The answer
    ☐$_3$Rule 12 motion
    ☐$_4$Amended complaint
    ☐$_5$Rule 26(f) conference
    ☐$_6$Early pretrial conference
    ☐$_7$After initial disclosures
    ☐$_8$After fact discovery
    ☐$_9$After contention discovery
    ☐$_{10}$ At summary judgment
    ☐$_{11}$Post-discovery pretrial conference
    ☐$_{12}$At trial
    ☐$_{13}$At multiple points
    ☐$_{14}$At no point
    ☐$_{15}$I can t say

57. In your experience in federal court, at what point, if any, in the typical case do you think that the disputed issues central to the case are adequately narrowed and framed for resolution? (Check one)

- ☐₁ The initial complaint
- ☐₂ The answer
- ☐₃ Rule 12 motion
- ☐₄ Amended complaint
- ☐₅ Rule 26(f) conference
- ☐₆ Early pretrial conference
- ☐₇ After initial disclosures
- ☐₈ After fact discovery
- ☐₉ After contention discovery
- ☐₁₀ At summary judgment
- ☐₁₁ Post-discovery pretrial conference
- ☐₁₂ At trial
- ☐₁₃ At multiple points
- ☐₁₄ At no point
- ☐₁₅ I can t say

58. The disputed issues would be identified at an earlier point in most cases if plaintiffs were required to plead more than "a short and plain statement of the claim showing that the pleader is entitled to relief." (Check one)

Strongly Agree	Agree	Neither Agree nor Disagree	Disagree	Strongly Disagree	Can't Say
☐₁	☐₂	☐₃	☐₄	☐₅	☐₆

59. Even if raising the pleading standards would help to identify and frame disputed issues at an earlier stage in litigation, the added burdens for plaintiffs would outweigh any benefits. (Check one)

Strongly Agree	Agree	Neither Agree nor Disagree	Disagree	Strongly Disagree	Can't Say
☐₁	☐₂	☐₃	☐₄	☐₅	☐₆

One proposal is to develop simplified procedures for the federal courts. These simplified procedures would require more detailed pleading and enhanced disclosure obligations, at the beginning of a case. They would also restrict discovery opportunities beyond the initial disclosures. Additional provisions would reduce motions practice and require an early, firm trial date. The principal argument for these simplified procedures is that the current system puts too much emphasis on discovery.

60. The Federal Rules' system of notice pleading and expansive discovery disproportionately increases the cost of litigating in federal court in relation to the system's benefits. (Check one)

Strongly Agree	Agree	Neither Agree nor Disagree	Disagree	Strongly Disagree	Can't Say
$\Box_1$	$\Box_2$	$\Box_3$	$\Box_4$	$\Box_5$	$\Box_6$

61. Heightened pleading standards and restrictions on discovery would discourage litigants from filing cases in federal court. (Check one)

Strongly Agree	Agree	Neither Agree nor Disagree	Disagree	Strongly Disagree	Can't Say
$\Box_1$	$\Box_2$	$\Box_3$	$\Box_4$	$\Box_5$	$\Box_6$

62. The federal courts should test simplified procedures, with all parties' consent, in a few select districts to determine whether such an idea is feasible. (Check one)

Strongly Agree	Agree	Neither Agree nor Disagree	Disagree	Strongly Disagree	Can't Say
$\Box_1$	$\Box_2$	$\Box_3$	$\Box_4$	$\Box_5$	$\Box_6$

63. If such simplified procedures had been an available option as part of such a test program at the time the named case was filed, would you have recommended that your client choose them over the existing Rules? (Check one)

$\Box_1$ Definitely would have recommended
$\Box_2$ Probably, depending on circumstances
$\Box_3$ Probably not, depending on circumstances
$\Box_4$ Definitely would not have recommended
$\Box_5$ Not enough information to answer the question

64. If such simplified procedures were an available option as part of such a test program, would you **generally** recommend to clients that they choose them over the existing Rules?

☐₁ Definitely would recommend
☐₂ Probably, depending on circumstances
☐₃ Probably not, depending on circumstances
☐₄ Definitely would not recommend
☐₅ Not enough information to answer the question

VI. The Federal Rules

For the questions in this section, do not limit your responses to your experiences in the named case, but please base your responses on your experiences in your federal cases and with the Federal Rules of Civil Procedure ("Rules").

65. Litigation in the federal courts is more expensive than litigation in the state courts in which I primarily practice. (Check one)

Strongly Agree	Agree	Neither Agree nor Disagree	Disagree	Strongly Disagree	Can't Say
☐₁	☐₂	☐₃	☐₄	☐₅	☐₆

66. Discovery in the federal courts is more expensive than discovery in the state courts in which I primarily practice. (Check one)

Strongly Agree	Agree	Neither Agree nor Disagree	Disagree	Strongly Disagree	Can't Say
☐₁	☐₂	☐₃	☐₄	☐₅	☐₆

67. Discovery in federal courts leads to more reliable and predictable case outcomes than in courts with more restricted discovery. (Check one)

Strongly Agree	Agree	Neither Agree nor Disagree	Disagree	Strongly Disagree	Can't Say
☐₁	☐₂	☐₃	☐₄	☐₅	☐₆

68. The Rules should be revised to limit discovery in general. (Check one)

Strongly Agree □₁	Agree □₂	Neither Agree nor Disagree □₃	Disagree □₄	Strongly Disagree □₅	Can't Say □₆

69. The Rules should be revised to limit electronic discovery. (Check one)

Strongly Agree □₁	Agree □₂	Neither Agree nor Disagree □₃	Disagree □₄	Strongly Disagree □₅	Can't Say □₆

70. Attorneys can cooperate in discovery while still being zealous advocates for their clients. (Check one)

Strongly Agree □₁	Agree □₂	Neither Agree nor Disagree □₃	Disagree □₄	Strongly Disagree □₅	Can't Say □₆

71. The Rules should be revised to enforce discovery obligations more effectively. (Check one)

Strongly Agree □₁	Agree □₂	Neither Agree nor Disagree □₃	Disagree □₄	Strongly Disagree □₅	Can't Say □₆

72. The Rules should be revised to require additional mandatory disclosures. (Check one)

Strongly Agree □₁	Agree □₂	Neither Agree nor Disagree □₃	Disagree □₄	Strongly Disagree □₅	Can't Say □₆

73. The Rules should be revised to provide for routine sharing of the costs of producing electronically stored information when the burdens of production are not equal. (Check one)

Strongly Agree □₁	Agree □₂	Neither Agree nor Disagree □₃	Disagree □₄	Strongly Disagree □₅	Can't Say □₆

74. The Rules should be revised to encourage more judicial case management. (Check one)

Strongly Agree ☐₁	Agree ☐₂	Neither Agree nor Disagree ☐₃	Disagree ☐₄	Strongly Disagree ☐₅	Can't Say ☐₆

75. The Rules should be revised to discourage judicial case management. (Check one)

Strongly Agree ☐₁	Agree ☐₂	Neither Agree nor Disagree ☐₃	Disagree ☐₄	Strongly Disagree ☐₅	Can't Say ☐₆

76. The outcomes of cases in the federal system are generally fair. (Check one)

Strongly Agree ☐₁	Agree ☐₂	Neither Agree nor Disagree ☐₃	Disagree ☐₄	Strongly Disagree ☐₅	Can't Say ☐₆

77. The procedures employed in the federal system are generally fair. (Check one)

Strongly Agree ☐₁	Agree ☐₂	Neither Agree nor Disagree ☐₃	Disagree ☐₄	Strongly Disagree ☐₅	Can't Say ☐₆

78. In the typical case in federal court, the cost of discovery should be no more than the following percentage of the total litigation costs of any party: _____%

79. Discovery is abused in almost every case in federal court. (Check one)

Strongly Agree ☐₁	Agree ☐₂	Neither Agree nor Disagree ☐₃	Disagree ☐₄	Strongly Disagree ☐₅	Can't Say ☐₆

80. Responding parties increase the cost and burden of discovery in federal court through delay and avoidance tactics. (Check one)

Strongly Agree ☐₁	Agree ☐₂	Neither Agree nor Disagree ☐₃	Disagree ☐₄	Strongly Disagree ☐₅	Can't Say ☐₆

81. The cost of litigating in federal court, including the cost of discovery, has caused at least one of my clients to settle a case that they would not have settled but for those costs. (Check one)

Strongly Agree ☐₁	Agree ☐₂	Neither Agree nor Disagree ☐₃	Disagree ☐₄	Strongly Disagree ☐₅	Can't Say ☐₆

82. The cost of litigating in federal court, including the cost of discovery, has caused at least one of my clients to abandon a claim that they would not have abandoned but for those costs. (Check one)

Strongly Agree ☐₁	Agree ☐₂	Neither Agree nor Disagree ☐₃	Disagree ☐₄	Strongly Disagree ☐₅	Can't Say ☐₆

83. It would be better if more cases went to trial. (Check one)

Strongly Agree ☐₁	Agree ☐₂	Neither Agree nor Disagree ☐₃	Disagree ☐₄	Strongly Disagree ☐₅	Can't Say ☐₆

84. Please enter any comments you may have on the subjects addressed in this survey in the box below:

Thank you!

Please mail or FAX the completed survey to Emery Lee, Federal Judicial Center, One Columbus Circle, N.E., Washington, D.C. 20002 (FAX: 202-502-4199). If you have any questions, please contact Emery Lee at elee@fjc.gov or 202-502-4078, or Tom Willging at twillgin@fjc.gov or 202-502-4049.

Appendix D: Attorney Comments

Table of Contents

Introduction	111
Respondents Representing Primarily Plaintiffs	
Discovery Abuse/Attorney Conduct	111
Discovery Costs	115
Discovery Process	117
Electronic Discovery	122
Federal Court Practice	123
Judicial Management	127
Rules	130
Summary Judgment	132
Rule 12 and *Twombly*	134
Civil Rights/Employment Law	138
Miscellaneous	139
Survey Comments	141
Respondents Representing Plaintiffs and Defendants About Equally	
Discovery Abuse/Attorney Conduct	143
Discovery Costs	145
Discovery Process	146
Electronic Discovery	149
Federal Court Practice	150
Judicial Management	152
Rules	153
Summary Judgment	155
Rule 12 and *Twombly*	155
Civil Rights/Employment Law	158
Miscellaneous	158
Survey Comments	159
Respondents Representing Primarily Defendants	
Discovery Abuse/Attorney Conduct	161
Discovery Costs	164
Discovery Process	166
Electronic Discovery	169
Federal Court Practice	173
Judicial Management	176
Rules	178
Summary Judgment	180
Rule 12 and *Twombly*	180
Civil Rights/Employment Law	183
Miscellaneous	184
Survey Comments	186

Introduction

At the end of the questionnaire, respondents were prompted to "enter any comments you may have on the subjects addressed in the survey in the box below." The following are the comments entered, arranged by the three categories of respondents used throughout the report and by the dominant subject matter of each comment. Many comments, of course, touched on multiple subjects but to avoid repetition were placed in one section. In a few comments, specific information that might identify the respondent has been deleted.

Respondents Representing Primarily Plaintiffs

Discovery Abuse/Attorney Conduct

My overwhelming experience as a plaintiff's attorney who has litigated dozens of cases in the Federal system is that Defendants routinely game discovery and pre-trial practice.

After practicing for 22 years, I've learned that lawyers can get along and cooperate and still be advocates for their clients. Most lawyers I deal with understand what is discoverable and what is not.

In my experience, the vast majority of opposing counsel have been cooperative and professional in managing discovery, which has resulted in decreased discovery costs for all parties.

Insurance companies have an advantage over the average insured when it comes to discovery. They abuse discovery by spending an inordinate amount of time and money to harass and over burden plaintiffs.

The insurance company's tactics in this case antagonized the jury and turned a $150,000 - $200,000 case ($125,000 actual fire loss) into a $1.2 million dollar case (without punitive damages.) Those tactics included combating discovery abuses.

There should be a limit on document production requests just like the limit on interrogatories. Large law firms are regularly abusing the fact that there is no limit and may propound ridiculous numbers of production requests that may take an inordinate amount of time.

Courts should put more resources and emphasis on ADR programs, which most parties disregard when court-sponsored. Judges should sanction lawyers who play too many games in discovery. The courts should recognize that in general defendants in civil cases have access to most information they need, while plaintiffs have access to nearly nothing. Summary judgment is granted almost as a matter of form in employment discrimination cases--only 5% of plaintiffs prevail.

Defendants' abuse of motion practice is the single largest contributor to the delay in reaching a resolution of a civil case in federal court.

Defendants are the parties that obstruct discovery and make it more complex. If 26(a)(1) disclosure was mandatory to include documents and ESI as well, it would make the process easier and less expensive.

Discovery abuse is the most stressful and time consuming problem with federal litigation. The federal judges with whom I regularly interact are too slow to react to discovery abuse, place too much burden on the requesting party to try to "amicably" obtain responsive discovery before allowing the court to become involved in discovery disputes and fail to sanction non-producing parties regardless of the unreasonableness of the non-producing parties' discovery responses and excuses.

Discovery is its own animal. The practice of assigning a magistrate judge to oversee discovery is a good one and should be encouraged. Cases (like mine in this instance) in which no magistrate is assigned tend to be the source of abuse because the federal judges do not have the time or commitment to pay attention to the discovery issues and often end up making decisions based on the sound bites in briefs rather than on substantive bases.

Discovery of records in [medical malpractice] cases and [personal injury] cases should be easy and there should not be a lot to fight over. With many defense attorneys there is cooperation. Unfortunately with a few everything is a fight.

Docket control orders that require a plaintiff to propound a settlement demand to the defendant early in the pretrial period; however, the requirement is a complete waste of time if the order does not require the defendant to tender a reasonable response consistent with a reasonable assessment of litigation risk, subject to judicial sanctions. Under our current system, the defendants always reply to early settlement offers by rejecting the plaintiff's offer (no matter how small) stating that additional discovery is needed before a response to the offer can be made. So long as there are no consequences to a defendant for conducting extensive discovery attempting to support a meritless defense, solely to delay the resolution, litigation in federal court will continue to be very expensive and protracted.

Federal Courts are generally a much better place for my clients than State Courts. The rules of civility make the Federal system a better forum.

For small firm practitioners representing individuals, federal court is generally a burden. Large defense firms representing large corporations routinely remove cases that can be tried in state court in order to increase the burden on plaintiffs. Strict and sometimes unyielding scheduling orders make some cases nearly unmanageable for small or solo practitioners that do not have an army of associates or large staff. I make every effort to keep my cases out of federal court.

I applaud your efforts to reform the federal litigation process. The vast majority of my federal cases are complex product liability cases. In such cases, the resolution is greatly influenced by the judge and his/her willingness to appropriately address discovery abuse by the corporate defendants. Simply put, unless the court will punish the recalcitrant defendant for discovery abuse, there is little incentive to comply with discovery requests and reveal information that can force early resolution. It seems that fewer and fewer federal courts are willing to do so. Thus, cases are now far more expensive and time consuming than necessary.

I appreciate the opportunity to participate in this survey. In the case in question, I had opposing counsel who ignored nearly all communications from me, who did not respond to discovery requests, who ignored letters requesting responses to discovery, and who at the pretrial denied receipt of the foregoing. Nevertheless, they stipulated to entry of a judgment in favor of my client at the pretrial.

I believe that because defendants attorneys generally are paid by the hour, they abuse the discovery system by holding depositions of witnesses that have little or nothing to add to a case. I have flown across country to attend a deposition of a non-party witness whom an east coast plaintiff testified he played golf with when the plaintiff used to live on the W. Coast. Why should a court permit that? That is just an example....Defendant's attorneys should be encouraged to bill on a contingency as do plaintiff's attys. Maybe that will help the system too.

I feel ordering mediation or an initial assessment to early on in the case is not helpful. The parties could not settle the case on their own and thus needed to file suit. There should be some minimal discovery allowed before the parties are ordered to mediate. Then information is available which should encourage reasonable settlement. I also feel there are no penalties for discovery abuses such as speaking objections and instructing clients not to answer. There should be clear rules on these types of issues with sanctions which would save the resources of the parties and of the Courts.

I have actively practiced [for] 51 years. I spent a great deal of time in Federal Courts in most of the coastal cities of the U.S. doing maritime and Jones Act litigation and product liability cases. Cases moved expeditiously when both counsel and their clients behaved properly, courteously and honored the rules. I believe tighter and more severe sanctions are needed to require litigants, especially corporate parties. Class action litigation Rules should be separately developed with really tough sanctions if parties withhold or play games.

I have recently, in the past two years, been so disgusted at the failure of the US government, when they are a defendant, to follow the rules of discovery. I have repeatedly requested electronic discovery.

I primarily sue parties represented by large law firms paid by the hour in employment cases. The defense attorneys have zero incentive to be efficient with discovery and thus drag things out. They are often rewarded for their tactics b/c many plaintiff's attorneys don't have the time/money to force the issue. My firm does, but it is still very irritating. The courts tend to back up the big firm lawyers. Maybe there is an assumption that they know what they are doing. But my experience has been that it is all about their legal fees - not their client's best interest. In addition - the defendants have in their possession all the important documents. I often wonder how much I am not getting that I will never know existed.

In general many lawyers fail to comply with the rule requiring initial disclosures. When a party does comply, the initial disclosures are barely sufficient compared to what is obtained based on the written discovery requests. If any rule should be changed it is that documents should be produced with the initial disclosures, not simply listed. Some lawyers will agree to produce, but most will not. Finally, in my experience, waiting until after the scheduling conference to be allowed to propound discovery delays discovery four to six weeks.

It has been my experience that delay, unwillingness to penalize parties for failing to follow the rules, and shortened time periods have made it much more difficult for people who bring cases to have a fair shot at resolving claims.

Many defendants play unnecessary games in responding to discovery requests. They especially abuse the meet-and-confer process by withholding documents until they absolutely have to produce them to avoid a motion to compel.

Much of the time and energy I expend in the pursuit of discovery from insurance company defendants (in insurance coverage matters) is targeted at materials that should properly have been produced as part of the initial disclosures. In my experience, corporate defendants generally (and insurers in particular) do not take seriously their obligation to make meaningful initial disclosures. Moreover, no one is policing this aspect of federal practice.

Spurious and excessive objections are the biggest problem with federal court discovery. Judges should deal harshly with page after page of blanket, general and stock objections. Objections should be set aside if they do not have specific merit to the discovery request in question and courts should do everything possible to discourage this practice.

The current rules would be improved greatly of the federal courts would discourage the abuse by counsel through unnecessary objections and stalling (especially in production of documents electronic or paper). There was a period of time when counsel were professionals and co-operated with each other while still being advocates for their clients. For several years now, the larger firms have used discovery as a means to inflate litigation costs thereby bogging down not only the litigants but also the Courts. No matter what changes are made, until this gamesmanship is stopped and a return to the professionalism that federal court was known for happens no rule changes will be effective.

The defense counsel needs to address the case and not focus on the generation of billable hours. Most cases can be settled early on. It was best when the court took an active roll in settling cases early on without huge amounts of time and costs expensed

The first 17 years of my practice was in defense and now I am primarily a plaintiff's attorney. Wealthy defendants and insurers through delay and abusive discovery techniques unduly increase the cost of litigating.

The poor have no records; the rich do, but can delay and delay, hiding behind commercial privilege. It's not the cost alone, it's the delay that destroys my clients.

Too many respondents attempt to evade their discovery responsibilities through bad faith practices

When defense and indemnity claims exist for a defendant, that defendant should be required to claim earlier on that claim, because tardiness of those claims slows down plaintiff's litigation, by inducing continuation of trials due to newcomer attorneys' conflicts with the original trial date. I wish there were a particularized rule or set of rules to handle summarily, early on, these scenarios. Some defense attorneys intentionally, dilatorily, abuse the current rules, in this situation.

My practice is limited to FELA litigation and most railroad lawyers generally get along well; there are not many electronic data disputes.

Until 2005, my practice was 50/50 plaintiff and defense. Now, since Hurricane Katrina, the practice has been primarily plaintiff oriented. Much can be done to avoid uniform discovery abuses by defendants.

Discovery Costs

I have primarily a section 1983 practice against a large municipality, and find that delay, lack of responsiveness to necessary discovery, and failure of the courts to adequately enforce discovery obligations is the greatest cause of increased costs of litigation.

Litigation costs would be substantially reduced if parties were forced to discuss settlement early and often.

More timely decisions by the Court on motions to dismiss and for summary judgment would have a greater impact on reducing costs, and defining the issues to reduce discovery burdens than most of the issues addressed in this survey.

The biggest expense in civil cases is experts. Requiring reports by experts and then producing them for deposition causes the client to incur more than double the expense. Electronic discovery is not the problem with expenses. Detailed expert reports are the problem because then you are forced to pay for their time in deposition. That is why I try not to file anything in Federal Court. That and the God complex of the Federal Bench.

The current restrictions on discovery (e.g., number of depositions, 7 hr depositions) are skewed in favor of defendants. The cost of litigation in federal court is NOT unduly increased by discovery.

The single best way to reduce litigation expense is by setting an early trial date and early discovery cutoff date.

42 USC 1983 litigation with police defendants is entirely too expensive for both sides. See *Mercy v. Suffolk County*, 93 F.R.D. 520, 524(E.D.N.Y. 1982) (Appendix to Order re model Discovery Order) Protective Orders are routinely sought without good cause. Discovery decisions are largely left to the whim of individual judges. See *Sullivan v. Glock, Inc.*, 175 F.R.D. 497, 505 (D.Md. 1997) -- as at "Alice's Restaurant, "one can find what one wants" by researching the law of discovery in the federal system.

Any changes to the federal rules should take into account that most corporate defendants have vastly more resources than individual plaintiffs. A fair system should make sure that disparity of resources does not deprive either party of justice.

"Costs of discovery" is too broad a term encompassing too many variables to address by simple survey.

Early ADR and settlement conferences in my experience are the most effective judicial tools to reduce discovery and litigation costs, and lead to the most satisfactory outcome of a case from the point of view of the client.

Expert depositions are very expensive. When you have to pay for the defendant's expert deposition and your own expert for trial, it can get very expensive. I was wondering if the federal courts ever considered some type of fee schedule for expert depositions. On the plus side, the judges and magistrates are very prepared. I like having a set time for conferences so I don't have to sit around in court. I like phone conferences; they save a lot of time.

Federal court has become very expensive for relatively small federal claims which cannot be filed in alternative forums e.g. civil rights and employment claims.

Federal court is more expensive than the State Courts in which I practice. There is more useless hearings, motions etc and less practical case management.

Generally, the discovery procedure and costs are better in the Federal Court than the State Court. However, the federal procedure may still be streamlined by more enforcement and case management of discovery/production obligations to avoid unnecessary discovery disputes and motions that increases the cost of litigation. Additionally, initial mandatory disclosures should be expanded and enforced. Initial conferences should be expanded to narrow facts in disputes and those not in dispute (based on initial disclosures), so that any subsequent discovery, including depositions, should be limited to facts in dispute.

I currently represent low-income clients in special education cases where discovery is typically limited. It is particularly difficult for low-income clients to pursue meritorious cases in Fed Ct. due to concerns re costs of discovery and requirements for in-person (instead of telephonic) status conferences.

I would like to encourage all districts to institute mandatory ADR proceedings at a time in the case process where it can be most effective before the costs of discovery and motion practice may make it very difficult to settle.

In my experience, controlling discovery costs means controlling the number of depositions and deposition exhibits. The defense bar does not fully comply with 26(a)(1); nor do they ever give a straight answer to an interrogatory. Plaintiffs are therefore required to depose more people, which drives up discovery costs. Enforcing discovery rules should be easier and faster. All the federal magistrates are too busy to enforce the discovery rules. I think the trial judge should appoint a local attorney as a special master to resolve discovery disputes, much the same way local attorneys act as mediators.

Mandatory expert witness reports are expensive, burdensome.

More mandatory initial disclosures would help reduce discovery costs.

The cost limits for expert witnesses should [be] removed and actual costs awarded to the prevailing party.

The Rules regarding subparts for Interrogatories are ridiculous. More discovery could be accomplished in written interrogatories if the Defense Bar didn't consider every semi-colon and comma in a single interrogatory as a part of the "included subparts" that counts against the total of 25. This leads to businesses paying increased costs, costs created by their own lawyers, for discovery that results in a motion to compel that is completely unnecessary. Rule 26 needs more liberality in allowing for the obtaining of information, not less.

U.S. Magistrate Judges in my experience are the single major factor in keeping discovery disputes and costs down. Southern District of CA. Magistrate Judges are very experienced in managing discovery disputes and they have excellent mediation skills. The human factor is much more important than the content of the discovery rules.

The reason discovery was so expensive in my case is that the plaintiff employed the "name every conceivable defendant" strategy.

Discovery Process

From the plaintiff's prospective expansive discovery is not needed. If a plaintiff needs discovery to make his/her case the contingent nature of the agreement militates against bringing the matter in the first instance. Thus, discovery is oftentimes completely unnecessary from the point of view of the plaintiff's prima facie case.

In the David vs. Goliath cases the discovery practices of Goliath virtually always create an inherent disadvantage to David. Mandatory comprehensive disclosure at a certain period in the litigation process will make all litigants aware of their requirement.

Limiting discovery is not the answer. Defendants oftentimes do not take Rule 26 disclosure obligation seriously. We spend too much time trying to get complete discovery responses, delaying our ability to effectively proceed in discovery.

One change that would make a difference in turns of costs is to require the party conducting depositions to provide at least electronic copies at no cost to opposing parties.

In my opinion, the problem with the Federal justice system is not related to discovery rules or procedures--even though they are too onerous.

Access to the courts, including the ability to have a full and fair trial of the issues, is important. Limiting discovery hampers the parties' ability to have a full and fair trial of the issues.

Allow discovery to start at the time the answer is served. It will speed up cases. Allow a Plaintiff to proceed by jury as of right in the event of default of a party. That will discourage intentional defaults which are on the rise.

Any efforts to limit parties' powers of discovery would be utterly misguided, and would severely limit parties' access to the truth. Moreover, any effort to 'allocate' discovery costs between the parties could cripple individual people's ability to bring cases, and would unfairly tilt the scales of justice in favor of large corporations.

Considering average size and level of resources of plaintiff vs. defense firms, it would be more fair to have defense counsel carry relatively more of the burden of paperwork, especially the obligation to draft the joint pre trial order.

Discovery is an important part of the litigation process and should not be limited in any way.

Discovery needs to be more uniform with regard to scheduling. In similar cases, one judge will allow 90 days of fact discovery and another judge will allow 9 months. This is unfair to litigants with a substantial litigation case load, such as myself.

Discovery should begin within 30 days of service of the Complaint. Waiting around for the Rule 26f conference merely allows the evidence to grow stale and delay prompt resolution of the matter.

Each effort to facilitate discovery only seems to make matters more complicated. The process has become cumbersome for most cases. Simplify the discovery process for most cases to reduce the cost and burden.

Eliminate interrogatories as a matter of right!!! Require court order for interrogatories.

Eliminating initial disclosures for forfeiture cases was a very good idea and reduced the risk of compromising on-going criminal investigations.

Fundamentally, the present mechanisms concerning discovery represent a fair balance that enables cases to proceed towards adjudications that promote justice. The worst injustices are those in which relevant materials are not produced and only become discovered later. Those are the instances which bring the legal system into disrepute. Most notably, I believe (and no question appeared to address this) that the federal courts, in recent years, have become significantly better in moving discovery along expeditiously and reasonably. As has often been the case, I feel the various proposed rule changes of late are behind, by at least a few years, the curve of learning and practice.

Generally, I believe that lawyers are not given enough time to conduct discovery on federal cases, especially civil rights cases, and truth in lending cases. The case I tried in which this survey questioned me on was a straightforward accident case against the Post Office. I have found on other cases, especially civil rights ones, that the Magistrates are not giving enough time for discovery. In state court, we get at least 450 days of discovery for such cases, and can extend with consent for another 60. The federal courts should give a similar amount of time, instead of pushing cases too fast. If both sides agree to a slower and more time to do proper discovery, I think justice is better served.

I am a plaintiff's side solo handling commercial litigation; but I worked for many years as a large-firm litigator. I've seen both sides of discovery abuses, and have a pretty solid understanding of the issues. For me, the biggest issue is disproportionate resources (both legal and economic) when I bring meritorious claims against large multi-national entities. The phrase "dump-truck discovery" and "tidal-wave litigation" are applicable to me. The rules provide for cost-shifting in light of perceived discovery abuses, but (at least in D. Mass) are almost never enforced except in egregious cases. More robust enforcement of existing cost-shifting provisions would be welcome. From a personal perspective, a recognition of the parties' relative financial resources would be appreciated, particularly when dealing with discovery delays.

I believe in facilitation and we have been very successful at resolving disputes in this fashion.

I strongly disagree that Rule 8 prevents issues central to resolution from being identified. In my experience, Defendants refuse to resolve cases until they have taken the Plaintiff's deposition and forced the Plaintiff to take one or several depositions.

I think all Federal Courts should operate with the "automatic" discovery orders and procedures that we have installed in the Eastern District of Texas.

I think the Judges are overburdened. Though discovery process could surely be streamlined somewhat, motion practice seems to be more of a delay. On the whole however, I am constantly surprised how well, in the end, the system works.

In my consumer protection practice, the defendants have virtually all of the information required to prove the claim while plaintiff has very little discovery. Limiting discovery would allow defendants in such cases to win by default. Limiting discovery only makes sense when you have two equal parties with equal information about a particular claim.

In my experience, firm trial and discovery cut off dates, coupled with enforcement of discovery rules pushes cases to settlement. Stronger enforcement of depositions going forward would help settle disputes more efficiently. Most notably, burdensome rules regarding motions to compel (i.e., the local rules of C.D. Cal.) make enforcing discovery more onerous for all (including the Court) but do not have the intended result of encouraging cooperation. If the process to get the actual information needed were simpler and quicker, parties would be more frank at the outset of the cases and disputes would resolve much quicker.

It would have been helpful for the Judge to take an active role in requiring and ensuring cooperation in discovery and requiring the federal agency involved to preserve and produce documents and bear the onus of providing a thorough explanation of how and where electronic documents were maintained and should be reproduced. Avoidance and lack of responsibility or coordination between the US Atty and the federal agency counsel resulted in destruction or loss of documents which did not meet an intentional standard, but was nonetheless harmful to the plaintiff's case, and is likely to continue because it serves defense strategy.

My practice deals mostly with administrative law cases so I do not deal with discovery very often. But discovery costs would be a big burden on my clients if it was a big part of a case because all my clients are non-profit organizations. Therefore, we purposefully try not to bring cases that require lots of experts and discovery for this reason.

Our division has successfully used local rules to streamline the procedural requirements of administrative review claims such as ERISA. The FJC might consider the formal adoption of less stringent procedural and discovery requirements in these cases.

Parties with a long-standing litigation relationship should be excused from the more formal case management rules and permitted to engage in discovery on their own, only seeking court involvement when a dispute arises. I practice FELA law and most FELA plaintiff and defense lawyers cooperate in discovery and do not need close court supervision.

Please include data about the judiciary and its role in the discovery process. Much discovery abuse is by defendants who abuse discovery to force resolution to cases.

Strong discovery must be available to insure that most litigants will comply with discovery obligations. A few will abuse the system and the court should treat them harshly and impose sanctions more often.

The disclosures are a joke. They require more work than normal discovery. Early mediation is also a joke it costs us too much money for a no offer we need to streamline and have responses to normal discovery with teeth and more RFA's since they narrow the issues finally what ever happened to trying cases? Seems it used to be cheaper and quicker.

As for my trials 100 med mal and products so they are complex cases but still too much crap and not enough trials.

The system generally works and does not need wholesale change.

The time limits placed on discovery are much too restrictive. In the case I was contacted about, my motion to file an amended complaint was denied because it was 21 days before the end of discovery. The court felt there was a "public interest" in seeing speedy resolution of cases. Then, it took that court 14 months to rule on summary judgment. So much for the public's interest when the court has time constraints.

There should be no hold on discovery before the ENE. it would be more productive if there was a mandatory disclosure before the ENE.

Whether discovery is more or less expansive, each District throughout the Country should have UNIFIED procedures. For attorneys who practice in multiple jurisdictions, which is an increasing phenomenon, it is ridiculous that the rules of procedure vary so widely, in courthouses less than 100 miles from each other.

You can't try a case based on voluntary discovery as no party will voluntarily produce information that is adverse to it. There needs to be stronger requirements of privilege logs for information withheld and stronger scrutiny of those logs with more *en camera* examinations.

My practice is primarily plaintiff's medical malpractice claims. The discovery required of both sides is fairly straightforward and consistent, case to case. The parties usually have a clear understanding of what records and documents are needed in the case. These are produced without question. I have not had a motion regarding a discovery question in federal or state court for about 8 years.

Rule 26 disclosures not adequate due to evasion, generalizations, incorporation of opposing parties' disclosures. Better enforcement, i.e. follow-up conf. with judge, could save costs and time in discovery.

The current disclosures required by Rule 26 are not meaningful and only serve to delay substantive discovery. My experience with electronic discovery is limited and will likely increase this year.

The Rule 26 (a)(1) voluntary disclosure requirements need to be taken more seriously by all the federal judges should show zero tolerance for the "usual" objections of "vague", "overly broad" and the like when answering interrogatories and request for production. If you do not understand what I am talking about, take a look at the first-round written responses from some big firm in a product liability lawsuit!

The Rule 26 disclosure obligations are too often skirted by cases that hold that a 4 factor test applies to whether an untimely designated expert can testify. Rule 37(c)(1) should be applied as written.

FYI: Our discovery requests were disputed. A settlement was reached in which plaintiffs withdrew their request in exchange for an agreed upon discovery schedule pending outcome of the court's ruling on 12(b) motions.

Electronic Discovery

As a Plaintiff's attorney, I find that corporations drag out discovery with objections rather than voluntarily producing discoverable information, especially electronic discovery. It is more likely that a Defendant will charge a Plaintiff for copies of documents than it is for a Plaintiff to charge the Defendant.

Delaying and stonewalling tactics by defendants, coupled with short and firm discovery and trial deadlines imposed by Judges who are concerned about statistical reports about their number of pending cases, combine to cause injustice for plaintiffs who typically cannot prove their cases without thorough discovery from the defendant.

Efforts by a State Gov't entity to enforce outrageous contractor costs of electronic discovery against a plaintiff in an employment (EEO) case served to constitute punitive litigation measures; Courts and parties are NOT dealing with electronic discovery correctly or timely, especially the cost components.

Electronic Discovery costs are often a phantom excuse. Defendants will say the information doesn't exist or would be expensive to produce when they just want to block the road. A database query can be cheap and damning. A D will just neglect to ask the employee who knows how to formulate the query.

Electronic discovery is potentially a cheaper, more effective and more reliable way of discovering the truth in civil litigation than many other methods now in use.

I do not have extensive experience with electronic discovery, but have heard horror stories regarding the amount of work caused. It seems a better balance should be struck regarding need for information and burden and cost.

In line with "guns don't kill people, people kill people." I think the opponents and attorneys make for good or bad discovery. If someone with a total lack of electronic knowledge tries to do electronic discovery it is going to be a problem no matter the rules.

Most of my cases in federal court are Jones Act cases. Electronic discovery is not substantial. All fees are contingent.

Plaintiff discovery of electronic information, either pre- or during litigation, is a joke. Defendants will never voluntarily provide damaging email or other digital data; and

Plaintiffs are powerless to compel such production unless they have the extremely unlikely equivalent of a smoking gun to demonstrate Defendant concealment of electronically-stored information.

The majority of my case load deals with personal injury cases. I represent plaintiffs who have been injured. Electronic discovery that I have received in the past usually involves company manuals.

Federal Court Practice

The majority of my Federal practice is in representing citizens aggrieved by law enforcement, usually false arrest (42USC1983). As a result, our discovery is rather limited.

The Eastern District of Virginia in Norfolk always favors government and business.

#1: More Magistrate Judges [or use of a panel of neutrals] are needed in every District to enforce the "Initial Disclosure" Requirements of FRCP 26 & 37. "Initial Disclosure" requisites under the Civil Justice Reform Act was a good idea - but, since too many litigants ignore their R. 26 duties, and there are too few Magistrate Judges to enforce their R. 16.1 [Early Meet, Confer, Exchange Discls.] Orders, over-worked USMJs and lack of time for oversight has led to unfairness for those who do comply, as we must & do.#2: More Magistrate Judges = better, faster and equal Justice under FRCP 1.

As a plaintiff's attorney, I like almost everything about litigating in federal court, including the professionalism of staff and from the bench, the more detailed procedure, the quality of the courtroom......the one thing I do not like is the requirement of unanimity with jury verdicts. In our state courts, 9 out of 12 is needed...the federal court burden is too tough and allows one dissenting juror to potentially hold the others hostage....should be 5 out 7 in civil cases but I won't hold my breath...that will never happen.

As an Oregon practitioner and primarily an appellate practitioner, my responses may differ from attorneys who do more trial work. Oregon is a congenial place to practice. We generally work out a lot of issues without court intervention.

Cases would be handled more fairly in District Courts if the judges were not so concerned that civil cases clog their criminal docket. Perhaps civil and criminal divisions should be employed in District Courts so that those judges handling civil matters will be vastly more familiar with the Civil Rules of Procedure and will be freed from the need to provide speedy trials in criminal cases.

Civil litigants are at a disadvantage in fed ct due to criminal docket.

Federal courts here in the Fifth Circuit are viscerally and unremittingly hostile to regular people -- not because of their race, gender, etc., but because people's last names don't end in "INC." or "CORP."

Federal practice is far superior than in state courts.

Federal procedures are too hard on Plaintiffs.

Generally speaking, I believe the system works well except for the fact that it is too slow, which I believe is the result of case load.

I appreciate being included in the survey. My experience in Federal Court with both the court and counsel has been generally positive.

I greatly prefer the state court system over the federal court system.

I have been practicing for over 35 years in the Southern District and Northern District now almost exclusively there as I find that the law, judges, magistrates, attorneys and court facilities are far superior to State Court practice. I consider myself very fortunate that my practice permits this choice.

I only bring my cases in Federal Court because Federal Court strongly enforces discovery against municipalities that I am suing. State courts let things slide.

I practice primarily in Arkansas where the federal judiciary does an admirable job of case management, the practicing bar is cooperative and well controlled by the Court, and the Court fairly administers justice.

I think that federal cases are too micromanaged by the court. Many good trial lawyers that I know will not practice in federal court for that reason.

It costs more to litigate in federal court than it does in state court because the federal system imposes too many rules and technical procedures. That also results in less fair outcomes. I tend to avoid federal court as a consequence of the above.

Limiting discovery favors corporate defendants, which are already at a significant advantage in District Court.

My practice is in the area of ERISA benefits litigation, and the Federal Courts around the country have yet to determine the scope of permitted discovery. An amendment to ERISA explicitly stating that a Federal ERISA action is like any other federal action would be appropriate.

No disrespect intended but lawyers who practice plaintiffs' air crash litigation say in private that voluntarily filing an air crash case in the Federal Courts is the commission of legal malpractice.

Now a case rarely is sent to Magistrate for settlement conference, even if that method is selected by the parties. If it is not an option, remove it and leave parties to choose other ADR methods at the Scheduling Conference.

Some of the questions I either could not answer or was not comfortable answering. In a nutshell, the federal system already dramatically favors corporate defendants, for a whole host of reasons beyond the scope of this limited email. Suffice it to say, tilting things even further in their favor by limiting discovery and by heightening burdens on plaintiffs would only serve to make an already unlevel playing field that much more slanted.

The amount of work required of counsel, solely for the Court, post discovery and pre-trial (such as bench binders, etc) is oppressive and too costly. It is a huge deterrent for smaller monetary cases.

The case upon which my participation is based is not a representative case. Overall the federal system is stacked against the individual and favors the $$.

The Courts of the Northern District of Illinois maintain a high standard for the lawyers who practice before these courts. Therefore, the issues presented to the court are often resolved without the necessity of constant management by the court. Further, the Federal Rules of Procedure and the Local Rules of the Northern District enable the parties to litigate without burdening the court, thus reducing the expenses to both the plaintiff and the defendant. The formality and high standards of the Court increases the ability of all parties to expeditiously and fairly resolve disputes.

The Federal Courts are already, in general, too Defendant friendly and place too many burdens on Plaintiffs. The last thing that the Federal Courts need is too place more obstacles for Plaintiffs in obtaining information from Defendants though discovery. The big problem from my perspective is that there are too many instances when Defendants offer false and misleading information in the discovery process and there is no real penalty for what amounts to perjury.

The federal courts need to experiment with alternatives to traditional litigation, involving serious (perhaps mandatory) ADR methods including the appointment of a serious (empowered) neutral to monitor discovery in real time (sit in on depositions).

The Federal courts need to actively limit discovery to match case size and structure. Huge cases and ordinary ones need separate discovery plans and more aggression at drawing distinctions.

The Federal System is pretty good as it is. Far, far, far better than our state system, and it starts with quality of the judges.

The Federal system seems more concerned with clearing its docket than providing justice for the "people". It also appears that it favors the rich and government over less fortunate citizens.

The Federal system works fine.

The judge's pretrial handling of exhibits made the trial go smoother than any previous one in federal court.

The majority of my work in Federal Court is ERISA disability cases. The system works well in the Middle District of Florida as we now have limited discovery. [Names deleted].

The model plan the Eastern District of Texas used several years ago on a trial basis required more mandatory disclosures and worked well.

The only time I am in federal court is when I am removed. I dislike federal court, not because of discovery, but because of the FRCP 56 standards.

The principle difference between the federal courts and the state practice in my area involves the depositions of experts. In state court, we rely exclusively on expert reports, and the absence of expert depositions reduces the costs associated with discovery by more than half. Moreover, I have cross-examined more than 50 experts at trial, and have never felt I needed a deposition in advance in order to do so effectively.

There are too many cases eliminated at an early stage without sufficient discovery being produced. The disclosures should include all documents maintained by the parties.

There should be more seminars sponsored by the Courts for attorneys. Also, I often feel that Federal Court practice with its requirements favors bigger firms and not the small firm or solo attorney.

This was an unusual case factually. My answers to the case specific questions certainly do not reflect my experience in other "garden variety" plaintiff's personal injury cases that I have litigated in Federal Court. Generally, the lawyers seem to get along well and discovery rarely becomes contentious.

We predominantly handle Plaintiffs' wage and hour cases under the FLSA. Unfortunately, the Florida District Court Judges have responded to a high influx of these cases by narrowly interpreting jurisdiction to hear said cases which has led to the dismissal of approximately 40% of the case load. See the THORNE case out of the 11th Cir. and its progeny. Rather than implementing this draconian method to reduce a high case load, I always felt that the District Courts of Florida should designate special divisions or Judges who only handle wage and hour cases. This would be a fair solution to the "issue" without, in effect, sterilizing the effect of the Statute (FLSA) via the judiciary.

We still have so matters pending in the case so I could not answer all of the questions. I generally think the streamlining that seems to be on the table would be a denial of justice to most people, especially if mandatory.

Too much motion practice in fed court. Too rigid on deadlines in some fed courts.

Early mandatory mediation would be helpful. Thank you for your interest.

My only complaint about litigating in federal court is that the mandatory E-Filing system is NOT user friendly. An attorney (and particularly a pro per plaintiff) who is filing in federal court generally needs significant prior experience in the E-Filing system in order to understand the esoteric requirements. Each time I have filed, I end up having to talk to a clerk to determine how to wade through the filing process. The process should be set forth online in a much more simplified manner.

Judicial Management

The defendant admitted to destroying all of the evidence which they claim existed at the time of her termination and failed to search backup and storage of those files. The District Court granted motions *in limine* to exclude mention of the destruction of evidence, the wiping of the computer hard drive of the decision maker and numerous other significant pieces of evidence.

Biggest concern of mine is that Judges can have a dramatic effect on the outcome. Though I generally have a high respect for the federal judges in Hawaii, I am aware of at least one state judge who will intentionally trip up plaintiff's attorneys to help the defense.

The Local Rules provide for a good framework where I practice--Middle District Florida. Judges need to realize that sometimes additional discovery time is needed, and should grant additional time more frequently.

Add judicial temperament and practices to the inquiries to come closer to real life answers.

Almost all of my cases were removed from State courts. All of my clients would have preferred to stay in Yuma County. Appearing in Court in Phoenix is what really increased our costs. Judges were not willing to allow us to appear by telephone on simple pretrial matters. This necessitated pulling young children out of schools to appear before the judge. I have always felt that the judges and distance from Yuma is what caused our costs to skyrocket. I greatly prefer the system used in our state courts. Federal judges tend to be too involved in discovery and in pretrial procedures.

Especially in employment cases and cases, generally, defendants companies should be rebuked by the court for their discovery abuses. Judges are often reluctant to punish defendant companies, represented by large law firms, when the attorneys engage in delay tactics.

Federal courts offer several mechanisms by which discovery matters may be resolved and settlement facilitated. On the other hand, I believe that currently Plaintiffs face an uphill battle to avoid their cases being gutted by Judges with heavy dockets rather than allowed to proceed to trial.

Generally, the federal system works well and efficiently. The problem I have encountered is the politicization of the federal judiciary where conservative judges are appointed for the specific purpose of minimizing the impact of civil rights laws.

I enjoy practicing in Federal Court. Judge Phillips gave us a fair trial and was courtesy to counsel on both sides, allowing us to do have a fair trial and present our evidence to the jury.

I have been an attorney for 32 years and do my best to stay out of Federal Courts, (a) the judges are at best temperamental and or abusive, (b) there is no simple rule book to follow, like starting at rule 1 and going to rule 2, then rule 3, etc. and (c) it would be nice if we did not need a unanimous verdict in Fed Court

I think the biggest issue in this case was the delay. Years and years for a resolution. The courts kept extending the deadlines. It would have been better if the discovery had been done as it was but in a much shorter time frame.

If the courts would stop favoring big corporations and start enforcing discovery rules against them, and prevent defense counsel from playing games in discovery through their incessant practice, trial litigation would go much smoother.

In federal court, my greatest problem is with getting prompt judge attention to the case. I do not find that R. 16, in fact, causes the judge to figure out what the case is about and impose rulings based on that knowledge. Slow judicial action on briefing is also an issue. My clients are Sierra Club and the like; they are looking for injunctive relief and declaratory judgments -- damages are not relevant, but much of federal procedure is geared to monetary damages. My clients are harmed by the mere passage of time -- a few thousand dollars a month for months and months drains their resources.

In my opinion, the Judge assigned to each case has a very large impact on the issues addressed by this survey. A reasonable, fair, yet strong handed Judge who takes an active role in the cases can keep a case, and discovery, on the right track, as long as personal bias is left out of the equation.

In the Northern District of Alabama I believe the judges have found the appropriate level of judicial management. I do think lawyers should be held to a higher standard in complying with initial disclosures.

Judges should be more willing to grant summary judgment if the law is clear and the facts support the decision. Much unwillingness to grant summary judgment seems to stem from fear of political consequences and is not based upon a desire to see justice done.

Judges should: Hold early trial conferences and sternly caution lawyers against strategic behavior in discovery and particularly enforce the Rule 26 early disclosure provisions on core evidentiary documents.

Less judicial intervention there should be no discovery timetables that restrict the time attorneys have to perform pre trial discovery for less than one year

Mississippi federal courts are in terrible shape currently. They have been "hi-jacked" by rogue, "pro-business" state Supreme Court Justices.

My firm encounters situations with relative frequency wherein federal court judges fail to rule on motions in a timely matter. As a result, the entire case unnecessarily comes to a complete stand-still. There should be a procedure in place to ensure that district court judges are attending to the matters on their dockets and ruling on both motions during trial and post-trial motions.

Some federal judges are overly enamored with their power to impose their personal views on cases. Minnesota state court judges are more respectful of litigants and their attorneys.

Some of the Justices need to be more understanding of the restrictions that attorneys who are sole practitioners or from small firms have to deal with in terms of availability etc.

The cost of appellate litigation is greatly increased by the failure of the district court to entertain the claims against all parties and requires too many instances of remand and other appellate fees, thereby increasing litigation costs. It appears many federal judges do not review de novo the objections to the magistrate's recommendations as required by statute and increases the cost of litigation and loss of time.

The Eastern District of Texas used to have mandatory disclosure of all relevant documents, which made things much faster, easier, and cheaper. That is a good way to go. Things get expensive in discovery because everyone objects to every request and Judges seem unwilling to hammer someone for those objections. If that happened, things would also move quicker. Generally, I am seeing Judges who seem overworked, underfunded, and understaffed. This is why it takes longer and longer to get to trial, and why more and more pressure is put on the parties to settle. Trials are a good thing and should be more accessible.

The fairness of the procedure and the quality of the outcome depends largely upon the integrity and skill of the judge in applying the rules, not in the letter of the rules. Judges need more specialization in their workloads so that they can bring expertise to each case and not reinvent the wheel in each civil action. Too often the wheel comes out square.

The federal court is so isolated that it is difficult for clients to have a realistic understanding of what is going on in their case. It is clear that the federal court does not want to actually see or hear civil litigation, since everything is done on paper. Most of the judges refuse to hear summary judgment motions, and having a trial is almost unheard of. The system would greatly improve if these dispositive motions were heard, rather than read, and having more trials would encourage settlement.

The Federal system tilts toward a recovery for corporations and government-state and Federal. Actually Federal Judge will ever understand how a sole individual will feel. I have known many Federal Judges, and they do not understand the discovery process.

The judge should be more accessible to quickly resolve discovery disputes without all the unnecessary paperwork and hoops to jump through.

The most frustrating part of Federal Court is the inability to have hearings in court, and the inflexible Federal Judges that will not allow parties to agree on discovery, even when the party's agreements would not interfere with the ability to try the case as the court schedules.

The temperament and interest of the Judge greatly affects the tenor of discovery, the quantity and timing of discovery, the cooperativeness of counsel and the timeliness to trial. Whether the rules are less or more restrictive, an experienced and fair judge has the greater impact on the process.

Too many federal judges come across as angry. The judiciary cannot demand or expect "civility" between attorneys when the judges far too often fail to set a good example. One need not be a jerk to be a great judge. Please share that with ALL of the judges!

More liberal discovery rules may make it more worthwhile for plaintiffs in employment cases to litigate in federal courts however recent precedent has made federal courts hostile to plaintiffs' employment claims. My clients avoid federal court as much as possible because of the federal judiciary's blatant hostility towards plaintiffs.

My practice is limited to employment discrimination law. A recent Harvard study showed that plaintiffs in job discrimination cases prevail only 18% of the time, compared with 51% of plaintiffs in other civil actions. This suggests that current judges are grossly unfair to job discrimination plaintiffs. This fact affected a few of the answers I gave in this survey.

The bias in Federal Courts for employment cases is the abuse of Summary Judgment by many Judges. Certain Judges are a nearly automatic win for employers, regardless of the merits.

Rules

A survey on the usage of Rule 56 Summary Judgment motions is also warranted.

I believe the rules for an offer of judgment should be revised so that there are consequences to the defendant for failing to accept a reasonable offer of judgment. As the rule is now written the offer of judgment is only a toll for the defense.

I think the automatic disclosures in Rule 26 are very helpful. I think they should be expanded.

Many of the cases my firm handles are simple Section 1983 claims that require minimal discovery and two to three depositions. On these cases justice would be advanced with a file to trial time line of six months or less. The rules are too cumbersome for the simple cases.

My client experienced an inordinate delay in receiving his settlement funds. There should be a 30 day requirement to tender the funds followed by sanctions if not provided within the time period.

My experience is that the rules associated with the conduct of trial are more onerous than discovery. Discovery is necessary to ferret out the truth, and hampering discovery by the responding party requires the flexibility to make further inquiry. Current rules unduly limit access to information due to time limitations imposed preventing "serial" discovery requests.

One very serious problem connected with the uniformity envisioned in rules 1 and 2 is the ad hoc deviation from critical rules is certain areas such as ERISA litigation without any coherent explanation why such cases should be treated differently.

Perhaps it is my age…67. But I don't think the rules need any change.

Revising the rules - as hinted at in the survey would disproportionately benefit large corporate defendants. I would be opposed to the suggested revisions.

Rule 11 should be thrown out because seldom if ever will a judge impose sanctions even when clearly warranted.

The rules relating to courtesy copies seems burdensome and unneeded.

The rules should allow depositions by videoconferencing as a matter of course. Right now if your opponent refuses to agree to depose by videoconferencing, a motion to authorize videoconferencing is required. Litigants refuse to agree in order to create barriers to taking depos. This should be changed to allow depos by videoconferencing just like the rules allow depos to be recorded by video merely upon notice.

The single worst discovery rule is the rule which prohibits any discovery prior to the Rule 26(f) conference. It is not unusual for key witnesses to move or disappear during the 3 or 4 month period that occurs after a case is filed but before the rule 26(f) conference is held. I like federal court better than state court, however, I have actually filed several cases in state court (rather than federal court) because I did not have the luxury of waiting for the rule 26(f) conference to occur before I conducted discovery. Cases are like crime scenes - - you need to immediately be allowed to depose witnesses and gather information. This information can be lost when you are required to wait. It is incomprehensible that this waiting period is required.

The system isn't broken for the great majority of cases, and the Federal Rules as applied are fair. I don't understand the motive for tinkering with them. In a small minority of cases, if discovery is too expensive in the opinion of the parties, they should pursue ADR, and not take away the justice that people can obtain with broad discovery and mandatory disclosures.

This survey is a blunt instrument, but I appreciate the opportunity to complete it. The bottom line is that the rules are only as good as the care, sophistication, and neutrality of the judges who enforce them, and the civility and sophistication of the attorneys who work with them.

Summary Judgment

The last section - I wish I could have commented after each selection - that would give you more insight why I feel the way I do. Overall, I prefer to be in federal court with the exception of the high % of summary judgments being granted.

11th Circuit will not allow employment discrimination cases, other than those with direct evidence, to survive summary judgment.

Costs of $1,000 should be required as a deposit to be paid to the respondent in the event of an unsuccessful MSJ to discourage groundless filings.

Expand time limit for opposing summary judgment motions. California state law now requires 75 days notice.

Federal courts over rely on summary judgment, causing the parties to emphasize gamesmanship in the discovery process. Discovery is not a preparation for trial but part of the summary judgment preparation process in too many cases.

I believe that summary judgment is used too often to reduce dockets rather than seek justice. If discovery rules were enforced more so, then summary judgment proceedings would at least appear fair. In the Southern District of Alabama, discovery disputes are not often resolved in a manner suggesting fairness. And then summary judgment proceedings are use to end litigation.

I think the Federal system would be better served with a greater focus on actual trial as opposed to pretrial motions. This is especially true where, in my opinion, the summary judgment proceedings are clearly abused. In virtually every one of my cases, the defense attorney files a Motion for Summary Judgment causing an unnecessary inflation of litigation expenses even where there are clear genuine issues of material fact. I also believe the Federal system would be greatly stream lined and improved if the Rules required the attorney and party filing a Motion for Summary Judgment to separately certify their affirmative belief in the merits of the Motion presented. Rule 11 does not do enough in that regard. As a consequence, the plaintiff bears the brunt of time and expense in opposing what are essentially non-meritorious motions burdening the entirety of the judiciary.

Limiting summary judgment would limit discovery abuse. Most defense discovery is aimed at summary judgment, not merits. Limit summary judgment and discovery will almost automatically become more reasonable and appropriate when aimed at trial or settlement.

Much more cases would be settled if summary judgment is limited and cases are scheduled for trial, after completing discovery.

Summary Judgment is abused and too readily--all too readily--granted. We should have system of Magistrate Judge based "Claims Sifting", whereby after fact discovery, the parties can present short "Ready for Trial Claims List" to the presiding Magistrate Judge. Parties would likely reach significant agreement in that 30 to 45 day period; any remaining claims would go to trial if parties agreed they were viable--and, only disputed claims would be the subject of a streamline summary judgment procedure. Thus, we would first have a sort of "Pre-Summary Judgment" before the District Judge was involved in laborious briefing.

Summary judgment is over-used in the federal court system and is often improvidently granted. This unnecessarily increases litigation costs as every federal case has a summary judgment motion filed, with no consequence to the defendant, even if there are clearly disputed issues of fact. This over-use of the Rule 56 motion by large defendants against individual plaintiffs must be constrained.

Summary judgment is too freely granted when important issues of fact should be decided by a jury

Summary judgment practice in federal court increases the cost of litigation and discourages settlements, particularly in employment cases. Rule 56 needs revisions and some retreat from the principles announced in *Celotex v. Catrett.*

The biggest problem with federal litigation today is the explosion in summary judgment since the three 1986 Supreme Court decisions. Despite statements to the contrary, Courts are resolving factual issues that are better left to a jury to decide.

The improper and liberal use of summary judgment allows parties to roll the dice. If more cases went to trial, more cases would probably settle.

The propensity of the courts to unfairly grant summary judgment in favor of defendants in employment discrimination cases should be reviewed and corrected.

The single most abused aspect of federal litigation is summary judgment, which should be severely limited.

The single most unfair aspect of federal litigation is summary judgment, because a defendant need allege next to nothing in the motion and the plaintiff is required to present evidence to support every element of plaintiff's claim, including defendant's state of mind where it is an element. Federal judges too often seem to use a combination of procedural devices and summary judgment to clear cases off the docket and avoid trial.

Rule 12 and *Twombly*

In the context of employment discrimination litigation, any steps to increase pleading requirements and decrease plaintiff's access to relevant discovery would preclude many plaintiffs and plaintiffs' advocates from pursuing meritorious claims.

I would strongly argue against changing Rule 8 or limiting parties' ability to conduct discovery. Doing away with notice pleading would only increase litigation costs, as defense attorneys would have additional ammunition to bring in 12(b) motions.

Depositions by Skype or similar web based video can save costs. Electronic discovery in NOT expensive, but easier. PDF makes document production effective. Confidentiality is generally a waste of time and should not be granted and is instead used as an excuse not to produce. 12b6 motions are abused because the Court never decides them for MONTHS and sometimes YEARS killing re-pleading and statute of limitations. EARLY trial dates must be adhered to and will allow resolution of disputes whether through trial or settlement.

I do not believe that simple notice pleading should be abandoned to simply the process in federal court, because that would result in making the courts less accessible to the public. Lawyers tend to abuse the discovery process, particularly in defense firms, so they can up their hourly fee collection.

In this case, one of the sets of lawyers were very professional, whereas the other attorney was difficult to the point of rudeness. Unfortunately or fortunately, his client won at Rule 12(c) motion so that I did not have to deal with him much. I would like to see Rule 56 amended to require statements of uncontested material fact that are backed up with specific references to documents and testimony as well as responses. See Rule 9.10 of the Louisiana Rules for District Courts.

The case which brought me to be asked to participate in this survey was a dispute between attorneys regarding a large fee in a personal injury action. The defendant attorney, from another jurisdiction moved to dismiss for lack of personal jurisdiction. His motion was denied. Once that occurred, both parties quickly reached a settlement as both were very familiar with the costs of litigation and discovery in particular. I don't think anything different would have occurred if the case had been brought in state court. To me discovery itself is not that costly, it is attempts by opposing parties to delay and avoid it that make it so expensive. If sanctions with real teeth were placed in the rules to prevent delay and avoidance I think the cost of discovery would moderate. Fact pleading may help, but making plaintiffs plead facts in their complaints is no substitute for detailed discovery.

There are unfair burdens on plaintiffs in the federal court system. I do not think the suggestions of requiring more demanding pleading and setting tougher discovery requirements will be helpful to litigants. In my experience, under the existing system I think the judges and the magistrates do a good job in managing discovery and deadlines in my cases. A lot depends on the attorneys involved. I think that bad behavior discovery behavior should be dealt with quickly, which would help to promote professionalism and greater cooperation.

In all but the most complex cases, the abolition of notice pleading and the full discovery process will only assist the defendants. As to notice pleading, the facts relating to most cases are possessed by the defending parties.

As a sole practitioner doing small business litigation and discrimination cases in Chicago Fed Ct the system is sensible and should not be altered to require fact pleading and cost shifting to small businesses or individual plaintiffs. To coin a phrase, it ain't broke, so don't "fix" it.

But for the parties being allowed to give non-specific answers in discovery pleadings, I see no major problems with he Federal Rules of Civil Procedures.

Enforcing a heightened pleading standard in civil rights cases would prejudice plaintiffs and give an unfair advantage to defendants. In such cases, defendants almost uniformly have a disproportionally greater amount of evidence including the identity of individuals, documentary evidence such as policies and procedures, and physical evidence like photographs and video footage. Forcing plaintiffs to meet a heightened pleading standard would restrict plaintiffs' access to the courts and would render many claims impossible where the plaintiff may not even know the identity of the government or company officials involved. In such circumstances, plaintiffs can only guess at many of the facts which will ultimately come to light during discovery. I would strongly oppose a heightened pleading standard in civil rights cases.

I am a big fan of federal court. I always have been. I think state courts should adopt the federal rules and proceed more like the federal system. Notice pleading is fine. By and large I think federal court yields the most fair outcomes. They are more responsive and take the system more seriously than do state courts (hence the survey).

I do not believe that anyone, attorney or judge, understands the most recent Supreme Court case concerning the requirements of pleading. If anything needs to be clarified, it is this.

I represent plaintiffs in Section 1983 actions alleging police misconduct. I am a sole practitioner. We already have a heightened pleading standard in the 11th Circuit. We rarely have discovery disputes. The rules are fine. Any additional burdens will affect sole practitioners like myself more than the large firms that defend my lawsuits. I have absolutely no staff. I feel that what I do is important. It is also difficult. Please don't make it any more difficult, so that I can continue to ably assist my clients.

I think generally that the rules of discovery are good, and need not be changed. The responding parties need to respond, to avoid excessive litigation costs. The pleading rules and Summary Judgment rules are very good as they are, and I support NOT changing them.

It is my experience that notice pleadings and discovery are necessary because many tort and contract cases involve issues in which one party (usually the defendant) has more knowledge about the subject so the other party has to find the full facts through discovery which leads to an amended complaint to clarify the issues and claims.

Survey questions combine pleading & discovery issues as if they are not separate. Expert discovery in federal courts is a big expense and discouragement. Pleading issues are not an issue at all. The more pleading requirements, the more wasted time and money on whether pleading is adequate BEFORE parties even know the facts of the case. Streamline production of records, then depositions can occur and lawyers will know their case. Then, they can re-plead, if necessary. Notice pleading is good for just, speedy and inexpensive determination of the action. The key is getting the facts out on the table early and efficiently.

The scope of discovery should not be curtailed, it should be expanded. Mandating more of a heightened pleading standard may close the courthouse doors to deserving litigants.

I believe that cases would settle faster and more fairly -- or get tried more efficiently -- if the federal courts made two changes: First, require a slightly higher pleading standard than notice pleading -- but not so high that it leads to a motion ever.

The goal should be to resolve cases on the merits and not get tied up on pleading and discovery issues.

The present system evens the field for non corporate plaintiffs. The effort to please more specifically rather than notice pleading only benefits the defendants -- usually corporate or government. The federal forum has always been the forum that promotes discovery of the truth and full disclosure, rather than "tricks of the trade. Its success is the reason state courts are adopting notice rather than specific fact pleadings.

Twombly has already heightened the pleading requirements, rendering another change right now unnecessary. Should the Committee consider changes to the pleading requirements, however, it would probably make sense to allow a little more time to see if *Twombly* has a significant impact first.

The discovery rules are adequate. Notice pleading and fraud pleading are appropriate. Conley v. Gibson and now Bell are sufficient as to Rule 8. Judges fail to properly enforce the existing rules. I currently have a case in Federal Court with 250 docket entries. Four Federal Court Judges, KS and now NY, have denied 26(a) disclosures after two years of litigation. 26a disclosures and proper discovery would settle the case. The problem is that Judges allow parties to hide behind various arguments that have little or nothing to do with a case, when the true merits can be determined by following the existing rules. Proper 26a disclosures would have settled the case I referenced in June of 2007. Staying discovery over a 25 page loan file has allowed the alleged fraud to continue with the multiple pleadings.

There were a number of questions about heightened pleading requirements for complaints--but in my view, defendants routinely commit more egregious violations of the pleading rules in their answers. I routinely see a laundry list of affirmative defenses that have nothing whatsoever to do with the case, along with denials like "the allegations of paragraph _ refer to a document that speaks for itself, and no answer is necessary." Or, even better, "the allegations of paragraph _ constitute a legal conclusion to which no response is necessary." I have started filing motions to strike in many cases, but this should not be necessary. I am fortunate to practice in the EDVA, where gamesmanship and obstructive discovery tactics are generally not tolerated. This is largely the result of tight discovery deadlines, which are good for everyone concerned.

I believe that routine stays of discovery while Rule 12(b)(6) motions are pending result in substantial delays, and often result in substantial miscarriages of justice. The misapplication of the *Twombly* case by certain federal courts to dismiss cases that, until recent years, were routinely adjudged meritorious, and that require discovery in order to prove the claims asserted, appears contrary to the terms of both Rule 1 and 8, as well as to be working a fundamental change in our civil justice system that favors defendants, regardless of the actual merits of the case.

Increasingly, and then a marked increase post *Twombly*, it seems impossible to put enough into many complaints to withstand Rule 12 motions. Too many cases are dismissed on Rule 12 motion even before discovery is obtainable.

My case may not be appropriate for this survey. The case was a Rule 20 multi-plaintiff case filed after a decertification of another FLSA collective action. The District Court initially adopted a Magistrate Judge's recommendation to deny a Rule 12(b)(6) dismissal motion. The case was stayed for approximately two years while the Court of Appeals adjudicated a procedural issue germane to the case, and upon the lifting of the stay the parties engaged in further briefing on the central procedural issue and participated in a hearing convened by a Magistrate Judge. The case was dismissed when the Court adopted the Magistrate Judge's recommendation to dismiss the case following the hearing. Therefore, the parties did not even convene a scheduling conference or conduct any discovery in the case.

My cases are filed against the U.S. government so many of the questions did not apply. Having said that, I find notice pleading to be very effective for me to make my claim and define the issues in the cases I file.

The case upon which you have asked me to comment is not a helpful one. It was an entirely frivolous action brought by pro se plaintiffs. I was immediately given permission to make a Rule 12(b)(6) motion within days of service of the Complaint and the Complaint was promptly dismissed thereafter. I would be happy to discuss another case where I can be of more help.

Civil Rights/Employment Law

I practice in the area of civil rights and employment where the actions challenged occur behind closed doors and my client is seldom privy to essential information.

In individual employment cases, most of the information is in the hands of defendants/employers who have many more resources than the individual plaintiffs.

My general experience is that the courts have become increasingly hostile to Plaintiffs and civil rights cases. I attribute this to a number of factors, not the least important of which is that many judges come to the bench from a prosecutorial or civil

This was a difficult survey to complete given that my clients are primarily individual employees that sue for discrimination or other civil rights violations.

I represent plaintiffs, who are generally low income, in civil rights litigation. The major stumbling block to resolution of my cases is the failure of defendants to provide much that is useful in their Answers and Initial Disclosures. Not until we have gone through several rounds of discovery, motions to compel production and depositions do they get serious about settlement.

I was appointed as the attorney for a pro se litigant in an employment discrimination case - attorneys should not be appointed to represent pro se litigants in employment matters, they have unreasonable expectations. I do not think that employment cases are the type of cases that were anticipated when the rules for appointing attorneys were created.

In employment litigation the plaintiff is always disadvantaged in discovery. The defense has all the information and control of most of the witnesses. Early, mandatory, comprehensive disclosure would serve to begin to even the playing field.

In practice, many judges have become fact finders at the summary judgment stage of a case, especially in employment discrimination cases. Discrimination cases involve questions of intent and motive that should be decided by the jury.

Limiting discovery in employment discrimination cases makes it even more difficult for plaintiffs to prove their cases, since they have to prove what a decision maker was thinking when he made the challenged decision. The proof is almost always exclusively in the possession of the defendant. (This is also a problem in arbitration.)

Many of the questions were not relevant to my practice because I engage in civil rights litigation under Titles II and III of the ADA, which have fee and cost shifting provisions. My clients never pay for costs or fees. My recovery of my fees and costs comes from the defendants.

On civil rights cases I haven't had discovery problems with the government defendants. They generally cooperate and produced fully, if not always promptly. The costs of litigation on constitutional rights litigation is the almost mandatory summary judgment motion. Dispositive motions are virtually required by all pretrial orders in these cases. Defendants will not settle unless they lose and judges will not encourage settlement before these motions are at least filed.

Our practice is limited to representing Plaintiffs in employment matters. We have to be very efficient in the use of financial resources. The costs associated with the use of consultants and/or experts to retrieve electronically stored information are relatively high.

Miscellaneous

For years I have had one or more civil cases being litigated in federal court, so I have some actual experience with these issues. I want to briefly share a couple of observations.

Over the years, I have noticed the issuance of orders sometimes that are subtle unlabelled essentially final orders undermining and dismantling my client's case if not immediately appealed as a protective measure.

The case of interest was dismissed for lack of personal jurisdiction in the ED of Mich.

The most bothersome issue for me in this litigation was the prospect of the actual physical getting all the boxes of materials past security and into the court after 8:00 a.m., but before the 9:00 a.m. docket call.

Discovery costs were not a factor in the outcome of my recent case. Most of the Plaintiff's discovery material was exchanged prior to formal requests. Defendant's discovery material was provided in response to Plaintiff's initial discovery material.

I have been involved for 25/28 years in the federal courts and would be glad to speak with a surveyor or some one from the court system to give me overall views.

I have responded to another survey regarding a case involving the federal government. However, in this case, the AUSA was more cooperative and discovery was not obstructed. However, the case is on appeal to the Ninth Circuit.

I practice federal tax law. My clients are taxpayers who litigate their federal tax liability in US district courts, the US Court of Federal Claims, or the US Tax Court. These facts shape my answers to the general questions above.

I presume "federal court" included bankruptcy court.

I was the local counsel for the [deleted]. I was released after the case was transferred to [deleted].

If you're seeking feedback on specific proposals, I would be happy to respond after learning more. Some questions seemed to reference ideas where the details make all the difference.

In the case I had it involved housing discrimination and settlement discussions were started immediately after the complaint was served. Voluntary discovery of investigation reports of the plaintiff helped to further the settlement thus no further discovery or supervision of the court was required.

Many of my initial answers were specific to this ERISA case in which discovery is limited to the administrative record.

My most recent case in federal court (SD Ill) was aided immensely by the participation of the court (via its magistrate judge) in mediation

Sorry for the delay!

The case in question was one where damages were the primary question. An early mediation greatly helped to resolve it.

The options for the nature of the fee arrangement did not allow for the arrangement in the referenced case, i.e., contingent based upon hourly rates and outcome, not based on percentage.

The subject case was referred to mandatory arbitration. As plaintiff's counsel, this is an excellent method of resolving a case as it allows parties to try a case in a quick and summary format without expending significant costs. Further, the quick time line for arbitration reduces discovery costs by no prolonging discovery. The parties are either content with the result at arbitration, or the dissatisfied party may appeal but know exactly where they stand in relation to an eventual result by trial. This additionally causes cases to settle, as in this instance. I would recommend that tort cases be referred to mandatory arbitration with no jurisdiction limit on damages.

There should be a 1 day mini trial in an attempt to reach a settlement before the trial date. Similar to NH.

This case was small dealing with an Insurance policy procured through the Pl.'s job; Employer failed to provide info. to H re: need for insurability Cert. from W's dr.--Workplace took premiums from H's ck. for 2.5 years; W dies & carrier wouldn't pay death benefit. Case settled for $75,000.00 of $84,000.00 policy.

We are a plaintiffs' injury firm. Our Federal Court in Chicago is a great forum to move a case along quickly, the discovery deadlines are enforced as are all the rules, when compared to our state system. The jury pool is not great though.

Unfortunately, my practice has been almost exclusively limited to state court so my input may not have been very beneficial.

Survey Comments

One point I would like to make, is that a number of the questions lumped heightened pleading requirements (doing away with mere notice pleading) with restrictions on discovery to streamline cases.

The survey did not address the 2 largest costs to plaintiffs 1) delay between case filing and resolution and 2) requirement of physical presence of the plaintiff in the district for deposition.

There is a fundamental problem that it will be hard to address in such a survey as this. Business and life in general get more complex with passing time.

This survey omits an important question regarding a major void in the Federal Rules of Civil Procedure. A specific Rule is needed to implement, fairly and uniformly throughout the Federal court system, 42 U.S.C. 2000e.

A couple of thoughts: 1) In the case I was contacted about, my client was class of plaintiffs. The options for the question about how would I best describe my client didn't allow for that. Representing a class is very different from representing an individual.2) I'm not sure what you meant when you asked what percentage of the "costs" should be discovery costs. Did you mean to include "fees" in the "costs"? I think you might get different answers from different lawyers, depending on their fee arrangements with their clients.

No reflection on the survey, but I found many of these questions extremely difficult to answer.

Some questions were so generalized that a competent and responsive answer was not possible. On occasion the choices of agree-disagree in degrees seemed restrictive.

Survey is a bit long.

Thank you for allowing me to participate.

Thank you for allowing participation

Thank you for including me in the survey. The case you have asked about settled at a court-sponsored settlement conference. Parties had exchanged paper discovery responses, but depositions had not been taken.

Thank you for taking the time to inquire about these important issues.

The survey did not have enough questions about how defense counsel drives up costs and causes delays.

The survey needs to let the "taker" know how far along they are in the survey (i.e. 40% complete).

The survey seemed to focus on electronic discovery issues, which are rarely if ever experienced in my practice area - Section 1983 litigation.

The survey seems to be at least, in part, written to assist the big corporations try to limit their exposure in discovery and e-discovery. I believe the rules in Federal Court are already much more strict than in State Court and do not need to be amended. The system works well and should not be changed. If anything, Federal Courts could relax their standards a little. Less discovery would allow more defendants to avoid liability.

This survey was too long and I think you need to better explain who you are and why you are doing this survey.

This was too long.

Your survey failed to address any ADR tools such as mediation, early neutral evaluation, etc.

I strongly disagree with the purpose of this project. The idea of requiring Plaintiffs to more specifically articulate claims at the inception of litigation, will only permit defendants to further manipulate discovery.

Generally, I found this survey to be biased-in a clear way- to encourage responses that would support greater limits and more cost sharing of discovery cost, which in turn disproportionately would adversely impact plaintiffs.

Good and thoughtful survey-would be interested in the results.

I hope the participants can be sent the results of the survey. Thanks.

I would have liked to qualify many of my answers.

In review I take issue with the survey, because it seems to present a skewing towards accepting form over function. Thank you.

Respondents Representing Plaintiffs and Defendants About Equally

Discovery Abuse/Attorney Conduct

Attorney antics (improper and exasperating) in discovery; and the general hesitation on the part of the court to involve itself in discovery disputes, and aggressively stop obstructionist behavior, has caused unreasonable cost and delay in many of my cases.

One of the major problems that impedes justice and causes unnecessary delay and expense is the unwillingness of judges to do the detail work to enforce discovery rules and curb abuses by the small minority of lawyers who abuse the rules.

Dilatory and careful parsing of discovery answers are used to obfuscate the truth more often than reach it. There should be prompt and severe sanctions against parties/attorneys who use discovery to bludgeon the other side and who refuse to truthfully and fully disclose relevant information.

Generally, attorneys work well with each other on discovery and other aspects of the case. Once deadlines are set, courts need not get involved unless the parties cannot reach an agreement or it would disturb the trial schedule. I rarely need to seek court assistance in federal court for discovery disputes.

I prefer litigating in federal court however get discouraged by the gamesmanship employed by litigants/attorneys in discovery and motion practice. I would love to see Rule 26 sanctions increased for bad faith actions of attorneys and litigants. Thank you for letting me participate in this survey.

I try cases on both sides, but by far the increased costs are caused by the defense side when they are charging by the hour. Thus the abuse is inherent to the fee/compensation structure in the system. When I started practicing law, with little exception, there was no discovery in state court; trials came quickly, moved quickly and good, fair results were obtained at a reasonable cost to the client. Discovery as it is applied in modern practice is nothing but a way to bill clients, subsidize otherwise out-of-work attorneys and thus increase costs. Limit discovery, limit the use and number of experts and allow people to testify about that which they know and the cost will go down, justice will be served. Please remove the gamesmanship and excessive cost from litigation.

If your concerns are truly to ensure a simple and legitimate process, the area of discovery abuse on defendants, especially corporate entities, and their large firm counsel should be explored. Despite the well versed fallacies of bogus lawsuits creating waste in the system, the most expensive, time consuming, and exasperating aspects of discovery are the abuses perpetrated by well-moneyed and large defendants and large firms. Whether it be specious claims of privilege over discovery requested of them, long and/or unnecessary depositions used to churn billable hours and as a harassment tactic along with numerous and extensive discovery requests, with extended sub parts to get around limitations in the Rules, large defendants and their counsel tend in a large part to unnecessarily increase the time and money needed to pursue a legitimate claim.

In my experience most civil litigation involves larger law firms that commit vast resources to the discovery process. Each person or party that has a remote connection to the dispute must be deposed. Rarely if ever do these tangents produce anything meaningful and drive up the litigation costs considerably. There is also a perception that federal court cases take on greater importance than state court cases. This is also used as a justification for the commitment of resources.

My 42+ years of experience has persuaded me that discovery in the Federal Courts is abused often by firms whose firm members are compelled to produce billable hours. I have considerable experience in labor relations matters which are often arbitrated by professionals or heard in federal courts. Most cases can be prepared by attorneys without intrusive and extensive discovery designed to enhance the bottom line. Early bench involvement helps considerably. I have represented both management and labor and feel I have the experience to make this point.

My sense of the survey is that you are exploring the relationship of discovery burden and fairness. One of the problems is that the burden of discovery varies most depending upon the behavior of the attorneys and the willingness of the Courts to intervene. I think the courts would find that if they required any in-court discovery management conference with the court early on that is a meaningful planning session, many motions would be avoided. Where motions occur, the court should move away from the practice of long briefs on issues and instead resolve the issues on oral argument promptly. Too much time and money is wasted in briefing discovery issues that are pretty plain from a simple discussion. Also, parties are more willing to file motions if they think the court will be slow in responding.

The cooperative conduct of counsel is the number one driving factor in the cost of litigation. If all sides are reasonable in their requests and are willing to work through issues in a cooperative fashion the federal court system works well. However, discovery fights for fighting alone brings down the whole litigation process. Professional cooperative counsel reduce the cost and litigation risk for our clients.

The great majority of discovery abuses and problems arise from the conduct of the attorneys and are not caused by the Rules. The Rules are generally fair, I rarely have discovery fights with reasonable opposing counsel.

The motion practice in the federal court clearly favors big corporations and big law firms. It unfairly makes Judges the Judge and Jury. It is said that big law firms will bury you in discovery, and I believe that the volumes of discovery have unfairly led to dismissals on summary judgment motions in favor of big law firms for their big corporations.

The particular case that was the subject of this survey settled after the defendant, whom I represented, filed an answer but before the Plaintiff replied. In my experience, a party can use discovery and motions to delay resolution and increase cost of the litigation to force a settlement. In my experience, judges tend to be lenient when parties abuse discovery or motion practice.

There are two problems with discovery: (1) requesting parties want too much; and (2) responding parties often do not disclose relevant and important information. The only remedy that I can see is to more narrowly tailor the scope of discovery to relate more closely to the causes of action pleaded and to impose sanctions -- costs, exclusion of evidence, etc. -- on parties that unnecessarily delay or fail to disclose relevant discovery items. Thanks for letting me participate in this survey and I would be happy to work with any group toward improving the rules of civil procedure.

How a case goes through the system is more dependent on the attorneys involved and the judge than the actual "rules".

Discovery Costs

Litigation costs would be greatly decreased if attorneys were courteous and cooperated with each other, while still protecting their clients and looked to reach a fair resolution.

Costs in federal court increase as a result of the multiple layers of disclosure and reporting now in vogue. Further, the discovery period is too short to work within the framework of the rules and the courts' ability to address discovery issues in a timely way.

Courts should be encouraged to address cost shifting at the end of a case based on ultimate outcome and conduct of the parties in discovery.

Federal cases in my area are more efficient and less costly than state cases under the current rules. Federal Judges will rule on discovery issues quickly and are not shy in granting summary judgment when appropriate. This is not the case in state court. Mandatory mediation and other rules which force settlements are going so far as to leave young lawyers without trial experience and create compromises when there should not be any.

Getting a handle on reducing the costs and burdens on e-discovery is welcome!

I would recommend more early case intervention - mediation, for example. For lower-valued cases, arbitration should be required, to keep costs down.

My answers to this survey were influenced by the fact that the named case was commenced in 2003, before Electronic discovery came into effect and also strongly influenced by the fact that during the nearly six years that the action was pending, we never once had the opportunity to either see or hear our judge (although we did have a magistrate judge rule on discovery twice and a special master recommend summary judgment). Had there been case management, the action would have been resolved much earlier and at a much lower cost.

The up-front paper and conferral burden in federal court before disclosure (to prepare for Status Conferences) is too high and presumes both sides know the other's case-which is not true. Requiring settlement conferences before disclosures/discovery is an expensive waste of time.

This survey is too long. The system works as it is. Changing it would increase costs.

While I don't believe that lawyers generally abuse the discovery process, there is still too much discovery. Lawyers will take whatever discovery is allowed simply to avoid being questioned if there is an adverse result. Allow less discovery and require more disclosure earlier. If you really want to reduce costs, you need to also look at motion practice. Too many judges sit on motions too long. Issues that should be eliminated or narrowed continue in cases (causing more discovery and more costs) because motions rot in chambers. May also want to look at limiting motions to dismiss/motions for summary judgment.

Discovery Process

I think the level of detail in the current pretrial disclosure and conference rules force judges to apply management techniques that may be necessary for some big, complex cases, but just impose unnecessary busy-work in smaller or simpler cases.

Make more discovery mandatory; court-propounded Interrogatories and RPD. Eliminate general objections to discovery and mandate definitions of words such as 'document'; 'person'; 'your'; etc.

The single best reform idea I have heard is requiring both parties up front to AGGRESSIVELY search for and PRODUCE any and all documents potentially relevant to any claim or defense in a case within the first 30-60 days of service, unless otherwise agreed

A revision of the discovery rules will benefit the legal procedure. While there is a balancing act, often courts are unwilling to sanction attorneys or parties but greater enforcement would make the judicial much more efficient.

Case management by Magistrates adds too much time to ordinary discovery which could be handled by a Standard Case Management process by Rule with exceptions carved out by motion when required.

Discovery is the Achilles heel of any civil action in any court.

Early court involvement in framing the issues and the discovery process, tailored to the type of case and likely requirements, would greatly save the parties and the court time and resources. Judicial oversight at the early stages of the case with follow-up case management conferences would yield much greater efficiencies. Changing the rules of civil procedure will likely yield much less efficient case resolution than judicial involvement and oversight at the early stages of the case.

Early settlement opportunities (e.g. ENE) followed up with limited discovery to facilitate another ENE makes the most sense.

Faster and firmer trial dates, faster judicial response to motions, required use of telephone conferences for discovery disputes would all help greatly.

Federal courts are viewed as being highly disdainful of "small" cases and therefore against the filers of diversity cases and "small" federal issues such as Fair Debt Collection Act cases, and this is very troubling and unjust. Most of my clients are "small" parties and they always struggle for fairness in the federal system, where big firms and big clients roam.

I believe that discovery should be allowed to commence before the Rule 17 Conference. The conferences are merely setting a schedule to conclude discovery and there is a lot of dead time waiting for the conference.

I have found that settlement conferences performed by magistrate judges early in the life of cases are very effective. However, experience has shown that parties are reluctant to share information prior to the settlement conferences, which hinders the ability to settle. I would contemplate a system under which the settlement conference judge would determine at a pre-trial conference with the attorneys what information is necessary to facilitate their respective clients' position on settlement and, if appropriate, to enter an initial disclosure order specific to the case requiring each party to divulge particular information in order to facilitate settlement conferences.

I would favor a tiered system that allowed for more discovery for larger cases and a methodology to make such an evaluation and to revise it during the litigation process. I would also favor mediation or other methods to narrow discovery and trial costs early in the process rather than just as a tool to settle cases.

If it is the recommendation to employ increased mandatory disclosures, perhaps practitioners should be polled on what kind and categories such disclosures might be.

Immediately after the Rule 26 disclosures, (or some time after) each party should propose key facts that will be established by the evidence, opponent must respond accurately to each separate fact.

In my view, the Court should require expansive disclosures with firm and fair motion and trial dates to allow the parties to conduct discovery. The biggest problem in Federal Court is that the parties often do not have sufficient time to complete fact discovery given the Court's case management orders.

In order to manage litigation, a judge should set reasonable deadlines for the completion of discovery, motions and expert opinions. No extensions, unless just cause can be demonstrated and a trial date kept in place.

In our district several judges have a chambers rule that parties must file for a "pre-filing conference" prior to filing a dispositive motion. I think this is rather pointless because it adds additional work and the Judges never seem to be able to get parties to abandon weak claims or defenses. I understand in theory what the Judges are trying to do, but in practice it just results in more work without any benefit to the litigants.

In the named case, the parties agreed to an early pre-discovery mediation and a voluntary exchange of documents. The case settled for less than the cost of defending through trial. In most civil cases, I think that mandatory pre-discovery mediation would be productive, as the costs of litigation are still in front of both parties.

Mediation should be required at an early stage in every case.

More streamlined discovery and mandatory disclosures up front would encourage settlement and lessen costs.

Much of the required discovery in Federal Court is duplicative and seems to serve no purpose, such as initial disclosures and pre-trial disclosures. These seem to be "busy work" rather than productive work. Also, the high cost of depositions makes it hard for individual parties to be on equal footing with corporate defendants. For example, in this case I was asked about, my client could not afford to take the depositions of the defendant's proposed experts.

Requiring parties to meet and confer and prepare "joint" discovery motions as is done in the Central District of California is a waste of time and leads to additional attorney shenanigans not less. Similarly requiring court order to extend discovery deadlines when parties agreed to same leads to traps for the unwary and gives an advantage to the unscrupulous. Parties who jerk around other parties are rarely taken to task, encouraging jerking around.

The parties should have to appoint a discovery administrator who should be required to attend a 1 hour class on discovery obligations.

The quality of the discovery process is dependent on the quality of the judge supervising it.

The scope of discovery allowed differs too much from Judge/Magistrate to Judge/Magistrate; Courts need to consider the law governing discovery in foreign jurisdictions when a party is a foreign national.

There should be harsher punishments for disregard of discovery obligations by municipalities.

Electronic discovery

In large, complex commercial litigation, the key documents are often communications which are only stored electronically; I can think of many cases that would have been lost for a plaintiff if electronic discovery was not available.

The new revisions to the discovery rules regarding electronic discovery are being actively used by most defendants to avoid producing discovery and/or falsely claiming cost burden.

Courts should regularly use rule 26b2C(iii) to limit electronic discovery.

Electronic discovery is the biggest single long-term issue in civil litigation. Its demands will make litigation impossible for all but the very richest. It needs a great deal of attention and a great deal of thought and a great deal of oversight.

I consider myself fairly knowledgeable regarding e-discovery in complex cases (I practice 100% patent litigation). Nonetheless, I found some of the survey questions regarding ESI informative enough to print so as to insure I am asking these questions of my client and opposing counsel. I think it would benefit the courts to have a more concrete set of rules regarding e-discovery. For example, in my opinion, it would be helpful if there were consistent e-discovery local rules that outlined the issues and topics that need to be discussed. Even courts with more progressive rules (e.g., USDC KS) were not as extensive as the survey questions.

I hope this was helpful. Our case started in 2003 and didn't settle until 2008. Over that time, the parties had to adapt to new rules and information about electronically stored information and this led to a number of disagreements. In general, however, the attorneys in most cases did resolve their differences based on cooperative discussions and reasonable compromises.

In general I disagree with the proposition of limiting discovery. It gives parties an incentive to hide information. But I do think that electronic discovery should be limited or at least managed by a magistrate judge.

Our case involved an immediate ex parte request for expedited electronic discovery, which was granted. Getting and enforcing that order proved expensive.

The area of greatest cost/abuse in the federal discovery procedure is electronic discovery, its costs and burden. This should be addressed. Also the delay in discovery required by rule 26(d) (until after the rule 26(f) conference) often causes unnecessary delay and should be eliminated so that discovery can begin early.

The subject case was filed prior to the e-discovery rules. I needed to take CLE courses and computer courses to learn basic e-discovery and, unfortunately, it seems to have developed a cottage industry of former attorney "e-vendors." These "e-vendors" are quite expensive. I am concerned that these costs are basically "blackmail" for settlements.

Federal Court Practice

(1) In Florida, motion practice in federal courts increases the cost of federal actions over similar state court actions. If motion practice could be reduced or made more streamlined, costs would come down.(2) When mandatory disclosures were introduced, it forced parties to cooperate and communicate more and thus move the case along, helping to increase the likelihood of an amicable settlement.(3) In my opinion, any improvements should be in area of streamlining motion practice, encouraging more mandatory exchange of information between the parties and encouraging more cooperation between the parties.

At this point in my career, I am disposed to regard the Federal courts as instruments of injustice, and the ever-proliferating rules as one means (though far from the most important means) by which that injustice is made more and more manifest.

Generally speaking I avoid federal court. I do not think you are given as fair a forum as in state court. We need more judges and we need to not place so much a burden on attorney with scheduling orders and requirement that do not affect the outcome.

I am generally impressed with the federal courts, the federal rules of civil procedure, and the federal bench. I think the early neutral evaluation conference is priceless. I also like the electronic filing system.

I have found Federal Court, with its case management system, to be much more efficient than State Courts. This efficiency spans from discovery through trial and post-trial motions.

I much prefer the predictability of federal court but believe all *voir dire* should be conducted by the attorneys except to the extent they ask the Court to conduct portions.

I practice in AZ, ND and MN, all state and federal courts. AZ state courts have implemented mandatory disclosures requirements which are greater than those under the federal rules. The AZ state court Rules are a disaster in comparisons to the federal rules. A whole new area of litigation/contest has been created which has made cases in AZ state courts far more expensive, more contentious, and protracted. Do not consider the AZ "solution"!

I prefer practicing in federal court because the outcome is more predictable than in state court. In general, the rules in federal court are expected to be followed and are enforced by the court when they are not.

In the Eastern District of Texas, we generally have mandatory, broad disclosure requirements where the attorneys are required to produce all relevant documents without the need for requests for production. Because of this simplified discovery procedure, my firm generally files plaintiff's cases in federal court whenever possible.

It is more expensive to practice in Federal court. Rule 26FRCP makes discovery more expensive. That being said, the quality of the District Court Judges is superior to state Judges.

Lower case loads to federal judges and mandatory in-person conferences requiring judicial participation would enhance the result and shorten the time from complaint to resolution. Over burdened judges push away necessary case management tasks that only exacerbate the litigation and prolong the case - in the long run consuming judicial resources.

The biggest injustice is the DELAYS in federal court. This was not addressed in your survey. The case at issue settled because it would have taken almost three (3) years to get to trial, and my client could not wait.

The court in the Southern District of Florida where I practice is very diligent in quickly resolving and avoiding discovery disputes. Overall, the efficiency of the process depends on the caliber of lawyers. I would urge mandatory seminars on conducting discovery and on the local practice, as well as district judges routinely referring discovery disputes to the magistrate judge to resolve.

The efficiency and procedures of the federal court in which I practice are such that discovery abuse is practically impossible to get away with so there is little or none; the discovery summary judgment procedures are such that the issues are well framed for the court's decision by the conclusion of summary judgment (even if trial is required); the speed of the local court is such that costs are minimized compared with similar suits in the state courts; the local court's use of magistrate judgment in the settlement process is efficient and advantageous to early settlements.

The Federal Court system works well as is, but like all human activities timely review of and revisions to the system are appropriate.

The rules enable one party to use discovery to make the price of justice prohibitively expensive for an opposing party. Faced with the astronomical costs of discovery, litigants are forced to settle -- not based upon the relative merits of their claims or defenses -- but simply to avoid the cost of having to prove or disprove those claims or defenses. Such a settlement is not consistent with the ends of justice. Such a settlement, rather, is an injustice. Rules and procedures should require early mandatory full disclosures and key fact witness depositions so that cases can be resolved promptly, either on summary judgment or trial. Courts should have no position, interest in, or input on the question of whether one or both parties should settle a case.

The USDC ED Michigan does a good job of early-on involvement in discovery issues. These efforts are often undermined by boilerplate objections that typically then require a motion to compel for all issues including electronic discovery issues. Much of the cost and delay comes from those objections, the motions that follow, the referral to the magistrate the briefing process then a hearing. Might take 1 to 2 months that have now been cut out of the substantive discovery time.

This case settled pretty early on due to the active involvement of Magistrate Judge Anderson of the E.D.Va. Our client felt that it got a "hearing" due to his personal involvement. The E.D.Va. and its speedy docket should be a model for other courts.

When attorneys cooperate as stressed by the Courts in a reasonable manner, tremendous expenses and time are saved. The fact that most Federal Civil cases move as quickly as they do actually saves clients money on litigation in the long run.

Greater use of appearances by phone would be beneficial. Increase to 30 days the time to respond to a complaint or counterclaim.

Federal court judges are more patient than Arizona Superior court judges in resolving discovery disputes. Federal court judges seem to have more power to comment on the evidence to the jury. Federal Court judges are required to make findings of fact in every case and therefore do a better job. In the smaller Arizona counties the judges are still elected and these judges tend to rule in the manner that will get them the most votes.

Judicial Management

Federal Judges used to be the shining beacon of protecting the rights of little people. That has too long been lost to an urgency to clear the docket and utilize judicial discretion to tilt the balance of justice in favor of big government and big business. SMJ are handed out far too frequently. Even when a judge denies SMJ, the judge takes so many swipes in granting partial SMJ's that it becomes almost impossible to have a fair day in court on the issues that brought the client there in the first place.

For my clients, generally entrepreneurs and small businesses, the problematic costs of federal court discovery arise not from the Rules but from the inconsistency with which the Rules are applied. My experience has been the more involvement and consistency the Judge has during discovery, the lower the costs and more likely the case is to settle ahead of trial.

I appreciate the opportunity to answer your survey. Unfortunately, the federal courts favor the wealthy and the more influential firms that place partners on the bench and often receive more "justice" than the less influential firms.

I do not practice in any courts that have more restrictive discovery than the Texas federal courts. The unfairness I perceive in federal court is the inability to get an oral argument on any motion, the burden of the pre-trial order (which typically requires the briefing of issues that the judge summarily dismisses) and the inability to get a prompt ruling on a discovery dispute, which rewards delay and obstruction by the responder.

In my experience as an employment law litigator it is the judge or magistrate that makes the difference as to whether the federal rules of procedure work or not, and this will not be remediable by rule changes.

In the named case, we had a very "hands on" judge, who worked with the parties, required early submission of positions to him (confidentially), met with both sides together to facilitate an understanding of issues and costs, which I believe enhanced settlement discussions.

Judges and Magistrates should disclose any relationship to the parties (past or current), including any close family members that may have been employees or are employed by the parties. We need more phone conferences!!!!

Judges should impose monetary sanctions on lawyers who routinely abuse discovery. In extreme cases, the sanction of removing the lawyer from the case should be utilized.

So much of the experience of a case is influenced by the judge, not the rules, that it is difficult to focus just on the rules as a discrete element of a case. You could change the rules all you want, but that would not give you consistency in application across judges, if you get the point.

The attitude of the assigned judge makes all the difference.

The Courts give a lot of leeway to defendants to obtain un-needed discovery and waste time. The Judges should be more firm in cases, and a bit harsher on defendants to comply with the discovery orders and try/settle cases more expeditiously.

The overall efficiency of judicial administration will be greatly advanced if judges dismissed frivolous complaints and/or claims at an early stage of the proceedings. Litigants are too often forced to deal with claims without merit and with attorneys that gather the courage to prosecute the same without facing any consequences. When one presents a frivolous argument, theory or complaint there should be objective consequences for such behavior.

The single, greatest cause of increased litigation costs, especially in discovery, is the reluctance of the Courts to quickly decide disputes. The requests for counsel to "work it out" among themselves makes delay (and repeated incidents of disputes) inevitable. If the lawyers could work it out there would be no dispute for the Court to decide.

Any decision is better than no decision.

The time it takes for judicial decisions on motions slows litigation.

Magistrates arbitrarily deprive plaintiffs of proper discovery and allow discovery abuses by defendants.

Rules

The Rule 26 disclosures are a waste of time. They do not reduce the amount of discovery. They only add more tasks, create additional billing opportunities for attorneys paid by the hour, and become traps.

The rules in voluntary dismissals are cumbersome. Many times a plaintiff will wish to dismiss without leave of court and without permission of the other party. Much like in TN state court, the fed system should allow a "non-suit" that will put the case to bed without additional costs to the plaintiff. If the defendants wish to get costs from a plaintiff after a non-suit, they could have done that with Rule 11 sanctions if the case was w/o merit. As it is, the clause in the voluntary dismissal rules exposes plaintiffs to sanction-like measures.

The rules need to be revised to address a recent situation I encountered in the case that is the basis for this survey request. My client was sued by a huge corporation that alleged he copied their textbooks/ i.e., copyright violations.

I find that the Federal Courts tend to be far more scrupulous in their enforcement of the Rules of Civil Procedure than that of their Maryland State counterparts. It is the predictability of Rule enforcement (or the lack thereof) rather than the particular Rules themselves which have the greatest direct impact upon the cost of litigation/discovery. As long as the Rules are enforced faithfully by the Courts, costs can be kept in check and clients' expectations properly managed.

It would be helpful if litigants could exchange and agree on search terms prior to producing documents. Also, the search is the easy part of the process. The time consuming part is weeding through the search results for relevant documents. Because this cannot be done electronically, it leads litigants to either produce many irrelevant documents, including possibly privileged documents, or to expend a great deal of time (more than 30 days) to sort through the documents. The rules do not recognize this reality.

One of the primary causes of the increase in the cost of discovery are the stringent requirements of Rule 702 and the *Daubert* decision. As a result of the increasing number of *Daubert* challenges, often for no other reason than a challenging party upping the cost of discovery or padding their bill, experts are forced to spend three or four times as much of the client's money preparing *Daubert*-proof reports to ensure they are not precluded at trial. A portion of my practice is devoted to prosecuting and defending against *Daubert* challenges, and I have seen in the last five years an enormous increase in the cost of litigation surrounding efforts to preclude expert witnesses when there is really no basis to do so.

Standard rules regarding discovery cannot address the intricacies and nuances of an individual case. The attorneys involved need to be free to pose the inquiries they need to discover the parameters of the case.

The Federal Rules are a good but imperfect system rendered even more imperfect by the habitual failure of judges to make difficult decisions in response to competing discovery claims. The ability of the judiciary to understand the legal underpinnings of a case in order to structure discovery so that it is speedy and inexpensive is the main issue. Magistrate judges who handle discovery, but not substance, actually often fail to appreciate the interrelationship between the two things meaning that discovery goes on and on after the relevant legal issues are covered.

The only complaint I have about the Federal Rules are the rigidity of the schedules. The schedules should be a little more flexible to meet the attorneys' other obligations when they arise.

The rules should be amended to allow a party to take one substitution of judges as a matter of right. The courts also impose too strict of deadlines on discovery and motions. The courts often treat the attorneys as though the pending case is the only case the attorney is handling.

Summary Judgment

If Summary Judgment were not in play; discovery costs would be reduced. Too often defense firms run up costs and fees in discovery just to set up a summary judgment motion that they feel they 'have' to file. Summary judgment is arguably unconstitutional, and its use has become too many judge's tools for avoiding trial.

My biggest issue is that some Judge sit on motion for summary judgment for years. A summary judgment motion or motion to dismiss should be decided with a year's time frame.

My case was a trademark infringement case against an alleged counterfeiter who had mental health issues so my responses to most questions probably should be disregarded. Speaking more generally, the biggest problem with federal court, and my state court as well, is summary judgment. I favor abolition of summary judgment but, failing that rather modest proposal, a required conference of counsel to engaged in a good faith attempt to agree on the uncontested material facts. Also, from my limited experience with it, discovery of electronic data appears to be a logistical and financial nightmare. Good luck.

My main concern in the federal court system is the degree to which the court grants summary judgment motions as compared to state court. The ratio of summary judgment benefiting defendants is very large. In many cases, it essentially negates the right to trial and discourages early resolution of claims, since corporate defendants know they have a very strong chance of attaining judgment by motion even where disputed facts are present.

Summary Judgment motions should be encouraged more by Courts. It is my experience that summary judgment motions are often disfavored by judges especially early in the case. But summary judgment is the best way for Courts to dispose of cases early where possible.

Rule 12 and *Twombly*

Discovery is abused routinely in Federal and State court. Enforcement of rules of discovery and ability to rule on motions is much better in Federal Court and provides more certainty of [what] can be expected going in. A change in the rules to require more fact pleading should not be a burden to anyone. Claimants should be expected to know the facts on which they base their claims and amendment is liberally granted.

If more detailed pleading is required, I would be concerned that the initial stage of the case would get bogged in a series of "strategic" motions for more definite statement, motions to dismiss, demurrers, etc., that we tried to get away from when notice pleading was first adopted.

In my opinion, although in some cases discovery is abused under the current system, moving away from notice pleading and heightening initial disclosure requirements is not the solution. That change would only result in (1) complaints rife with "information and belief" allegations, which would unnecessarily complicate and confuse litigation, and (2) in some cases, abuse of the initial disclosure requirements. In addition, given the large amount of information that must be collected and reviewed given the ubiquity of e-mail, etc., there would be enormous practical problems inherent in complying with heightened initial disclosure obligations. Clients would be prejudiced if they simply did not have time to collect and review all evidence prior to initial disclosure deadlines, and were barred from using that evidence later in the lawsuit.

My experience in the specific case queried is not typical. It was a [deleted] personal injury case that went into default, judgment was entered on the default and the defendants attempted to vacate default and failed. The judgment was appealed and the matter settled during the appeal. Discovery played no role in this matter. With respect to practice in general, I have not so much a problem with the present rules as I have a problem with dilatory tactics, especially by the larger firms one encounters in federal practice. I believe more assertive case management would assist in dealing with these tactics which would be used no matter what the rules are. Notice pleading is essential to provide access to the injured and I find that many judges tend to use discovery as a weapon against pro se and small litigants to get their cases out of their courtrooms.

The most abusive procedure presently is the 12b motions for early dismissal. After the plaintiff survives two or three attempts they are without resources to continue the fight and discovery has not even started.

There is a need to refine the issues early in order to prevent discovery abuse. Under the current regime, the pleadings do not adequately refine the issues, leaving parties and non-parties exposed to answering questions in depositions that are, at best, marginally relevant to the cause, and at worst are totally collateral. One solution would allow counsel defending a witness broader authority to instruct the witness not to answer. For a good discussion of the problem of questions that go too far afield in deposition, and a comparison of the differences in state and federal court practice on how the lawyer for the witness may respond, see Judge Wettick's opinion in *Acri v. Golden Triangle Mgmt. Acceptance Co.*, 142 Pitts. L.J. 225 (1994).

I support heightened pleading requirements, less judicial case management, and more liberal discovery

More specific pleading rules would be more beneficial than additional mandatory initial discovery disclosures. Discovery is already difficult to collect from the client; additional mandatory disclosures would only increase the burden and increase motion practice. I also deal with a lot of pro se individuals who don't follow the rules anyway. Additional requirements would be burdensome on both parties. I struggle with following the rules while the pro se individuals do not.

Electronic discovery is killing litigation. The costs (and fear of spoliation claims) are forcing litigants to settle cases far to early. We've tried to come up with some creative solutions to avoid the costs (i.e. *Perfect Barrier LLC v. Woodsmart Solutions, Inc.*, 2008 WL 2230192 (N.D. IN)) but it's still a challenge. Not sure what the answer is. I like the idea of fact based pleadings.

1. The "named case" has not ended; we just had the ENE Conference. Thus, I skipped over the first few sections.2. When a Magistrate Judge has experience in the subject-matter, he/she often facilitates early resolution of the case. However, when a judge has limited civil-law experience, the cases do not settle early on. 3. I strongly disagree with any proposal to limit motion practice. Rule 12 and 56 Motions help dispose of unmeritorious claims.4. I strongly disagree with "early firm trial dates"--it is too expensive for smaller parties. Most cases settle, and a short pre-trial time-frame would result in prejudicing parties who are less wealthy than their opponents. More time allows for paced-out discovery, experts, and settlement negotiations. Thank you.

In my state, California, the absence of notice pleading results in sloppy, undisciplined pleading, and undue expense in pleading challenges that go nowhere. In my opinion, the FRCP is a work of collective genius.

My criticism of Federal Court is that there are too many rules. Every time a court tries to control litigation with broad policies, it ends up creating more work that may or may not be appropriate for all cases. The reason Fed Ct. cost more than state court is that parties have to get completely ready for trial too early (all the preparation money is spent), and all motions have to be in writing and supported by written briefs; all that formal briefing is expensive. In State court you can appear before a judge with minimal written pleading/motion/briefs and explain the problem and get a ruling. Process is less costly than the formal Fed Ct process. Frankly, defendants use the increased cost and formality of Fed Ct as an intimidation tactic against Plaintiffs.

The Rules work rather well now. I think it would unduly increase the cost of federal litigation to require more detailed pleading in the complaint and to further restrict discovery. The rules presently allow Judges and Magistrates to tailor discovery as fits the case before them and I think those rules should stay the way they are. Heavier sanctions for discovery abuse would lead to greater reform and compliance with obligations than changing the rules.

Notice pleading is not a problem since most good attorneys will go beyond the requirements of notice pleading in order to persuade the opposing party to settle. The final question was not well worded in terms of whether it would be "better" for more cases to go to trial. Better for whom? Better for the client, the court, or the public? Probably not. Better for the attorneys who are billing at an hourly rate? Most definitely.

Named case was disposed of on 12(b)(1) and 12(b)(6) motion prior to answer, prior to scheduling order and any discovery.

Civil Rights/Employment Law

Most of my federal work is plaintiffs' civil rights work in which discovery of electronically stored information is not especially significant. Government attorneys are fairly accustomed to the process and generally cooperative in reducing costs to both parties.

Miscellaneous

My named case was an improperly filed "removal" by a pro se party. We had to wait until the scheduling conference for Magistrate Watanabe to strongly convince the removing party that he had no basis for removal and fees would be assessed if he didn't voluntarily dismiss. This should have happened earlier.

I entered this case after discovery and initial motion hearings but before a trial. My client filed pro se. I discovered that there was an unresolved state suit still pending from 20 years ago on the exact same subject matter.

We very seldom see the trial judge in any of the Federal court cases until argument or trial. I believe that is a mistake. Phone conferences are not the same as a personal conference.

A U.S. District Judge appointed me to replace a retained attorney for a plaintiff who brought a civil rights case under section 1983, contending the police officer used excessive force in making an arrest, in violation of the 4th Amendment. The court overruled defense motions. The case was tried to a jury twice. The first jury was unable to reach a verdict. The court granted a motion for mistrial and reset the case. The second jury reached a verdict for the defendant police officer.

Answers assume that Rule 26 disclosures are not "voluntary" disclosures.

I was a law clerk to a very proactive federal judge, and I observed more than 70 trials in three districts on inter-circuit assignments.

If the survey was sent sooner after the conclusion of the trial, I might have remembered more of the information requested.

In my practice (federal tax litigation), there is often very little required in the way of evidence and many of our cases are resolved either on dispositive motions or by stipulation.

In the present case settlement was reached early on, as the client was not prepared to spend the money to proceed. We suffered economic coercion.

Justice is directly dependent upon the quality of the attorneys and the judge.

Let me know how we can provide additional service.

Many of the questions did not apply to this particular case, which was dismissed at an early stage with the other side refusing to provide any informal disclosure before Defendants' Motion to Dismiss was decided.

Needs more federal funding to increase the team of Federal Judicial Officers so as to allow more cases to reach the jury.

The named case settled at an early mediation conference ordered by the judge and administered by the magistrate judge. This early intervention dramatically decreased the costs of the case and was successful in bringing about a quick resolution.

The particular litigation about which you inquired is an admiralty case. I practice primarily admiralty law and get along well with the other admiralty practitioners in the state of Florida. We stream line discovery which makes litigation cost effective and beneficial to client.

Survey Comments

Most of these questions do not have simple yes or no responses. Each case varies with the subject matter, the parties and the attorneys. Some, unfortunately, make discovery burdensome, while others make the process less expensive and productive.

Some of the questions might have been answered differently if the choices allowed consideration of civility between adversaries and economic disparity of the parties.

Thank you for the opportunity to participate. The questions were good.

Thank you for the opportunity to provide my opinions of litigation and discovery in the Federal Courts.

The questions were generally clear; a blog with give and take, and a chance to provide context, may be able to provide added insight.

The survey data is incomplete without a question about the nature of the case.

The survey seemed to be drafted from the point of view that there is too much discovery.

Will be interested to see results.

Each case is really so different. It is difficult to answer generally for those questions calling for such an answer.

Respondents Representing Primarily Defendants

Discovery Abuse/Attorney Conduct

I am an employment defense attorney, practicing in the federal court for some 22 years. In areas such as Fair Labor Standards Act overtime claims, Plaintiff's attorneys abuse the discovery process to coerce settlement.

The best way to control costs is to insist that the discovery be designed to relate to the existing claim and not be a fishing expedition to discover what other matters you can use to expand or create new and enhanced claims.

A substantial part of my practice involves defense cases in which the Plaintiff's counsel seeks voluminous document requests in order to force the Defendant to settle the case rather than expend the man-hours to produce and/or fight the discovery requests. Many of the topics merely seek to obtain corporate governance documents or internal procedures or processes that have nothing to do with the case. The federal courts have little time to thoroughly challenge these "fishing expeditions" and in the SD Fla, some judges have even issued standing orders warning attorney's not to oppose discovery based on "relevancy." Corporate Defendants have little protection against "private" issues that have nothing to do with the actual claims in the lawsuit other than to force production and expense.

Courts should be more punitive, including dismissals of claims, for parties who fail to timely cooperate in discovery. The failure of parties to cooperate in discovery, especially via early written discovery such as interrogatories and requests to produce, cause delays and result in a ripple effect on scheduling orders entered by Courts. Often this prejudices the party requesting the discovery as it relates to future deadlines, such as dispositive motion deadlines. If the parties know that courts are going to enforce the rules that apply to discovery this should serve to relieve this problem.

Federal discovery rules are adequate. Problems arise from inadequate compliance or intentional stonewalling. Motions to compel are available but the time, cost, and ultimate swearing contest about who has what make this a less than attractive option. Our local Court uses a mirror version of the Federal Rules so the response to questions which assume a different state court system may be misleading.

Generally speaking one would hope that, when discovery puts information on the table, the parties would be able to reach settlement. I find it frustrating that responses to written discovery and answers are often relatively useless in terms of learning anything new because responding attorneys are so vague or use stock language with little application to the particular case in question.

Generally speaking, the discovery burdens are fair to both parties. I prefer court rules that permit informal letter briefs or letter requests to the court for resolutions on discovery issues, rather than filing discovery motions. On the other hand, I often find that plaintiffs' attorneys do not fully comply with Rule 26(a) disclosure requirements, thus necessitating meet and confer efforts. I would favor easy accessibility to a magistrate to resolve such omissions.

I believe the federal courts should adopt an explicit rule that discovery must be proportional to what is at issue in the case. The biggest abuse of discovery comes in cases where the parties have asymmetrical burdens. When the burden is essentially equal on the plaintiff and defendant, cooperation is most likely.

I generally represent defendants. While discovery is, of course, necessary in most cases, courts normally fail to recognize that a plaintiff by spending 30 seconds drafting a request which reads "Please produce all..." can cause a defendant hundreds of hours of work and great disruption of its operations. Similarly it seems to be the game of many plaintiffs' lawyers to propound voluminous discovery early in the game when the defense attorney has not really gotten a feel for the case or the nature of his client's records, and then become outraged and move for sanctions or exclusion of evidence because something is discovered some later time during the case-preparation process. The discovery game frequently seems more often directed toward not getting information (followed by the threat of sanctions) than it is toward actually getting useful information.

I have more trouble in some state courts with discovery abuse than in the federal courts.

In cases other than the specific case, we have seen very abusive, disruptive discovery requests requiring an inordinate amount of government time for no discernable purpose. Motions for protective orders narrow it somewhat but not enough.

In my practice, the plaintiff's side abuses the discovery process because I represent mostly large companies that hold all or most of the arguably relevant information and documents. I routinely receive 50+ document requests asking for year's worth of marginal or irrelevant data. The cost of wading through the requests becomes exorbitant. My clients typically can't make overreaching discovery requests because the individual plaintiff's on the other side simply don't have much information (beyond their personal testimony) that is relevant to the case. Courts ought to get involved early in asking the parties (particularly the plaintiff) what they plan on asking for in discovery and why, and then limiting the abusive tactics.

In our case, there had been a prior state court case that had been dismissed voluntarily by plaintiff. It was re-filed under a new theory and then removed to Federal Court. Much of the discovery from the prior state court case was used in the Federal case. The attorneys got along well. Some of the defense experts were company witnesses and there was a treating physician used by both sides.

In single plaintiff employment cases in my practice area the lawyers tend to cooperate in discovery and have very few disputes. I am not sure if that is because of the federal bench in Alabama or because of the temperament of the local lawyers.

More sanctions should be imposed upon lawyers who do not follow the federal rules. Federal judges should participate more in the litigation process.

My federal judicial district has good local rules and procedures. Lawyers here are generally reasonable and collegial. Frustrations of and expense to litigants would be reduced if all of the district judges in the district were diligent and efficient.

My primary Federal Court litigation involves defending the municipality for which I work. As a salaried attorney, I do not deal with much of the discovery cost issues that others face.

Simple tort cases are not usually prone to discovery abuses. But corporate litigation cases are fraught with abuse.

The biggest abuse of discovery is unlimited requests by parties who don't want or need the documents, etc. that they are seeking, but only propound requests to drive up costs for opponents. Courts are generally not inclined to deal with discovery and other collateral disputes until and unless everything is way out of control.

The case in issue was a 1983 false arrest action, and the plaintiffs' counsel was more than happy to drive up the costs of discovery because she knew she would be able to recover them from the defendants if she were to prevail, via 42 USC 1988. We had a tough case to defend and were motivated to settle, but at the same time we did not want to reward her for driving up the atty's fees and costs, which bore no relation to the realistic "value" of the case - Also, until we had reached the second day of trial, she would not budge from ridiculously high settlement demands. We ultimately settled for a lump sum of $225,000, leaving it to plaintiffs and their counsel to allocate the fund between them.

The discovery abuses in my practice primarily involve excessive deposition hours. Our local practice is pretty good about this. As a government lawyer, litigation costs are not the driving force in settlement.

The plaintiff's personal injury bar is the biggest reason for discovery abuse. They do not plan wisely, and keep moving their clients from doctor to doctor when defense counsel paints them into an unfavorable position. The Courts should frown on doctor shopping which will reduce discovery costs (i.e. depositions).

The reasonableness of discovery costs is directly related to the reasonableness of the attorneys. No amendment to the Federal Rules can have a significant impact on that.

The specific case referred to had a plaintiff's attorney who was completely non-responsive and failed on multiple occasions to prepare the joint status report to the court which resulted in my client having to expend funds to file multiple reports to the court with declarations explaining the situation each time the court sent it back for a joint report. No sanction was ever levied on plaintiff for the failure to cooperate and the burden fell to my client, which was disappointing.

This survey is way too long. Everyone knows there is too much discovery in Federal Cases and way too much abuse of discovery.

I believe the rules are adequate. The hesitancy of judges to enforce the rules in a practical way to prevent lawyer abuses is the core of such problems as they exist. The bottom quartile lawyers get away with too much and that is what generally creates the problems.

Discovery Costs

The total costs of litigation were primarily based on the attorney hours of the 2 government lawyers representing the defendant in this case, using hourly rates of $108.75 and $166.88.

42 USC Sec. 1988 and other attorney fees provisions vastly increase the cost of litigation and provide an unequal incentive for plaintiffs to obtain settlement on non-meritorious cases. When attorney's fees are 5 to 10 times a compensatory damage award the system is broken. Attorney fees should not be the motivating factor in settling cases and unfortunately it is.

1. The particular case inquired about was judicially determined before the initial disclosure stage.2. Discovery is costly and often not well managed by the Court.3. Active case management, including considering staged discovery, would be helpful.4. Early setting of trial dates would also help avoid extended discovery costs.5. I think reform is needed and applaud your efforts.

Cost and witness/client convenience would be measurably advanced by giving up or limiting the practice (at least locally) of the 2 week trailing docket for trial assignment. While I recognize it's done to increase the Court's utilization of facilities and case management, it is extremely difficult to juggle schedules to accommodate the extra time needed for trial on an uncertain 2 week basis and particularly difficult with witness and client availability/scheduling.

Due to the liberal discovery rules, the cost of discovery is far disproportionate to the value of the case in almost all cases.

Federal court is way too expensive for most companies. Very academic approach generally - federal court summary judgment costs almost as much as a state court trial.

I strongly recommend more judicial oversight of discovery to limit the scope of discovery. Open-ended discovery requests, which result in large volumes of discovery (most of which is useless), are a real hassle, and are not worth the time and expense, from a cost/benefit perspective.

If I have one complaint with the Federal system (in general) it would be that, in some cases, the Judge's failure to rule on Motions to Dismiss and/or Motions for Summary Judgments (sometimes for 6 months or more) protracts Discovery and thus the costs of the case, which could have been limited by the Judge ruling in a timely fashion. I have had Judges who seemingly completely ignore Reminder Motions that have not been made on Motions filed.

In my experience, the costs of discovery are higher in state court because state court judges impose virtually no limitations on discovery while federal judges reliably impose reasonable limitations on discovery when issues are presented to them. That is one reason the plaintiffs bar in my state is turning to state court more frequently than federal court, which is disappointing.

In this case, the litigation costs and the costs of discovery were really a moot point because the parties settled the case very early through facilitation. Also, in general, I don't believe that the costs of discovery or litigation are too much. Most of my practice is defending sec. 1983 cases, and my complaint is that the threat of attorney fees being awarded to plaintiffs makes the cases settle for far too much. In the Moore case, it settled for as much as 10 times what it should have because of sec. 1988 attorney fees.

Some Plaintiffs' attorneys use expansive discovery to harass defendants and force settlement. The exorbitant cost of discovery, especially unnecessary long hours of depositions, sometimes force attorney to settle cases that are frivolous. Discovery requests should be narrowly tailored to address the issues raised in the complaint. Courts seem to be reluctant to limit the scope of discovery, even in instances where it is being abused by opposing counsel. There should be a limit as to number of hours a witness can be deposed, without leave of the court.

The case you asked about was an ERISA case, so discovery was not much of an issue. In most non-ERISA cases, discovery can be a big cost factor, especially where the judge/magistrate is not willing to make real decisions early on about the scope of discovery. A bigger problem that you should look into is the courts' inability or unwillingness to enforce deadlines once imposed, which drags cases out and also significantly increases costs for defendants. I'm not asking for judges to micromanage or to be unreasonable with requested extensions (attys need judges' cooperation), but when one side continually ignores deadlines, dragging the case out, the other side should be able to look to the court for relief.

This case involved ADA/Cal. state law disability access claims in a retail store. There are literally thousands of these cases pending in the California federal courts. Statutory attorneys fees is the primary purpose of these cases (since damages are capped by statute at $1K), and the prohibitive cost of discovery (which could potentially be awarded as attorneys fees) actually serves as a disincentive for defendants to litigate ANY of these cases, 99.9% of which are blatantly frivolous. If the cost of discovery were not so high, these cases would be resolved in a rational manner relating to the underlying merits, not the cost of litigation. The system is a disservice to all involved, and makes a mockery of the process.

Time problems are directly related to the number of parties and how many people have to "touch" the discovery, i.e. Answers to Interrogatories, Answer to Request to Produce and working around people's schedules for depositions.

Discovery Process

3-4 months to complete discovery in most cases is woefully inadequate and we almost always have to move the court for more time.

Discovery abuses, both in terms of excessive requests and failure to produce, are best resolved when the judge assertively applies the existing (as well as any revised) rules and takes a practical and realistic approach to discovery requests.

The most effective rule change has been the requirement of voluntary initial disclosures. In most cases, in lieu of identifying documents, I voluntarily produce the documents with the initial disclosures in the hope of narrowing discovery.

A discovery plan agreed to by all parties and approved by the judge would allow for a road map for the discovery process and a budget concerning the costs of discovery could be prepared for the client.

Alittle more flexibility and understanding regarding discovery deadlines; especially in regard to timing of mediations.

Discovery is broader, and is even more burdensome in state court than in District Court. The discovery "problem", if any, has nothing to do with the District Courts. Please do not attempt to cure any discovery abuses in District Court by turning the District Court into some sort of "rocket docket" with severe limitations on discovery.

Discovery is too expensive, burdensome and mostly irrelevant. Early pre-discovery summary judgment motions should be encouraged where appropriate, such as copyright cases where the motion is on ground of lack of actionable similarity. Parties should not have to go through discovery and only then be permitted to make dispositive motion when case can be revolved by motion without discovery.

Discovery procedures should be tailored to the type of case being litigated.

Discovery works best when the parties and their lawyers cooperate. The court's role is basically to act as a referee when they don't.

Discovery would be more efficacious if a realistic definition of relevance were used in the discovery process.

Federal Court's are more demanding but I think this leads to better and more efficient lawyering. A heightened complaint requirement will assist in narrowing the issues earlier. Unfortunately, a heightened requirement is not as easy for a defendant's attorney who is just learning of the case when it comes in the door. If there is such a heightened requirement, the 20 days to respond should be at least doubled. Thanks.

Generally, it is very difficult to say "all cases" should be subject to anything. I think the present Rules work in terms of identifying cases early on as "standard or complex" as limiting discovery accordingly. Blanket rules seldom work well.

I am adamantly against any further move toward requiring parties to identify and produce information to the opposing party for which the opposing party has not asked. The other side ought to be thoughtful enough to know what kind of information it wants and to ask for it and the original Rule 26, for example which required lawyers to determine what would be relevant to the case and turn it over to the other side, just put honest and conscientious lawyers at a disadvantage vis-à-vis sloppy or dishonest lawyers who simply would not exercise due diligence in complying with the rule. Moreover, requiring the lawyer on one side to try and determine the universe of information the other side or the court might deem relevant is overly burdensome and unfair.

I am admitted and practice in multiple Federal Courts. This survey was difficult because of the vast differences in court procedures among the various courts. In my experience, some work much better than others. In other words, some courts are very good at effectively and efficiently resolving disputes while others, frankly, create unnecessary and costly requirements, hurdles and roadblocks. So it's difficult to "evaluate" the Rules in any meaningful fashion across the various Federal Courts precisely because the "Rules" are not applied uniformly when it comes to actual cases. All in all I truly enjoy Federal Court cases and procedure (typically vastly superior to most State Courts) but like all things in life, Federal Courts are not perfect either.

I believe there should be focus on the matters that can be discovered. All too often, plaintiffs seek irrelevant information on issues especially document requests. I also find because there are very few trials anymore, depositions which should be used to ascertain what an individuals knows turns into lawyers doing trial cross-examination. Also, I find 90 per cent of transcript is useless because the lawyers ask question on issues that have no relevance to the case. I think what would help in discovery disputes is at the initial rule 16 conference the parties should stipulate to all facts that are not in dispute. From there agree to the disputed facts and then only allow discovery on those issues and place the burden the requesting party to show how certain information they believe exist is relevant to the disputed facts.

I defend local entities and their employees in civil rights cases. Any use of simplified discovery and case management would require the flexibility for a defendant to opt out of a compressed trial setting in order to get a timely pre-trial ruling on immunity issues. Cases which have pre-trial defenses such as immunity do not fit well within a one size approach to case management.

I practice extensively in Federal Courts across the country and before administrative agencies (NLRB) where discovery is not allowed. The quality of justice in Federal Court is not improved with discovery. The outcomes would be the same without discovery.

I strongly agree with the concept of broadened mandatory disclosures. For example, in some of my more complex cases in state court, the judge will order at the outset that the parties turn over their relevant documents and files to each other without formal discovery. This has proven to be an efficient way for both sides to evaluate the merits of the case early on and has led to early settlement.

I would like to see standard for complaints be higher. Too may times we defend cases which allege difficult to understand claims or claims that have no factual support.

If Initial Disclosures were to be expanded or increased, it would be important that there be more time for such disclosures.

In 1983 cases, discovery may be abused to increase attorneys' fees and apply pressure to settle cases. This may be a pattern where statutory attorneys' fees exist. It is not uncommon for the fees to far exceed the value of the case, and ultimately, summary judgment is awarded. Perhaps phased discovery should be mandated if the legal issues can be readily separated from the damages issues. Many Judges is this district offer phased discovery, but are cognizant that the case must be "timely" resolved and, as such, do not emphasize this option.

Initial Disclosures provide valuable info for case evaluation. I do not think discovery should be artificially limited regardless of the case. The rules are fine as they are. The costs of electronic discovery should fall on the party seek the information.

Liberal discovery has killed effective litigation and trial. Electronic document discovery has compounded the problem. The cost of discovery needs to be shouldered by the party seeking it, and in any event should be limited. Mandatory disclosures, enforced by a good faith standard, could streamline the discovery process and let cases go to trial.

Parties should have to turn over what they have that helps them and what hurts them. Most discovery is a waste of time and the major abuse is objections to doc requests and interrogatories.

Problems with discovery in the federal court usually arise from two sources - (1) overly liberal discovery, leading to significant disputes and (2) either the ruling of the disputes without formal motion, resulting in an adequate appellate record, or, failure to rule disputes in a timely fashion. Moreover, many parties fail to abide by the requirements of Rule 26 in Initial Disclosures, resulting in additional discovery being required. While the Rule is clear, it is largely ignored by most plaintiffs. The Rules should provide either with more specificity those items that are to be produced without discovery, or Judges should awards costs when discovery is required that would have been avoided had good faith disclosure taken place.

Thank you for looking into this important topic. I do think discovery has become too automatic and should be limited.

The case that I was involved in that resulted in my participation in the survey was pending in the Eastern District of Texas. The ED-Texas can be a very challenging venue from a discovery perspective for a corporate defendant. The venue and the judges within the division, probably more so than the discovery itself, play a very important role in our evaluation of a case.

The easiest way to address all of the Center's concerns is to amend the rules to permit the prevailing party to recover his/her attorneys fees ("costs"). Such costs should be assessed not as the useless R11 sanction procedure which requires that a party serve a copy of their contemplated motion, and not as a "sanction" under rule 37, but as a matter of course – i.e. costs should be awarded as a matter of course to the prevailing party on any non-consent matter that is brought before the court as the case proceeds - e.g. motions, and to the prevailing party at the end of the case. You would be amazed how many otherwise frivolous claims, cases and motions would disappear (and the court should be allowed to impose costs not only on the parties but their attorneys depending on the circumstances). Regards. Thanks for doing this.

The specific case that resulted in my participation in the survey was a pro=bono matter that we agreed to take on after the case was already filed and in the summary judgment stage. We ended up trying the case and obtained a good result for the client. Overall, I believe that far too many matters in federal court have too much discovery, the rules are too cumbersome and the courts take too much time to decide motions. Not every motion needs a 15-20 decision. The parties need quick decisions, whether they are perfect or not, so the litigation does not grind to a halt.

The system is generally fair but possibly could be more efficient if more initial disclosures were required.

There needs to be clearer black letter law regarding the scope of discovery, rather than judicial discretion which leads to expensive motions and prolonged litigation.

Written discovery, after initial discovery, is generally not very helpful.

Electronic Discovery

E-discovery and the process of what a corporation has to do is not understood by Federal judges. The costs associated with e-discovery are prohibitive and used as leverage by plaintiffs. Attorneys fees should be awarded to prevailing parties equally.

E-discovery is new enough in the courts in which I practice that, by and large, the magistrate judges and most practitioners are still struggling with figuring out how to handle. Incidentally, the case selected was a small case, with little or no ESI issues. There are been others in which I've been involved in which the costs to my clients of compliance have run into the hundreds of thousands of dollars and have required several hearings and motions to compel on both sides.

Electronic discovery addressed to constantly changing storage media is a heavy burden on parties required to respond and should be limited sharply.

Electronic discovery is a problem in one of my employment discrimination cases. The plaintiff's attorney is harassing my client in his procedures.

Electronic discovery is out of control. Courts should require plaintiffs to show what benefit they expect to receive from the discovery sought and the use they intend to make of the information before electronic discovery is permitted. Email discovery should be severely curtailed by timeframe and restrictive concatenated key word searches should be required to massively reduce the volume of email that companies must review.

Electronic discovery is too broad and burdensome on defendants, particularly non-profit and governmental entities with limited resources. The electronic discovery allowed should be severely narrowed, and provisions should be made to shift the cost of electronic and other discovery to the plaintiffs.

Electronic discovery rules need reform as they lead to overkill, unfair imposition of liability and responsibilities on counsel, and tactical use to increase cost on an institutional or municipal defendant, for instance.

Electronic discovery was not a large factor in the particular case at issue. However, generally speaking, it is an extremely burdensome and expensive part of the discovery process in employment discrimination cases on the defense side.

Good Magistrates and experienced counsel can make a difference when common sense and some consideration of substantive law is brought to bear in dealing with discovery-especially electronic discovery.

I am a veteran of many federal civil jury trials. The general limitations on discovery (# of interrogs, # of deps, time limits) have made things better not worse. Electronic discovery remains a concern, especially spoliation and cost. This is a good process to test the system. Keep it up.

I find that electronic filing has led to better judicial management of cases, which in turn makes discovery flow better. My experience in federal court is that the resolutions of the cases are quicker, and surer, than in state court.

I think initial disclosures are useless. Lawyers still engage in the same discovery. Unless we are to impose more limits on discovery, initial disclosures should be abandoned. Regarding ESI, the Courts should be more willing to impose the cost of production in the seeking party without regard to the corporate status of the plaintiff or defendant.

I think the rules on electronic discovery need to be implemented over a longer period of time- and their provisions enforced- before making any changes.

I think the use of electronic discovery can and has been abused in federal court. Said discovery should be limited and managed more stringently by the court.

In the central district of California there are limits on depos as to time and number which I think greatly reduces discovery costs between state and federal courts. However, no one is really addressing electronic costs up front and when you get a big firm going after a public entity they can drive up the costs dramatically and I have had them refuse to pay for any costs of electronic discovery even 50 dollars for the disc.

More clarity on what is expected as far as the collection and production of electronic discovery, when the costs are too burdensome and should be shared, would reduce a significant amount of expense in every case. That issue, in almost every single case, results in a contentious dispute, as the sources of information available these days are immense, and the requesting party's initial position is that every stone must be turned over, regardless of the cost to the other side. Clearer guidelines would reduce this universal point of contention that does not further the lawsuit, but simply adds expense.

My practice is devoted to the defense of clients under statutory law with fee shifting. Discovery is utilized in a majority of cases solely for the purpose of increasing fee claims for the benefit of plaintiffs' counsel. The increase in fees based on electronic discovery and the unwillingness of the courts to pay close attention to the reasonableness of these fees renders the legitimate defense of cases unduly costly, with no benefit to plaintiffs (only the attorneys seem to benefit). The material benefit of discovery is lost when weighed against the fee shifting costs and the willingness of the courts to grant such fees irrespective of the legitimacy of the fees.

The answers regarding this case are skewed as it was a PSLRA case that was decided on motion and, hence, mutual discovery never commenced. The discovery costs reflected in the answers above involved document preservation and initial review of some information, including gathering of ESI for preparation purposes. Having said that, the sheer cost of ESI discovery would have coerced a settlement here if the matter was not disposed of on motion.

The cost of responding to electronic discovery requests can be tremendous. This cost is onerous for most defendants. The party seeking electronic information should be required to meet some burden before being allowed to proceed, and the requesting party should be responsible for all costs. Parties should not be allowed to conduct fishing expeditions with electronic discovery. Thanks.

The electronic discovery in the case discussed in my responses here was limited, but in general, the electronic discovery burdens imposed by the federal rules are much too heavy.

The explosion of e-discovery has led to abusive tactics by plaintiffs when not constrained by judges inclined towards "wide-open" discovery. These problems are more prevalent in state, rather than federal, jurisdictions. Requiring the party requesting e-discovery to front the costs, with those costs being taxable as court costs at the conclusion of the action, would be a terrific deterrence to e-discovery abuse.

The rules on electronic discovery are a minefield for the practitioner and without a doubt should be changed to be less burdensome, less costly and less inclusive/intrusive. It is ridiculous to have to tell a client that everyone has to save everything from their cell phones, personal laptops, etc. No one does it so why have a rule that says you must.

Maybe in multi-billion dollar cases it makes sense -- in the routine case, it is beyond anything that anyone can say is reasonable. Everyone essentially disregards those rules in every case in which I have been involved -- i.e. we enter an agreement up front to not have to produce ESI except in PDF form. This is one rule that everyone agrees should be changed.

There is no question that something needs to be done about electronic discovery. The costs are incredible and burdensome, even to a multi-national corporation. The time and money spent finding, retrieving and reviewing the information sought is so far out of line with any benefit the information has ever yielded in any case in which I've been involved. That is, in no case has the benefit outweighed the cost.

This was a small case for a large client I have and the cost of potential discovery outweighed the cost of the case. I believe the case settled for less than $5,000 prior to getting into the real ESI production. In the other litigation we have for this client in federal court, this client generally spends over $500,000 per month on complying with ESI orders alone. And this cost has been ongoing for years. Other defendants are spending much more - our client is a minor player. This does not include other federal litigation the company is involved in. Since 2004, probably 90% of my time has been spend on discovery and a large portion on ESI including overseeing a team of people who have been working on ESI coding and production since 2004.

Unfortunately, the case you selected for consideration was a very simple, standard marine cargo damage case involving only a moderate amount of money and opposing attorneys with a long history of prior dealings so the case was simple and very civil compared to the average case.

Unsure if additional mandatory requirements are going to serve the needs of reducing the costs of litigation. Litigation needs to be tailored to the particularities of each individual case; to that extent, the involvement of a federal magistrate is helpful to potentially narrow the issues relative to the case or discovery.

You asked about a simple case. The new electronic discovery rules and issues create great abuse of defendants by competent plaintiffs attorneys and greatly increase the cost of litigation to defendants. At this stage the requirements are not well know to the average plaintiff attorney and it is not an issue in most cases.

Federal Court Practice

More judges are requiring the parties to discuss settlement at the initial scheduling conference in a case. Because Judges want to push settlement so early in litigation, clearer, more precise allegations in the complaint are required.

My federal practice deals mostly with defending claims of Fourth Amendment violations under 42 USC 1983. A major problem for the defense is that plaintiff's allegations, no matter how preposterous, are assumed to be true until a Rule 56 motion is filed.

The problem in federal court is not discovery (although the new electronic discovery rules are too burdensome). The discovery in federal and state court (Texas) is not meaningfully different to me.

This was an atypical case for me. Usually there is contentious discovery over police personnel records and lengthy Rule 37 joint motions. Judge Wilson is very efficient in getting matters to trial, which is atypical as well.

1. Individuals suing government should generally be required to file unsealing releases with the initial complaint.2. Municipal defendants should generally be afforded 90 days (rather than 20 days) to respond to an initial complaint.3. Judges should be permitted to require plaintiffs to provide an early settlement demand.4. Discovery not plainly related to the claims at issue should generally be barred.5. Guidelines should be established for determining whether plaintiffs should have to share the costs of producing discovery that is not plainly related to the claims at issue.

By far the biggest waste of resources in federal court comes from not deciding dispositive motions in a timely manner. If Courts would rule on motions, the parties would have more information on which to based settlement negotiations and would not engage in useless litigation and trial preparation in cases that should be dismissed on summary judgment.

For me, the main advantage of federal court practice over state court practice is that federal judges are not afraid to rule on dispositive motions (and to grant them where appropriate). Also the federal rules on offers of judgment are far more effective than those in state court.

For the most part with a few notable exceptions the Federal judiciary is Vastly more fair and even handed than in State courts. The costs and fairness to the litigants is much better in Federal Court. In most cases that I have in Federal court we find a safe haven from ideological and political favoritism in the State courts. There are far too many counties in TX. Where as a defendant you will NOT get a fair shake in the State court due to ideological and political considerations of the local judiciary. This results in massively higher bills to defense clients in those forums. The Federal courts do a 100 times better job in dispensing justice than do the State courts.

Generally, my experience in Federal Court has been very positive. There is more hands on case management in Federal Court than State Court, and I would be hesitant to revise procedures to include more judicial control, or to limit discovery. It isn't broken so don't tinker with it too much!

I am generally very pleased with the practice in the federal courts.

I believe that overall, the federal system is much more efficient and cost effective to litigate cases then the state court systems and in the last year, I have handled cases in Vermont, Rhode Island, Pennsylvania and New Jersey. Many times, in the state court system, discovery is much more burdensome and there is little judicial involvement or interaction. That is not the case in the federal system.

I have found federal court to be fair and more effective in litigating claims than state court. The rules are very fair as is. Rushing cases to trial is more burdensome and less effective than letting the case progress naturally since all cases are not the same. In my opinion the rules are good where they are now. I would urge those involved to tinker with the rules less and devote that time to adjudicating cases. There is confidence to be found in consistency, not constant change.

I hold the federal courts in high esteem. However, as in state courts, a more stringent application and enforcement of the rules would lessen the expense of litigation. Further, pro se parties are permitted to inflict substantial cost on other parties with little or no consequence.

I prefer litigation in the federal courts due to the availability of summary judgment based on use of depositions, which is not available in our state courts. While expense is greater, it is primarily related to preparing for and arguing summary judgment. Rarely are summary judgment motions argued in our state courts.

I think our federal system works well, though I think that there is too much emphasis on closing cases without enough consideration to the realities of busy litigators.

In this matter, my client voluntarily withdrew the complaint once it was assured that the defendant was out of business and had no assets. As to cost, it is not so much in complying with discovery, but rather that the federal rules require more things than state rules.

Litigating in Federal Court is a pleasure because the Court takes seriously dispositive motions.

My clients typically want cases in state rather than federal courts. Federal cases are more expensive despite the claims to the opposite.

My comment is specific to the jurisdiction in which I practice: The Northern District of Illinois. I have had matters in many other federal courts, and the Northern District is the only one, to my knowledge, that has a process for attorneys to physically "present" the motion and be heard for a briefing schedule. In my view, this is an unnecessary step, and added cost, to the process. Briefing schedules for motions are typically set by rule, upon receipt of electronic filing. Thank you.

My practice is primarily labor and employment. Generally speaking, I think the federal district courts in Arkansas do a good job of controlling their dockets and addressing issues that involve abuse of discovery under the current rules.

Of primary concern is the problem of local judges who have their own "local rules" which either change or abrogate existing Federal Rules. For example, many judges in the Central District of California require their own forms of Summary Judgment motions (joint motions) that require so much extra work as to be prohibitive and impossible (how does one require "joint facts" on an MSJ if the issue is whether the facts are undisputed?) Many judges are so reluctant to take cases they seek any way to get remand. The costs of federal court litigation is absurd.

Our firm represents insurance companies. When given the chance, we ALWAYS remove cases to federal court because federal judges are generally better (and not afraid) to follow the law on summary judgment motions. The extra discovery required in federal court is NOT a deterrent to our decision to remove cases.

Regarding costs, one other item which should be addressed is the amount of time/money which the parties have to invest in preparing a case for trial. Many federal judges require extensive pre-trial orders and pre-trial briefs. This should be streamlined and paired down so as to allow more cases to be tried.

State Courts are clogged, understaffed and incapable of fairly resolving complex cases. Our Federal courts are the Benchmark for the world. Please do not "over fix" them. They actually work now!

The actual case involved in this survey was one of the least complicated federal cases I have handled, with the fewest discovery issues--so it was not the norm for my practice. My experience is that Rule 26 disclosure is never sufficient, but I am skeptical that requiring more detailed voluntary disclosure will in any way lessen the need for interrogatories and requests for production. Our federal cases are ALL scheduled for trial not later than 18 months after filing. A very good system. I have spent many years on such issues, as I was a member of our state's Rules committee for 19 years.

The cost of notifying the class in a relatively large class action in federal court forced one client to bring matter in D.C. Superior Court, where fundamental nature of the complaint was federal. Frustrating.

The litigation costs of defending the case at issue in this survey were vastly increased because the Court took almost 22 months to rule on my client's summary judgment motion, requiring the parties to retain experts and prepare for trial.

The system in the USDC EDLA works extremely well. Some lawyers cause problems and seem to get away with it but overall we have an excellent hard working and efficient judiciary that causes things to work smoothly.

The thing that distinguishes use of federal court over state court is the quality of the judges. There is a presumption that if a case is filed in federal court, justice will be more intelligently administered, without any reference to discovery, electronic discovery or other things asked about in your survey. My experience is that most times this is true. It certainly makes counsel put on a better face.

There is no black and white answer to any of the questions posed. Discovery expense is typically not a concern. Rather, fairness of the judiciary and the appellate route is often an overriding concern. Federal courts are more cognizant of e-discovery issues. Accordingly, it is more likely to become an issue in federal cases. However, we have been able to work with opposing counsel in more complex matters to address e-discovery framework as part of or in advance of the Rule 26(f) meeting. It is our practice to involve opposing counsel in legal hold and key word process to eliminate potential disputes down the road.

We are fortunate to have magistrate and district judges who generally enforce reasonable discovery procedures which allows discovery to function as it should - to develop the case to allow the parties to make an accurate evaluation and proceed to trial or settlement. The process depends on the fact that most attorneys in this area are able to communicate directly and professionally. Many discovery "abuses" could be avoided by more attention to professionalism and less to enacting more rules.

We have a great federal judge which makes trying a lawsuit very efficient and enjoyable. She is an absolute pleasure to work with. She is very fair and always prepared. Even if she rules against your client you feel she has given you a very fair hearing.

Motion practice is vital to defending excessive force claims in federal court.

Judicial Management

The more significant discovery issue in my federal practice is the failure of magistrates to enforce relevant discovery requests. The more discovery the more likely the case will resolve as it should, because the more the parties know about the case.

As an attorney who defends insurance companies in bad faith cases, I like the federal system because of the ECF system, the judges have the case from start to finish, discovery is much more uniform and orderly than state court, and the judges are more involved in their cases. I also find that generally federal judges are more professional and polite. Most of my cases involve intense discovery battles. I find that federal judges to a better job than state court in managing and resolving the disputes in an orderly manner. I choose federal court because the discovery issues are easier to litigate there than state court. Thank you for the opportunity to be a part of the survey.

Federal judges are not consistent in managing discovery. Some set strict deadlines and others don't.

For sole practitioners and small firms with limited financial resources, practice in federal courts is, more often than not, prohibitively expensive and therefore risky. As a result, there is often an attitude among federal judges that if you are from a small firm, you are unwelcome in their court.

I answered the question regarding whether the rules and court system were fair in the negative because in comparison to most federal district courts the Western District of Washington is extremely plaintiff-friendly and unfriendly to government as defendants.

I believe discovery can be improved, the federal judges must not be so rigid in forcing matters to trial when the parties need more time to conduct discovery. Strict adherence to a trial date may be good for clearing a case off a judge's docket, in most cases it is not in the best interest of the parties before the court.

I do not find problems with the Rules of Civil Procedure. Unfortunately, they are not enforced on a systematic and regular basis. I see problems arising with ECF where it appears the Judges are not closely reading the orders prepared by the Law Clerks.

If judges would spend less time trying to force settlements of suits and more time trying them or disposing of them on motion, there would be fewer unmeritorious suits clogging up the courts and more time for legitimate cases.

In general, the courts seem to follow the rules of civil procedure, however when a judge allows the other party to totally ignore the rules and deadlines, there is little or no recourse to this abuse of power. Also, large and wealthy plaintiff's abuse discovery to increase their fees with abandon and the Court does not reign in this practice.

In my experience some federal courts go overboard with requiring parties to provide a multitude of reports (like a Rule 26f report) which do nothing to resolve the case, and are more form than substance, and only add to expense of litigation. Furthermore, judges rarely find that sanctions are appropriate for failure to cooperate in discovery, or enforce their own deadlines. Discovery would not be as expensive or as much as an ordeal if the courts would consistently enforce the rules.

Judge Lynn Hughes actively managed the identified case specifically to control costs, given the size of the claim. It went to trial six months after filing.

Judges forget that they were trial lawyers and set discovery deadlines which do not take into consideration that lawyers often are working on many cases at once; in this case we settled after inspection of machine and site of incident revealed it was largely caused by misuse of the product- Mandatory arbitration in the Western District of PA is too early and thus precludes a real chance to resolve the matter- but this case was the exception to that rule.

Judges should resolve discovery disputes quickly and easily without written motions. Judges should not force settlements. There is too much emphasis on cooperation. If a motion to compel is filed, the judge will likely blame the attorney for not cooperating. A cooperating attorney is usually taken advantage of by the average attorney that will not cooperate.

Judges should enforce the discovery rules we have, should pay close attention in discovery disputes to whether they are really in good faith, and should consider (as the rules permit) whether the discovery request is appropriate considering the amount at stake.

Lack of diligence by the courts in enforcing the mandatory Rule 26 disclosures in my district is not helpful.

My only real criticism with the Federal System is the inability to appeal a remand order and the lack of an extraordinary writ procedure to deal with maverick judges.

The case that prompted my receipt of the survey was a summons enforcement proceeding that did not entail discovery; I strongly believe that too many judges have an "a plague on both your houses" or "you go work it out yourself" approach to discovery disputes.

The most unpleasant aspect of federal litigation is judicial temperament. The imperial judiciary is alive and well in the federal courts, and the longer I practice, the more unpleasant it becomes.

The unwillingness of judges to grant dispositive motions and/or exercise strong control over abusive discovery practices encourages "scorched earth" tactics and turns the judicial system into a very expensive lottery. Most of my (employment) cases settle because the cost of going forward, even in meritless cases, can't be justified. It's like dealing with legalized extortion.

There should be more judicial involvement to discourage discovery battles.

When there is a discovery dispute which requires some court involvement for resolution, it can be difficult to get a timely determination within the timeframe for discovery. Especially where the parties have used some time to try to work it out themselves first.

Rules

Changes to the FRCP regarding costs awarded for prevailing parties might encourage litigants to forgo baseless claims. Costs for Westlaw research and many other areas should be recoverable. Good luck to whomever with this project. It is encouraging that someone is looking at these issues.

I believe the federal rules generally work well. In Wyoming, we do not see the discovery abuses we hear about occurring in other jurisdictions.

I'm not sure the Rules need to be changed, or the present Rules better enforced. What is tolerated in State court by way of evasiveness and unhelpful disclosure responses is less tolerated in federal court, but it takes a motion to get relief.

My recommendation would be a Rule 26 amendment stating that documents not produced during discovery and later produced are presumed to have been withheld and presumed not admissible. On Rule 56 I would add an amendment stating that renewed summary judgment motions based on information previously available during a first summary judgment motion are not favored.

One size fits all rules, particularly with regard to discovery and disclosure, should be reconsidered. Perhaps a tiered system, depending upon the nature and magnitude of a case, should be considered. Many cases do not warrant the degree of discovery which more significant cases require. As matters stand now, no distinction is drawn by the rules, to the detriment of parties and the court.

Overall I have found the Federal Rules to be far superior than those of the state courts I practice in. I would recommend more judicial involvement whether that be from magistrates or judicial referees so the process is monitored more closely and the outcome provides for a more fair process. Sometimes lawyers are too wary of upsetting judges with discovery disputes but in the end it should be about what is fairness and justice call for.

Rule 26 is confusing.

Rule 54 permitting the award of costs should be expanded as a way to shift more discovery costs to the losing party. I believe this was a Sedona Conference recommendation.

Rules should be more flexible; mandatory discovery should be streamlined; shorter Rule 16 plans; attorney fees should be recoverable for prevailing party in all suits.

The Court actually should have more flexibility in allowing necessary discovery than the amount allowed under the Rules. Some cases are more complex than others and the Court should not forbid discovery beyond the Rule limits just to meet the Rules - it should consider the issues/parties/circumstances involved in the case.

The Rule 26 expert disclosures seem to be the biggest expense and burden. I have yet to see such a disclosure obviate the need for an expert deposition.

The Rules work well. While I appreciate the effort to improve the Rules, the current rules allow for a fair presentation of the evidence to a jury, and juries almost always reach the right result.

There should be some consideration given to amending Rule 56 to require the district courts to set definite non-oral hearing dates for dispositive motions, preferably 60-90 days before a scheduled trial date. When district court judges fail to issue decisions on dispositive motions (A) until the Friday before a Monday trial start; or (B) after trial preparation has begun, it results in a huge waste of time for the Parties because no one knows precisely what claims are going to be tried until the court issues a decision. Post-summary judgment, if there are remaining claims, it helps dramatically reduce the time and expense of preparing for trial when one can plan witnesses, exhibits, etc., well in advance of trial.

Summary Judgment

Although not in the case at hand, too many cases are dismissed on summary judgment and affirmed on appeal.

Courts should give much more attention to summary judgment proceedings, as most cases which proceed to trial should have been dismissed on summary judgment.

I deal with a specialty area where cases are fully heard through an administrative hearing. The federal court is the reviewing body. Discovery is not favored in case law and it takes time to get the court up to speed. This has led to very awkward situations in federal court to shoe horn these types of cases in the case management systems concerning discovery instead of moving quickly to summary judgments based on the administrative record.

I personally think more summary judgments should be filed to limit the scope of issues at the trial level.

More liberal granting of summary judgments would be a more effective way of disposing of non-meritorious cases and limiting litigation costs than generalized discovery reforms.

Rule 12 and *Twombly*

I think the Supreme Court was right in establishing the *Twombly*, which should be extended and enforced in all civil cases.

Excessive discovery and overzealous practitioners are making litigation very expensive. In fact, it is making it prohibitively expensive for well-financed litigants and has nearly denied justice to most that are not financially well off. Discovery expenses are becoming an unnecessary burden and the theory that you must know everything that can be done is an anachronism of another era. Cost can be dramatically diminished by stringent disclosures rules and detailed pleading requirements of all facts that entail a party to a remedy. Moreover, stringent initial scheduling orders and conferences and active court supervision will shorten the time cases for cases to be tried, discourage discovery abuses and promote early settlements.

I believe that one of the rules that should be reviewed is the rule that requires all motions to be argued by brief and does not allow for hearings. If some of the discovery disputes could be resolved at hearings, especially the simpler discovery disputes, it might allow for quicker resolutions and direction to the parties that would provide a substantial savings in discovery costs. Also, more detailed statements of the issues, whether in initial pleadings or early pre-trial conferences, would assist in curtailing discovery costs and reduce the time it takes to move a case through the federal system. The cost of filing any discovery motion, the delay in a ruling on those motions and the time it takes to work a case through the federal courts causes additional discovery costs that can be curtailed with rule changes.

My criticism is the liberal notice pleading that is particularly unfair to defendants given the broad, expensive discovery.

Compliance with the Rule 26 disclosure requirement is a challenge, especially in Eastern District courts which require the disclosure of "all relevant information." Pleadings are often vague, making it impossible to know what the other side may deem relevant. Compliance with these orders is not realistic, and is often used by plaintiffs to try the case on sanctions, rather than on the merits.

Discovery is a necessary tool; one through which cases are won or lost. Discovery is essential however increased scrutiny of pleadings, increased required disclosures and increased judicial oversight of cases will increase the likelihood of pretrial resolution.

Federal Court is too formal - everything - absolutely everything - requires a formal motion or pleading. The law clerks and secretaries are almost never helpful even when the phone call is intended to aid the court and not foster *ex parte* communications.

I am concerned that more elaborate pleading rules and greater initial disclosures were lumped together as a "simplified approach", when these are very different ideas. Complicating pleading is a bad idea. Pleadings are too dense and full of superfluous allegations and argument already. Rule *'s mandate for a "short and simple statement" is routinely ignored. Complaints read like press releases - or novels! In pleading, less is more. Requiring greater initial disclosures is an excellent idea. With greater initial "automatic" document production (including electronic data) and standard interrogatories at the outset, discovery could move relatively quickly to depositions. Generous deadlines for paper discovery are a waste of time.

This survey is geared towards changes in the discovery process. I believe that discovery is useful to both sides in order to measure and/or prove the merits, weaknesses and strengths of each party's case; accordingly, I prefer having broad discovery. However, I do believe the pleading requirements should be less liberal as there are many meritless cases that proceed through the costly discovery and motion phase before the plaintiff is willing to settle or agree to a reasonable settlement.

While the case chosen did not have any electronic discovery, I have had cases where that has become a major issue and one which is very expensive with often very little gained by it. It seems to be used as a very, very expensive fishing expedition. I also believe that there should be more stringent pleading standards. Cases that often get decided on summary judgment could be dismissed at the pleading stage if the plaintiffs were held to a higher standard. Claims that are being filed now might not be filed with a higher pleading standard.

Notice pleading (and the rule allowing liberal amendments to pleadings) is an unfair advantage to Plaintiffs and unfair disadvantage to Defendants.

Overall, the Federal Court System is more efficient, fair and predictable than State Court. I do feel strongly, however, that by requiring more informative pleading from both plaintiffs and defendants, and requiring more expansive discovery at an earlier stage, the cost of litigating would be reduced.

The current discovery process generally provides adequate and efficient discovery. However, federal courts, in my experience, are overly lenient with pro se litigants and with represented parties that fail to respond to discovery. Stricter enforcement would make litigation far more efficient. Also, a heightened pleading standard would greatly reduce the frivolous claims filed in federal court and allow the court and counsel to focus on meritorious claims, and avoid wasting time and effort with "shotgun" type complaints that throw in every possible claim that an active imagination could dream up.

Judges need to better manage discovery and the 12(b) process. The Supreme Court has made it more difficult to pass muster under 12(b) for the reason that discovery is so expensive and that such complex trials in front of a jury are like playing roulette.

The main problem I see is judges refusing to get involved in the case until the end. Summary judgment should be granted much more frequently, and if the judge is wrong, there is an appeal. On occasion, the judge has not even read the briefs before the Rule 12 motion is heard. Where a party is caught in a violation, he should be sanctioned. Any sanction would be effective, no matter the size. Best of luck with your worthy survey.

The case referenced, in my opinion, was frivolous. I tried to utilize every rule to limit discovery and obtain an early resolution. I had limited success. I represent municipalities and police officers in Section 1983 litigation. The rules (7(a), 12(e), 12(b)(6) and local rules limiting discovery are not strictly applied. I would like to see more mandates to follow these rules in 1983 litigation. A lot of taxpayer money is spent litigating claims that are ultimately dismissed per an MSJ that could have been dismissed very early.

The Rules should state a maximum period of time for the court to rule on pending pre-trial motions. The Rules should postpone initial disclosures until 12(b) motions are ruled upon. The judges should tailor their orders to reflect the choices offered in electronic filing.

While I believe that rules covering discovery and notice pleading in could be improved, they are far superior to the systems provided for in State courts.

I think that the question about the Rule 8 standard may have been rendered moot by the *Twombly* and *Iqbal* decisions, which have emphasized the need, even under the current standard, to be more precise. I also feel that defendants in my area of practice (employment litigation) bear almost all of the burden and expense of discovery, creating unjust incentives to settle cases.

Thank you for the opportunity to provide input. Our firm is completely paperless and we routinely deal with electronic discovery. Among the benefits are various programs that allow for discovery and depositions to be integrated for easy access, coding and presentation. I am finding in Federal court that the *Bell Atlantic v. Twombly* case is serving to require much more specific pleading that ultimately helps frame the issues earlier; and consequently, reduces costs.

Civil Rights/Employment Law

I specialize in labor and employment law. In general, the federal courts do an excellent job of overseeing these cases (discovery, settlement, SJ and trial). However, I think streamlined discovery procedures would lessen cost and could still address each party's needs. Good luck!

Most of my cases are for governmental defendants in civil rights cases. I find that the Plaintiffs attorneys run up cost of discovery and numerous depositions to increase the possible recovery under §1988 fees.

My focus is in defending employment litigation. In virtually every employment case filed in federal court, the costs of discovery and litigation are used to leverage a settlement. In my experience, many defendants pay settlements in completely frivolous cases because the cost of litigation substantially outweighs fairness and justice. The present rules do not work for small and mid-size businesses that cannot afford to defend themselves.

Please eliminate procedures that require preliminary non-binding trials to magistrates or arbitrators, and that allow either party to simply object to the outcome and proceed to trial. The required preliminary non-binding trial is a great waste of resources and a cause of delay. Example is the rule in N.D. Ga. that all Title VII cases be tried to a magistrate -- but if you win, the opponent can still force a jury trial, and you cannot even tell the jury that you won before the magistrate.

Since most of my claims are representing municipalities and their officers in civil rights actions, the biggest deterrent to trying cases that have merit is the threat of attorney's fees.

The most significant problem I have encountered in federal cases (in the employment/discrimination area) turns on the availability of fee shifting, and the fact that the courts currently do not link the availability of fees to the reasonableness of the efforts.

The reason that my clients settle cases is because of the risk of having to pay Plaintiff's attorney fees, in the event even a small judgment is entered in Plaintiff's favor. While discovery is a significant cost to litigation. It is that "hammer" that causes most Defendants to settle rather than go to trial in employment discrimination cases.

Miscellaneous

As a fed government agency we generally produce all known responsive documents with private attorneys hiding the ball more often.

Generally, my experience has proven that some aspects of discovery - i.e., written discovery - do not benefit the parties. Written discovery produces many objections from parties that prevent parties from obtaining worthwhile information.

In this case, I had worked with the opposing attorney on a number of other trials. We were able to meet early on and work out an agreement that provided for the exchange of paper, not electronic discovery.

The case in question was an insurance coverage matter. In this case, the four attorneys (all of whom had known and respected each other for years) fully cooperated and agreed on a joint stipulation of all relevant facts.

A substantial cost to the litigants in the Federal courts not addressed in this survey are pre-trial preparation required by the court as well as post trial submissions to the court, particularly in bench trial cases.

Defendant admitted liability..court trial..case under submission far too long..verdict extremely low.

Discovery costs and but one important issue. More litigation is generated and forced to inequitable conclusions due to 1988 fee shifting.

I don't think I can disclose the actual cost of defending this case.

I had two other cases going on simultaneously so it was hard to remember what occurred in which case. The biggest dispute was over the need for a protective order, as there was security sensitive information involved. I took the deposition of Plaintiff's expert which I forgot to list above.

I'd be happy to participate in any advisory committees.

In terms of context, California state courts do not restrict discovery to the same degree as is the case in the Central District of California. My responses were somewhat governed by comparison to state courts here.

In this particular case, I filed a Motion to Dismiss or for Summary Judgment after receiving the complaint. The case was resolved before discovery became an issue.

Many of the questions were not applicable to the case in question, as Plaintiffs were proceeding pro se.

More trials would be better for me but not necessarily for the litigants.

My colleagues and regularly litigate maritime matters. We are very interested in this issue and would be glad to help the committee.

My experience litigating this case in the Western District of Pennsylvania was extremely satisfying to both myself and my client.

Opposing counsel in the listed case is a long time adversary, so we enjoy a mutual respect and civility in cooperating in discovery matters to gain more efficient results for our clients and so as to not burden the courts with discovery squabbles.

[Named case] was a pro se prisoner case against the State Parole Board so my responses reflect that fact.

Please examine the Northern District of Georgia's form submission to be completed following the Rule 26(f) conference, which I find to be thoughtful and well organized.

Some State courts, like Texas allow the Parties to select the discovery track of the case based on the issues and basic facts. This may work in the Maritime cases that that I generally handle.

Sorry, I do not have the total attorney costs on the case you asked for but estimate that it was approximately $36,000.

The case was sent to arbitration following motion to compel arbitration. [Illegible word] it would be good representative sample.

The named case was filed by pro se plaintiffs who are usually harder to work with than with attorneys - with exceptions. The court should provide more control over pro se plaintiff cases and litigious pro se plaintiffs.

The only criticism I have in this case is case specific. The ENEC was never held because the defendants kept continuing it due to unavailability. I believe we could have resolved the case even earlier had we been compelled to actually meet at an ENEC as is normally done. Instead we ended up resolving the case at a settlement conference. However, overall, I think the procedure for this insurance contract dispute was adequate and reasonable. This last statement has been true for the other cases I have handled in this Southern District of California and the Central District of California.

The subject case was a standard seaman injury brought under maritime law. The results of Discovery brought resolution. Without broad Discovery, the claim would have proceeded to trial.

The use of mediation was not addressed and would affect my last answer about more cases going to trial. Mediation is an alternative and has helped in many cases

There needs to be a better balance between the needs of the parties/their attorneys and the courts' dockets. Cases should be subject to judicial scrutiny before service of process on defendants is accomplished to help weed out the meritless cases sooner.

This was a hard survey for me to answer as the case which prompted the request was a pro bono Vets case involving a discrete legal issue. On the other hand, my work with corporate litigation prompted some answers regarding my overall experience that would bear further discussion. Thank you for your time.

Wish I knew more about the proposed changes in order to answer some of the questions.

Survey Comments

Some of these questions are loaded. Generally, I think we need to focus less on changing the rules and more on encouraging a more uniform approach to application of the rules among our judges and magistrate judges.

A lot of the questions are badly worded, so that it is unclear what you are looking for. Other questions are so vague and subjective as to be meaningless. The set-up is such that for one batch of answers, the "agree/disagree" spectrum is hidden as one gets to the bottom of the page, creating the possibility of confusion and responses opposite of what they should be. Obvious questions, such as the result of the litigation, are omitted.

Please be sure to inform me when the results of the survey are published on the web. Thanks.

Some of the questions were very ambiguous. For example, I think fewer cases should go to trial because judges should adhere to Rule 56, and not because parties should settle non-meritorious claims that withstand summary judgment. The summary judgment pro

Survey is too long. Don't need more rules on discovery--plenty of rules and court enforcement is available in timely and efficient ways.

Survey was too long. Suggest a more focused approach.

Thank you for addressing this issue.

Thank you for the opportunity to participate!

Thanks!

The survey is unreasonably long.

My case was a pro per Plaintiff alleging constitutional claims via 42 USC 1983 decided on a 12(b)6 motion; thus the nature of the responses herein.

There should be a choice "not applicable" rather than "unable to say."There was no question regarding sanctions ordered by the magistrate or trial judge and, if so, whether the sanctions related to findings of fact or were monetary in nature and or both. There should have been some type of classifications of cases, i.e., personal injury, product liability, police misconduct, labor and employment, intellectual law, etc.

We [are] a national group, which w/o judges and variations depending on the local court, manages discovery based on the different case types, applying rules consistent throughout the entire Federal Court system.

Well thought out survey

You have too much time on your hands.

Excellent survey.

Good luck with the review process. We look forward to seeing the results.

Good luck.

I found this survey very interesting and look forward to the results. I could not personally answer the technical questions about e-discovery but hopefully others could.

I would be interested in obtaining the poll results when they are complete. Thank you for asking me to participate. Very interesting.

[Named case] was a foreclosure case, which is not how a typical case is handled.

www.ingramcontent.com/pod-product-compliance
Lightning Source LLC
Chambersburg PA
CBHW080009210526
45170CB00015B/1952